discussions of specific works, both "secular" and avowedly religious, and their testimony about human existence. Christian drama is treated from the professional viewpoint of the director of T. S. Eliot's plays, E. Martin Browne. One chapter is then devoted to the voice of the poet in the city today and another to the peculiar problems and pitfalls that endanger the Christian artist in our time. Finally the symposium is drawn to a close by the projection of a "hope for literature" in years to come, by the notable Christian author, Chad Walsh.

The perilous and the promising, the degrading and the sublime, the whole assemblage of faces and masks in contemporary poetry, drama, and prose, all are explored with an urgency and audacity that may even touch on the prophetic. Nathan A. Scott, Jr., who is known as a pioneer in the coordinated study of theology and literature, provides the critical background as well as much of the inspiration.

The
Climate of Faith
in
Modern Literature

The Climate of Faith in Modern Literature

EDITED BY NATHAN A. SCOTT, JR.

New York

1964

Library of Congress Catalog Card Number: 63-9057
454-364-C-3
Printed in the United States of America

Acknowledgments

Grateful acknowledgment is made to the following authors and publishers for permission to use copyrighted material from the titles listed below:

Bollingen Foundation, New York—Henri-Charles Puech, "Gnosis and Time" in *Man and Time*, edited by Joseph Campbell, Bollingen Series, Pantheon Books, Inc.

Cambridge University Press, New York—C. S. Lewis, *De Descriptione Temporum: An Inaugural Lecture.*

Cornell University Press, Ithaca, N.Y.—Henry Alonzo Myers, *Tragedy: A View of Life.*

Doubleday & Company, Inc., New York—Richard Chase, *The Democratic Vista.*

Faber & Faber, Ltd., London—Edwin Muir, "The Poet" in *Collected Poems.*

Farrar, Straus & Company, Inc., New York—Francois Mauriac, *Mémoires intérieurs*, trans. by Gerard Hopkins.

Grove Press, Inc., New York—Samuel Beckett, *Endgame, Waiting for Godot.*

Hamish Hamilton, Ltd., London—Kathleen Raine, "Ex Nihilo" in *Collected Poems.*

Harcourt, Brace & World, Inc., New York—Hannah Arendt, *The Origins of Totalitarianism;* E. E. Cummings, "Pity this busy monster" in *Poems, 1923-1954*, copyright 1944 by E. E. Cummings; T. S. Eliot, *The Cocktail Party*, copyright 1950 by T. S. Eliot; "Burnt Norton" and "The Dry Salvages" in *Four Quartets*, copyright 1943 by T. S. Eliot; T. S. Eliot, "Love Song of J. Alfred Prufrock," "Burial of the Dead," "Preludes," and "What the Thunder Said" in *Collected*

Poems of T. S. Eliot, copyright 1936 by Harcourt, Brace & World; T. S. Eliot, *Murder in the Cathedral*, copyright 1935 by Harcourt, Brace & World; Wright Morris, *The Territory Ahead;* Virginia Woolf, "Modern Fiction" in *The Common Reader*. Reprinted by permission of Harcourt, Brace & World.

Harper & Row, Publishers, New York—Roger Hazelton, *New Accents in Contemporary Theology*; Dorothy Sayers, *Further Papers on Dante.*

The Hogarth Press, Ltd., London—Virginia Woolf, *The Voyage Out.*

Holt, Rinehart and Winston, Inc., New York—Denis de Rougemont, *The Christian Opportunity.*

P. J. Kenedy & Sons, New York—St. Therese, *Autobiography of St. Therese of Lisieux*, trans. by Ronald Knox.

The Kenyon Review, Gambier, Ohio—Leslie A. Fiedler, "Toward an Amateur Criticism," XII, No. 4, Autumn, 1950. Used by permission of the author.

Alfred A. Knopf, Inc., New York—Albert Camus, *The Writings of Albert Camus*, trans. by Justin O'Brien; Wallace Stevens, "The Emperor of Ice Cream," "Sunday Morning" in *Collected Poems.*

Little, Brown & Company, Boston—Stanley Kunitz, "My Surgeons" in *Selected Poems 1928-1958*, copyright © 1958 by Stanley Kunitz.

David McKay Co., Inc., New York—J. V. Langmead Casserley, *Christian Community.*

The Macmillan Company, New York—W. B. Yeats, "The Cold Heaven," "The Second Coming," in *Collected Poems*, copyright 1924, renewed 1952 by Bertha Georgie Yeats.

The Manchester Guardian, Manchester, England—Raymond Williams, "Eliot and Belief," December 9, 1960.

Methuen & Co., Ltd., London—Jean Anouilh, *The Lark*, trans. by Christopher Fry; Bertolt Brecht, *The Life of Galileo* in *Bertolt Brecht Plays*, I, trans. by Desmond I. Vesey.

Motive magazine, Nashville, Tenn.—Nathan A. Scott, Jr., "Faith and Art in a World Awry," November, 1961.

New Directions, New York—Friedrich Hölderlin, "Patmos" in *Some Poems of Friedrich Hölderlin,* trans. by Frederic Prokosch, copyright 1943 by New Directions; Thomas Merton, *New Seeds of Contemplation* © by the Abbey of Gethsemani, Inc.; Ezra Pound, "Canto XLV" in *The Cantos of Ezra Pound,* copyright 1934, 1948 by Ezra Pound; "Hugh Selwyn Mauberley" in *Personae: The Collected Poems of Ezra Pound,* copyright 1926, 1954 by Ezra Pound; Dylan Thomas, "This bread I break," "And death shall have no dominion," "Do not go gentle into that good night," "The force that through the green fuse" in *Collected Poems of Dylan Thomas,* copyright © 1957 by New Directions; Lionel Trilling, *E. M. Forster,* copyright 1943 by New Directions. Reprinted by permission of New Directions, Publishers.

Oliver & Boyd, Ltd., Edinburgh—G. S. Fraser, *Ezra Pound.*

Oxford University Press, New York—Kenneth Cragg, *Sandals at the Mosque;* Richard Eberhart, "A Testament" in *Collected Poems 1930-1960;* Christopher Fry, *Curtmantle* and *The Dark Is Light Enough.*

Penguin Books, Middlesex, England—"Hell" in Dante, *The Divine Comedy,* Canto III, trans. by Dorothy L. Sayers.

Princeton University Press—Francis Fergusson, *The Idea of a Theater.*

G. P. Putnam's–Coward-McCann, New York—William Golding, *Lord of the Flies.*

Random House, Inc.—W. H. Auden, *The Age of Anxiety,* copyright 1946, 1947 by W. H. Auden; "For the Time Being," in *The Collected Poetry of W. H. Auden,* copyright 1944 by the author; "Friday's Child," © copyright 1958 by W. H. Auden in *Homage to Clio;* "The Sabbath," © copyright 1959 by W. H. Auden in *Homage to Clio;* "To Reinhold and Ursula Niebuhr," and "To T. S. Eliot on his Sixtieth Birthday," in *Nones,* copyright 1951 by W. H. Auden; James Joyce, *Ulysses,* copyright 1914, 1918, and renewed by Nora Joseph Joyce; Ray Lawler, *Summer of the Seventeenth Doll,* © copyright 1957 by Ray Lawler; Eugene O'Neill, *The Ice-*

man Cometh, copyright 1946 by Eugene O'Neill; Robert Penn Warren, *Brother to Dragons*, copyright 1953 by Robert Penn Warren. Reprinted by permission of Random House, Inc., New York.

Rupert Hart-Davis Ltd., London—R. S. Thomas, *Poetry for Supper*, p. 28; R. S. Thomas, "Affinity," "The Minister," pp. 92, 114, "A Priest to his People" in *Song at the Year's Turning*; R. S. Thomas, "The Survivor" in *Tares*.

St. Martin's Press, Inc., New York, and Macmillan & Company, Ltd., London—William Temple, *Nature, Man and God*.

Schocken Books, Inc., New York—Franz Kafka, *Parables and Paradoxes*, copyright 1935 by Schocken Verlag, Berlin; copyright 1936, 1937 by Heinr. Mercy Sohn, Prague; copyright 1946, 1947, 1948, 1953, 1954, 1958 by Schocken Books, Inc., New York. Reprinted by Schocken Books, Inc.

Charles Scribner's Sons, New York—Ernest Hemingway, "A Clean, Well-Lighted Place" in *Winner Take Nothing*; Susanne Langer, *Feeling and Form*; Reinhold Niebuhr, *The Nature and Destiny of Man*, I; John Crowe Ransom, *The World's Body*.

Martin Secker & Warburg Ltd., London—R. Mallet, editor, *Correspondence between Claudel and Gide*, trans. by John Russell.

Sheed & Ward, Inc., New York—William F. Lynch, S.J., *Christ and Apollo*, © 1960 by Sheed & Ward Inc.

Student Christian Movement Press, Ltd., London, and Harper & Row, New York—Ronald Gregor Smith, *The New Man*.

Vanguard Press, Inc., New York—Edith Sitwell, "Clowns' Houses," "Gold Coast Customs" in *Collected Poems*.

The Viking Press, Inc., New York—Graham Greene, *A Burnt-Out Case*, *The Living Room*, and *The Potting Shed*; James Joyce, *A Portrait of the Artist as a Young Man*, Viking Compass edition; D. H. Lawrence, *Last Poems*, edited by R. A. Aldington and G. Oriolo, p. 11; D. H. Lawrence, *Women in Love*, Viking Compass edition.

Yale University Press, New Haven—Richard Sewall, *The Vision of Tragedy*.

Contents

Editor's Introduction

MANY YEARS ago, in the late forties, the distinguished French Protestant lay theologian Denis de Rougemont declared that

> . . . as a layman belonging to the Church and seeing the opportunity for action in the world and the call of need in our time, I expect . . . that the Church offer a type of livable cultural relationship; that it dare again to support and head an intellectual vanguard instead of keeping its retrogressive and suspicious position, a stance which is academic not only in the liturgical arts but with respect to the living culture. . . . Theologians should adopt a policy of participation instead of expressing self-righteous indignation toward new schools unprovided with principles of integration. . . . All the culture of the West—music, painting, philosophy, literature—came out of the churches and the monasteries but, alas, it also went out of them! It is time that we struggle to find it again and bring it back.[1]

And it may well be that the chief difference between the general mood of the theological community today and that of twenty years ago is defined by the intentness with which Christian thinkers have been learning M. de Rougemont's lesson in the intervening period. For whereas the new orthodoxies of the thirties and the forties, whether Catholic or Protestant, were busy promoting an embattled and polemical posture vis-à-vis the world of what was called "secular" culture, the new concern that one feels to be abroad today points toward reconciliation and *rapprochement*, toward what M. de Rouge-

[1] Denis de Rougemont, "The Christian Opportunity," in *The Third Hour* (New York: Morehouse-Barlow Co. Inc., 1958). Reprinted by itself (Holt, Rinehart and Winston, 1963).

mont called "a policy of participation," and the most authentic voices speak out in behalf of what we have learned to call "dialogue."

It is just here that what is perhaps the most basic shift in the theological sensibility of our period comes into view, at the point where the radical disjunctions that were drawn in an earlier time between the sacred and the secular, between the holy and the profane, seem no longer to do even a rough kind of justice to the great fact that the *whole* world is God's world and that Jerusalem cannot therefore afford skeptically to wonder whether it need have anything to do with Athens. And on none of the major frontiers of contemporary cultural life has the Christian community been more eager for instruction and exchange than on that where it is met by all the strange, difficult new idioms of the arts. Here we have come to feel—in our poetry and drama and fiction—is a kind of direct and immediate refraction of the human mystery that gives us an avenue into what is at once threatening and promising of renewal in this late stage of modern experience. And thus everywhere today, in the main intellectual centers of the Church, the painting and literature and music of our age are being made the subject of intense theological scrutiny.

It has also to be remarked, however, that this increasing alertness amongst the Christian laity and clergy to the arts, and particularly to the arts of the word, is accompanied by a parallel movement on the other side where, with an especial force in the literary community, the renascence of religious concern is one of the most noticeable features of the contemporary scene. In part this is doubtless a development that results from a reaction among younger literary scholars and critics against what is felt to be the excessive formalism that has characterized the central tradition in the literary criticism of our period. For, after a long period of having been taught that a work of literary art is or should be an absolutely self-contained and discrete set of mutually interrelated references, a newly emerging generation in criticism begins now to ask whether the mode of existence of imaginative literature is really characterized by such isolation from the other departments of experience. The direction which is now being aimed at was nicely suggested a few years ago by Leslie Fiedler in one of his spirited essays, when he said:

> The "pure" literary critic, who pretends, in the cant phrase, to stay "inside" a work all of whose metaphors and meanings are pressing outward, is only half-aware. And half-aware, he deceives; for he cannot help smuggling unexamined moral and metaphysical judgments into his "close analyses," any more than the "pure" literary historian can help bootlegging unconfessed aesthetic estimates into his chronicles. Literary criticism is always becoming "something else," for the simple reason that literature is always "something else." [2]

"Literary criticism is always becoming 'something else,' for the simple reason that literature is always 'something else.'" Which is for Mr. Fiedler to say that the work of art is involved in the total human experience, the experience from which it issues and the experience upon which it is, in some way or other, a comment. And all the more interesting fresh tacks that criticism has taken in recent years have represented various attempts to pay a kind of partial tribute to this fact and, more and more, to push literary analysis in the direction of a new philosophical and theological criticism. Such men as John Bayley, Murray Krieger, and R. W. B. Lewis are critics who do not, of course, publicly express allegiance to any kind of religious orthodoxy, and I do not intend even slightly to suggest that they are, in some sense, proto-Christians: indeed they would themselves perhaps be a little astonished, or even indignant, were it to be proposed to them that theirs is an effort that in any way trenches upon even an implicitly theological order of valuation. But whatever may be the terms in which they choose to understand themselves, these critics, and many others, are very definitely pushing beyond the kind

[2] Leslie Fiedler, "Toward an Amateur Criticism," *The Kenyon Review*, Vol. XII, No. 4 (Autumn, 1950), p. 564.

of territory which the New Criticism was so ably colonizing at an earlier time. They do not intend merely to abandon the rich result of those shrewd researches into the nature of poetic language and meaning and structure that were conducted by the New Criticism; but they are very much bent on complicating and deepening the poetics of the immediate past by more radically committing literary criticism to various types of "existential" analysis. They make us feel that, for them, the critic's vocation reaches far beyond subtle exercises in dialectic and in grammar and syntax, and theirs is a criticism that, increasingly, is being guided by the recognition that, though the literary work is a special sort of linguistic structure, that which holds the highest interest for us is the special seizure of reality which this structure is instrumental toward: the nature of literature itself, in other words, is felt to require the critic finally to move beyond the level of purely verbal and stylistic analysis to the level of metaphysical and theological valuation. And, when it is recalled that the new tendency in criticism has been accompanied by an even more decisive reinstatement of religious themes and preoccupations in the poetry and fiction and drama of the last twenty-five years, we are by way of taking some measure of how pervasive is the religious interest in the literary life of our time.

The world of faith and the world of literary art, in other words, are, more and more, converging upon each other, and their chief strategists are busily attempting to discover the lines along which it will be most fruitful for the dialogue to proceed. Among professional critics of literature who are guided by a theological orientation, one thinks, for example, in Roman Catholic circles, of the "anti-Gnosticism" of Father William Lynch,[3] of the existentialist personalism of Father Walter Ong,[4] or of the critique of "angelism" that Allen Tate was moving toward in the early fifties in *The Forlorn*

[3] See William F. Lynch, S.J., *Christ and Apollo: The Dimensions of the Literary Imagination* (New York: Sheed & Ward, 1960).

[4] See Walter J. Ong, S.J., *The Barbarian Within* (New York: The Macmillan Co., 1962), Part I.

Demon (Chicago: Henry Regnery Co., 1953). Among Anglicans, Father Martin Jarrett-Kerr's writings[5] and much of my own work[6] furnish examples of the critical effort being clearly undertaken from a theological perspective. And, in Protestant circles, Amos Wilder is the chief representative of an effort being carried forward by many others.[7]

It is significant too that theological education itself begins to be a part of this whole background of ferment and burgeoning enterprise. Over the last decade elaborate programs of study in theology and the arts have come into existence in the Divinity School of the University of Chicago, at Union Theological Seminary in New York City, and in many of the other leading centers of theological education. The younger clergy, one sometimes feels, are reading Faulkner and Auden and Camus as avidly as they are reading Tillich and Bultmann. In parish churches all over the country discussion groups of young people are to be found attempting, through the study of imaginative literature, to probe the issues of faith in relation to modern experience. And the various branches of the Student Christian Movement have, increasingly in recent years, been moving into this area in their study programs.

To all these developments in the Christian community there are also many significant analogues in the world of secular humanistic scholarship. In the English departments of many of our leading colleges and universities, specialist scholars are frequently today being brought onto staffs where their primary responsibility is for the conduct of studies in the religious dimensions of literature. A few years ago the English Institute, which meets annually for a week at Colum-

[5] Martin Jarrett-Kerr, C.R., *D. H. Lawrence and Human Existence* (London: Rockliff, 1951); *François Mauriac* (Cambridge: Bowes & Bowes, 1953); and *Studies in Literature and Belief* (London: Rockliff, 1954).

[6] Nathan A. Scott, Jr., *Modern Literature and the Religious Frontier* (New York: Harper & Bros., 1958); and *Albert Camus* (London: Bowes & Bowes, 1962).

[7] Amos N. Wilder, *Modern Poetry and the Christian Tradition* (New York: Charles Scribner's Sons, 1952); and *Theology and Modern Literature* (Cambridge: Harvard University Press, 1958).

bia University, devoted a series of sessions to an exploration of the relation between literature and belief, and the brilliant volume of papers which resulted from these conversations marks one of the most significant recent contributions to the growing literature in this field.[8] In the annual meetings of the Modern Language Association (the leading professional organization of college and university teachers of literature in the United States), there is now a regularly established section devoted to "Religion and Literature." And one could cite numerous other interesting expressions of how deeply the dialogue between faith and the literary imagination is taking root at the present time.

So it seems not at all inaccurate to say that one of the chief new frontiers of concern in contemporary intellectual life is that on which the central issue has to do with what is involved in the whole transaction between the Christian faith and the world of modern literature. And it is hoped that the several studies which make up this book will to some extent advance the inquiry that is now in progress. We offer them not at all as any sort of definitive statement but, rather, as an interim report on how the engagement seems presently to be moving. And it is also to be hoped that, if, in the next few years, they have become a period piece, this will be because the *rapprochement* between art and faith will have then surpassed anything that is here envisaged.

Finally, I should like to express my personal thanks to the contributors: they have, in every way, been helpful to me, and I am grateful for their generous collaboration.

NATHAN A. SCOTT, JR.

[8] M. H. Abrams, editor, *Literature and Belief* (New York: Columbia University Press, 1958).

The Climate of Faith in Modern Literature

Faith and Art in a World Awry

BY NATHAN A. SCOTT, JR.

IT MAY well have been established in another few years that the most significant development in American theological life during the 1950's was the displacement of an earlier social passion by a new concern for the more purely humanistic dimensions of culture. A brilliant young social scientist at the University of California, in a massive study of the American theological climate in this century, has suggested that theological thought has lately been attempting to impregnate and deepen itself with the themes of modern literature and the arts, because it has found the artist's methods of rendering "the dramas of childhood, of sexual life, of work . . . [to be] methods for correlation with theology that could help overcome the frustration" [1] felt by the religious enterprise in a time of fundamental political impasse. And here, unquestionably, is, in large part, the root of the matter. For the arts, and most especially the arts of literature, can "render and evoke experience in a detail, an intimacy, and an intensity both dangerous and almost impossible in politics." [2] And it may even be, as Professor Meyer suggests, that the widespread preoccupation with the modern arts today among Christian interpreters of culture bespeaks an intention to allow the heroic impulse to discharge itself in realms where creative risks of self-definition may be more safely taken than in the hot, explosive furnace of mid-century politics. It would, of

[1] Donald B. Meyer, *The Protestant Search for Political Realism: 1919-1941* (Berkeley and Los Angeles: University of California Press, 1960), p. 412.
[2] *Ibid.*

course, be unfortunate if this development were to encourage any simple abdication from politics in the religious community; but since it has not as yet, in any demonstrable way, had this effect, its advent surely deserves acknowledgment as a most wholesome sign of fresh redintegration in the Church's mission to a whole department of culture which for too long it ignored.

There is, however, one aspect of this insurgency which deserves to be put under some critical pressure, and it is the increasingly recurrent expression of confidence in the possibility and in the imperativeness of developing a "Christian philosophy of art" under whose standards this whole new development may gain its proper enfranchisement. I cannot on this present occasion proceed to explicate, within the compass of a brief essay, the theological grounds from which my own reservations about this kind of project stem. And so, therefore, it must simply suffice for me flatly to say that I do not conceive it to be the business of the man whom Kierkegaard called "the knight of faith" to bully the world into granting its suffrage to some special system of propositions of his own invention: he does not come into this world from another world, like a *deus ex machina*, with a marvelous formula that can unlock all the entanglements of human culture. No, he lives in the historical order like all his fellows: the resource on which he relies is simply that "new hope and strength which he is given in this world because of what has been done [of God] in and for this world." [3] And having this resource, his vocation is to live, as his Master lived, in solicitude for, and in openness to, the men to whom he is related by the particular moment in history in which he happens to stand.

The Christian scholar faces, in other words, the same world that is faced by all other men. It is, I believe, the most outrageous kind of arrogance for him to assume that his faith

[3] Ronald Gregor Smith, *The New Man: Christianity and Man's Coming of Age* (New York: Harper & Bros., 1956), p. 59.

provides him with some sort of privileged perspective by means of which he can integrate internally the various fields of culture, and then assign to each its proper place in some tidily comprehensive arrangement that will be a Christian map of the modern mind. Indeed, for him even to attempt to produce some special *speculum mentis* for his brethren in the faith is for him profoundly to misunderstand the nature of the intellectual situation in which he must today do his work. And, here, surely the endless multiplication of metaphors based on the "I-Thou" philosophy of Martin Buber is something which itself witnesses to a deep and pervasive intuition among the most sensitive men of our age, that the fragmentation of modern intellectual life commits us irrevocably to an ethos of encounter and to the stance of attentiveness and listening.

It is, I take it, the recognition of precisely this that lies behind Roger Hazelton's recent definition of what the theological enterprise must entail in our time. He turns to the physiological image of the systole and diastole of the human heart and suggests that the work of the Christian theologian is, in a way, analogous to the alternate expansions and contractions of the heart. "There are times," he says, "when Christian faith has to turn inward upon itself, asking what is authentically and ultimately its own kind of truth. Then theology becomes an essay in self-discovery and self-definition." [4] But then there are other times when "it becomes imperative for theologians to move out into the world again, on the basis of this self-understanding, seeking out and coming to grips with those modes of truth from which earlier they had strategically withdrawn." [5] And Dr. Hazelton is alert to the fact that it is into this second phase that the theological community is moving today. Nor does he see the reasons for this as being wholly cultural in character, for he takes careful

[4] Roger Hazelton, *New Accents in Contemporary Theology* (New York: Harper & Bros., 1960), p. 11.

[5] *Ibid.*, p. 12.

cognizance of what it is in the nature of Christian faith itself that requires the attitude of attentiveness and listening to the world of culture. "Living within the circle of faith," he says, "involves the most drastic sort of exposure to unwelcome experience and unfamiliar truth. It finds charity and hope to be not simply moral but also intellectual virtues." [6]

And since Christ is the Lord of all the world and not only of those who believe in his name, it would behoove the Christian in his intellectual existence not to segregate himself from anyone and not to suppose that he has been given exclusive charge of the truth about any segment of human reality. The Christian scholar, in other words, had better not come prancing into the forums of our cultural life with a Christian system of aesthetics or with a Christian system of psychology or with a Christian system of anything else. For the world is one, the same for the Christian as for all other men of whatever persuasion: if Christ is truly the *Logos*, then he is witnessed to in all apprehensions of truth, whether they occur within a framework of Christian concern or not. And, this being the case, the Christian theologian will not be in a hurry to sponsor any particular system as *the* necessarily Christian way of ordering the data in a given field of inquiry. For he will understand that the most fundamental issue for Christian thought pertains not to any conceptual structure at all but rather, as Professor Ronald Gregor Smith of Glasgow has recently said, to the question, "Whence do we receive?" [7]

So, then, rather than attempting to put forward anything that might be called a "Christian philosophy of art," it may well be that the more important task for a Christian philosophy of culture at the present time is, first of all, that of clearly discerning what in fact the function of art truly is and how it may co-operate with the kind of imagination of reality that is authentically Christian. Then, in addition to basic ques-

[6] *Ibid.*

[7] Ronald Gregor Smith, "A Theological Perspective of the Secular," *The Christian Scholar*, 1960, XLIII, 14.

tions of this sort, it may well be also that careful consideration deserves to be given to the particular respects wherein the present *malaise* of the modern artist is itself something which is pregnant with fruitful possibility for the religious situation in our time.

Now, when one bluntly asks what it is the ultimate office of art to do, it is important to avoid at least one of the answers which has continually recurred in the history of aesthetics; and this is the doctrine which, in one way or another, asserts that a work of art is an expression of the artist's subjectivity or, as it has often been put, of his emotion. The perennial attractiveness of this doctrine is doubtless in large part a result of the fact that we know both the creative process and the aesthetic experience to be suffused with emotion; and when, in a particular case, the work of art is of unquestioned greatness, it does indeed very often stem from, and elicit, emotion of the intensest sort. But, however much emotion may be a factor both in the act of artistic creation and in the act of aesthetic appreciation, the fact remains that, finally, all emotionalist theories of art are both internally illogical and essentially untrue to the experience that we actually have, when we are in the presence of a work of art that is capable of deeply engaging the imagination. The emotionalist theory is internally illogical because it succeeds in doing precisely what it is unreasonable to expect an aesthetic theory to do—namely, to dissolve itself into some field of discourse that is not aesthetical but something else. That is to say, in viewing the work of art as significant because of what it tells us about the emotional condition of the artist, an expressionist aesthetic is always tending to convert aesthetics into a branch of psychology and thus to destroy the vital nerve of its own integrity as an independent field of humanistic inquiry. And I speak of the emotionalist theory of art as untrue to our profoundest aesthetic experience because I am convinced that this is a kind of experience which we deem to be of such high importance not at all by reason of any information it conveys about the artist.

For what is exhilarating in the encounter that we have with an authentic work of art is always the clarification and deepening that we feel in our perception of the realities that constitute our world environment. The aesthetic experience might be said always to involve an experience of what Paul Tillich calls "the shock of being," [8] and this may be why Jacques Maritain tells us that "poetry is ontology." [9]

But, of course, when Maritain speaks of poetry as a kind of ontology, he does not intend to imply that the operation which the poet performs is identical, in its kind or agency, with the operation that is performed by the philosopher. For, unlike the philosopher, the poet does not deal with *generalizations* about anything at all: his mode of statement, as Susanne Langer says, is a "non-discursive" mode.[10] He does not talk, for example, about the mortality of the human creature with the funereal air of a young parson: no, Shakespeare simply says:

> Golden lads and girls all must,
> As chimney-sweepers, come to dust.

Nor does he talk about the internal complications of the mind in the labored, discursive manner of the academic psychologist: no, Gerard Manley Hopkins tells us:

> O the mind, mind has mountains; cliffs of fall
> Frightful, sheer, no-man-fathomed. Hold them cheap
> May who ne'er hung there. Nor does long our small
> Durance deal with that steep or deep. . . .

Which is to say that it is the poet's purpose to expose us to the stark irrevocability of things as they are. And "things" is the word we must use, for it is with things that the poetic transaction is carried on, since, as I suspect, it is in them that

[8] Paul Tillich, *The Protestant Era* (Chicago: University of Chicago Press, 1948), p. 85; also *Systematic Theology*, I (Chicago: University of Chicago Press, 1951), pp. 110-115 and p. 163.

[9] Jacques Maritain, *Art and Scholasticism* (New York: Charles Scribner's Sons, 1943), pp. 87-122.

[10] Susanne Langer, *Feeling and Form* (New York: Charles Scribner's Sons, 1953), Chapter 13.

Being has its location. If we may borrow an excellent term from Langmead Casserley, it might be said that it is the habit of the poet to be fascinated with "the singular" [11]—the particular event, the unrepeatable experience, the unique reality. "The texture of poetry is of actual things," says Father McCarron in his fine little essay, *Realization*.[12] And we should not forget that Homer dealt with the ocean and Wordsworth with the farm land and Hopkins with "the dearest freshness deep down things." And so too has the imagination of all true poets been captured by things, by that which is *other than* the human mind. Indeed, it is "the wonder and mystery of art," as it is also of religion in the last resort, that it "is the revelation of something 'wholly other' by which the inexpressible loneliness of thinking is broken and enriched." [13] Poetry, characteristically, handles not universals but, rather, the individual aspects of reality. It "uncovers for us the character of particular things in the starkness and strangeness of their being what they are." [14] And this is why the scientist and the philosopher who conceives of philosophy as a handmaiden of science tend to view the poet with misgivings, for he remains incorrigibly devoted to the celebration of that rich complexity of the singular which always resists domestication within the abstract systems of scientific and philosophic ideas. We have long said that poetry's great gift to man is what the Greeks called *katharsis*, and it may well be that that experience involves, fundamentally, the profound relief that is to be had when we succeed in simply contemplating the intractable givenness of reality, as it transcends all our scientific, philosophic propositions about it and our efforts at poetic evocation of it, making its majesty known through what Hegel called the "concrete universal."

[11] J. V. Langmead Casserley, *The Christian in Philosophy* (London: Faber and Faber Ltd., 1949), *passim*.

[12] Hugh McCarron, *Realization: A Philosophy of Poetry* (London: Sheed & Ward, 1937), p. 35.

[13] H. D. Lewis, *Morals and Revelation* (London: George Allen and Unwin Ltd., 1951), p. 241.

[14] *Ibid.*, p. 212.

Now, of course, modern aestheticians since Kant have often said something quite different about art—namely (as A. C. Bradley put it), that "its nature is to be not a part, nor yet a copy, of the real world . . . but to be a world by itself, independent, complete, autonomous." [15] And this too is true. Indeed, we here come upon what is perhaps the central paradox that art presents. For, on the one hand, we must never forget that it does establish a world of its own and, as Bradley said, "to possess it fully, you must enter that world, conform to its laws, and ignore for the time the beliefs, aims, and particular conditions which belong to you in the other world of reality." [16] But then, on the other hand, it is equally true (and true perhaps in a very much larger order of magnitude) that the greatest and most vital art always drives us beyond itself and makes us contemplate anew, with a shock of discovery, the permanence and glory and strangeness of the circumambient world. Its purpose is to stir and quicken within us an awareness of realities that impinge upon us from beyond ourselves. It wants, as it were, to make all things new, in order that we might marvel at the sheer thereness of them, at the fact that they exist in one way rather than in a thousand other possible ways. "To know facts as facts in the ordinary way has, indeed, no particular power or worth. But," as Professor H. D. Lewis says, "a quickening of our awareness of the irrevocability by which a thing is what it is has such power, and it is . . . the very soul of art." [17] For the artist, as Marianne Moore puts it, is a "literalist of the imagination" who presents "for inspection 'imaginary gardens with real toads in them.' " [18] Which is to say that, though he creates a kind of fiction, it is a fiction intended to be a vehicle by means of which there may be enforced upon us a haunting

[15] A. C. Bradley, *Oxford Lectures on Poetry* (London: Macmillan and Co., Ltd., 1909), p. 5.

[16] *Ibid.*

[17] H. D. Lewis, *op. cit.*, p. 241.

[18] Marianne Moore, "Poetry," *Collected Poems* (New York: The Macmillan Co., 1951), p. 41.

sense of some "otherness in reality" [19] which impinges upon us and with which we must risk a confrontation.

Now I wonder if it is not precisely this sense of "otherness in reality" to which religious faith itself conduces. Ronald Gregor Smith tells us that our ultimate theological concern has to do with what is not ourselves, "with what [we] . . . do not and never can possess at all . . . with what comes to [us] . . . all the time from beyond [ourselves]." [20] And this is indeed the import of vital religion. Becket, in T. S. Eliot's *Murder in the Cathedral,* says at one point:

> . . . Only
> The fool, fixed in his folly, may think
> He can turn the wheel on which he turns.[21]

And it is some such realization as this that all great religion promotes: it brings us news of a reality beyond all the extremities of human thought and calculation, and it speaks of a world which moves to "a rhythm which is neither the strophe nor the antistrophe of our mortal music." [22] So, though a certain kind of philistine hostility to the arts may sometimes fob itself off as carrying some sort of religious sanction, the truth of the matter is that both art and religious faith share a common intention to summon us into the presence of what is other than and transcendent to the human mind; and in this, they provide each other with a kind of mutual confirmation.

But, in the particular kind of faith that Christianity posits, it is not simply sheer *otherness* that is confronted, however much the early teachings of Karl Barth may have seemed to represent this as being the Christian's situation. For, in the world of Christian experience, the *otherness* which confronts and which challenges man becomes luminously trans-

[19] H. D. Lewis, *op. cit.*, p. 242.

[20] Ronald Gregor Smith, in *The Christian Scholar, op. cit.*, p. 15.

[21] T. S. Eliot, *Murder in the Cathedral* (New York: Harcourt, Brace and Co., 1935), p. 24.

[22] M. Chaning-Pearce, *The Terrible Crystal* (New York: Oxford University Press, 1941), p. 143.

parent in the incarnate Word of God which was Jesus Christ himself. Which is to say that, for the Christian imagination, the ultimate reality—which is the reality of God—is disclosed in the person and in the life of Jesus Christ. And this means that, when human life is understood within the terms of the Christian faith, the primary axiom of all thought henceforward becomes the premise that the full grandeur and mystery of man are known only in Jesus Christ and that indeed the infinite majesty and graciousness of God are fully known only in Jesus Christ. In him all Christian reflection finds its basic fulcrum, for he is the transparent center and focus of that disturbing *otherness* which surrounds us and pursues us and requires of us an appropriate acknowledgment.

Now there is no one in recent years to whom I have been more indebted for deepening my understanding of this central reality of Christian faith than to Dietrich Bonhoeffer, the gifted young German theologian who was executed by the Nazis in the spring of 1945. And what above all else I owe to Bonhoeffer is the realization that what we meet in Jesus Christ is not the old metaphysical riddle of how the two natures, the divine and the human, could coinhere in one person. Nor should it be supposed that Bonhoeffer's refusal to fidget over this ancient puzzle was the result of any intellectual indolence which made him want to find excuses for evading the hard, exacting labor of reading the history of Christian theology. Indeed, it was just as a result of the most careful study of the theological tradition that he reached a conclusion the revolutionary consequences of which for Christian thought in our time are only beginning to be felt. And that conclusion was that, on this one point, the tradition has often been woefully misguided: for, said he, what we meet in Jesus Christ is not a metaphysical enigma but the simple fact of a human life that was totally pledged in responsibility for others, a life indeed so concentrated in the selflessness of its concern for all other life that it had the consequence of disclosing to the community of faith the tremendous fact that in his life the essential structure of all life had been revealed. And to this essential structure of responsible life as bound to man and to God, Bonhoeffer applied the term "deputyship." For this, he declared, is the form that life takes when it is lived responsibly: one person or one group of persons acts *for* another: when a "father acts for the children, working for them, caring for them, interceding, fighting and suffering for them . . . in a real sense he is their deputy." [23] Indeed, whenever and wherever life surrenders itself in obedience to the needs and claims of other life, there you have "deputyship." And here, said Bonhoeffer, is the essential truth about Jesus Christ, that he "lived in deputyship for us as the incarnate Son of God," and, since "his living, his action and his dying was deputyship," in him we have "the responsible person *par excellence*": "in him there is fulfilled what the living, the action and the suffering of [all] men ought to be." [24]

So, then, when St. Paul in his epistle to the Philippians (1:21) tells us that "to me to live is Christ," he is simply saying, both for himself and for other men, that insofar as we do truly live, we live in and through Christ, for he *is* life. Which is to say that life is deputyship or, as it is put by Martin Buber, with his remarkable, intuitive sense for things implicitly Christian, real life is "meeting." [25] This is what Christ reveals the fundamental form of reality to be, and faith, as Bonhoeffer taught us to understand, is not so much believing difficult propositions about something or other as it is life lived in "correspondence" with the form that Christ disclosed reality to have: the real man is "the man for others."

Now I have spoken of the dimension of otherness into which we are brought by both art and religious faith. But, as I have said, in the Christian apprehension of reality, this is an otherness whose secret is disclosed in the person and in

[23] Dietrich Bonhoeffer, *Ethics*, trans. by Neville Horton Smith and ed. by Eberhard Bethge (New York: The Macmillan Co., 1955), p. 192.

[24] *Ibid*., p. 195.

[25] Martin Buber, *I and Thou*, trans. by Ronald Gregor Smith (Edinburgh: T. & T. Clark, 1937), *passim*.

the life of Jesus Christ. For in him the Christian imagination beholds the fundamental form of reality—which, adopting a central term of the late Charles Williams, we may call "exchange";[26] or, following the Jew Martin Buber, "meeting"; or following Dietrich Bonhoeffer, we may call "deputyship," or, as he sometimes spoke of it, "life together."

When, however, we move from any authentically Christian account of things to that which is recorded in the most important art and literature of our period, it becomes immediately apparent that here a quite different form of reality is presented as normative in human experience. Not "life together," but life fractured and broken into isolateness and solitude and loneliness—these are the realities which make up the special kind of pathos that we meet in the representative art of our time.

From the painting of this century one recalls, for example—and inevitably—the great Cubist canvases of the early Picasso in which the human image is either shattered utterly or is forsaken altogether for the *pastiche* of newspaper clippings and odd bits of junk extracted from some scrap heap. Or there are those dreadful and wonderfully fascinating double-faced images which he was painting in the 1930's and which figure forth the awful dragons of the inner life which must be captured in us all. And then there is that beautiful and horrible immensity in black and white, the *Guernica* mural, which brings to a kind of climax the scenes of disorder which the artists of our time have painted, a canvas which is ostensibly about a particular moment in the modern agony but which, once we have really confronted it, makes us know that it is about the whole eschatological furnace of our age. It has sometimes been said that what is most essential in Picasso is a "taste for paroxysm," but, in a way, this seems also to be what is most essential in such men as Kokoschka and de Chirico and Beckmann and Rouault who were his

[26] Charles Williams, *The Image of the City—And Other Essays,* selected by Anne Ridler (London: Oxford University Press, 1958), Section V.

contemporaries and in the generation of Pollock and de Kooning and Francis Bacon whose vision is felt with especial immediacy at the present time. Indeed, these and many others have often been navigators negotiating a voyage that has skirted most narrowly the brink of the chaos which has threatened to overwhelm us all.

And not only have our painters fought battles with the dragons of the inner life, but so too have our poets and our novelists. It is "a century of homelessness and exile, of nervous disorder and persecution, of actual enslavement and barbaric cruelty."[27] And it should therefore be no occasion of surprise when these are the things that we encounter in our literature. Here is a sentence, for example, from a novel (*On This Side Nothing*) by the English writer Alex Comfort, and it takes us immediately into the kind of ethos which the representative writers of our age have been exploring: "I saw the same fear in her face that I should have felt if a stranger called at night, the world-wide twentieth-century fear which one sees wherever one knocks unexpectedly at any door." And this is the face of the contemporary hero, whether one encounters him in the plays of Beckett and Ionesco or in the novels of Camus and William Golding and John Hawkes or in the poetry of Robert Penn Warren and Gottfried Benn. There are, to be sure, here and there, a few writers—like Eliot and Edith Sitwell of the older generation, or Auden and Christopher Fry of the middle generation, or Robert Lowell of a slightly younger group—who are sustained and governed by a traditional faith. But by far the great majority of those on the contemporary scene who exemplify "our period style" are writers who live in much the same *ambiance* as that with which we associate the great classic moderns, Kafka and Pound and Joyce and Hemingway. For the fundamental form of the human reality, as they report upon it, is that of disruption and anxiety and nostalgia and loneliness.

[27] Ralph Harper, *The Sleeping Beauty* (New York: Harper & Bros., n.d.), p. 15.

So when, therefore, the Christian community faces the whole body of testimony issuing from much of the great art of the modern period, it is confronted by a diametrical opposition between the form of reality that it knows to be the true norm of human existence and that which tends generally to be cited by the artists of our time. Yet surely it would be a great mistake for churchmen simply to reject this testimony and to withdraw into the certitudes of those theologians who write systems of Church dogmatics and who expatiate on "the divine-human encounter." Indeed, were this to be the prevailing Christian response to the modern movement in art, nothing would more tellingly indicate that ours is today a Church which has forgotten the Cross and all that it implies for Christian participation in the life of culture. For if the Church is an "extension and perpetuation of the Incarnation in the world" [28]—and Bishop Gore's formula has, I suppose, at best but a limited usefulness[29]—then its relation to the world must be wholly governed by God's relation to the world, as this was disclosed in Christ himself, and most especially in his Crucifixion. The Church, in other words, is the community that lives under the Cross—which is to say that it is the community which knows the fundamental form of reality to be that of deputyship, of living and acting for others. It is, of course, the community in which there is knowledge of the "last things," of the fact that the final and ultimate word to be pronounced on the human situation is that man shall be justified by grace and faith alone. But, when it seeks the kind of profound identification with the world that the message of the Crucifixion demands, it may then, for the very sake of the ultimate truth about human existence, choose not to speak about the last things but rather to open itself up to what Dietrich Bonhoeffer called "the things which go before

[28] Charles Gore, *The Incarnation of the Son of God* (London: John Murray, 1891), p. 219.

[29] The formula's usefulness is limited because, though it does a rough kind of justice to the doctrine of the Mystical Body, it very seriously fails to make adequate provision for the Church itself being under judgment.

the last things"—that is, to those penultimate expressions of humanity which are the real *preparatio* for the Gospel of Jesus Christ.[30] Indeed, the Christian community should never fail to heed Bonhoeffer's wise warning against speaking of the last things too soon. "I don't think it is Christian," he said, "to want to get to the New Testament too soon and too directly."[31] And what he meant is simply that, if the Christian community closets itself in safety away from what is broken and problematic in human life, then the ultimate message of the Gospel will never be grasped in its *relevance* to man's deepest predicaments. Christ's coming in grace, in other words, is, to be sure, the very last thing, but we shall perceive the power and the appositeness of this ultimacy only insofar as we remain attentive to everything that is penultimate in the human story.

So, therefore, on the particular frontier of culture which is here in view, the task of those who are custodians of the Christian faith in our time is not, I think, to invent something called a Christian *philosophy* of art and thus to add to the babel of conflicting *philosophies* which so much oppresses us today. We shall want, I should think, a vigorous Christian criticism in the various fields of art, and there are signs, particularly in the field of literature, that this effort is beginning to be undertaken with intelligence and discrimination. But a Christian philosophy of art, in the sense of a systematic phenomenology of aesthetic facts which consistently proceeds from Christian presuppositions—this is hardly an immediate prospect; and there may well be difficult jurisdictional questions of a theoretical order that in principle rule out even the possibility of such a project. But, were it theoretically possible and were it something which we might expect the best theological intelligence of our day in time to deliver, I should still, from a strategic standpoint, question its real value

[30] Dietrich Bonhoeffer, *op. cit.*, pp. 84-91.

[31] Dietrich Bonhoeffer, *Letters and Papers from Prison*, ed. by Eberhard Bethge and trans. by Reginald H. Fuller (London: SCM Press Ltd., 1953), p. 79.

at this particular juncture of our cultural situation. For that which is, I believe, most needed is for theological interpreters to keep the Church alive to what it is in the nature of its own faith that requires it to be attentive to all the somber reports and prophecies and maledictions which the arts in our time are uttering. And, if this effort is attended with success, so that the Christian community does really appear once again to be a community of *deputyship*, of those who are *for others*, then it may well be that the artist may be persuaded to move beyond what is *penultimate*, to the things that are really *the last things*.

Theology and Literature: The Terms of the Dialogue on the Modern Scene

BY JOHN MC GILL KRUMM

CHRISTIAN FAITH and all forms of cultural creativity are closely allied expressions of the human spirit, and their innumerable interactions and interpenetrations are of the keenest interest both to the theologian and to the creative artist. This is so because of the nature both of the Christian world outlook and of the aim and ambition of the serious creative artist. Christianity, by its teaching about creation and redemption, commits itself to sympathetic and genuine interest in whatever fascinates, exercises, or excites the human mind. The ultimate aim is, of course, often stated in imperial terms, as when St. Paul announces bluntly, "We make every mind surrender to Christ's service" (II Cor. 10:5, Knox translation). But in the service of Christ there is perfect freedom, and Christianity proposes not to impose a crippling inhibition upon culture but to enable it to see more clearly the whole truth about man and his world and to express it more sensitively and compellingly. Inasmuch as it is a religion of the Incarnation, Christianity is obliged to accept the setting of the intellectual and cultural situation in which it finds itself as the divinely ordained milieu in which to preach, to teach, to convert, and to save. Dr. Cragg has said recently: "The Gospel of the Word made flesh must be intelligibly told. Those who tell it must be prepared to reckon with the mental world of other men in which it is understood or—as often as not—misunderstood. From that world, the listener's world, comes the framework of ideas within which, at least initially, the new thing is judged. If witness is really translation, speaking to one realm the riches of another, it must attend like all other translations, both to what it says and how it goes." [1] Christianity does not prescribe in advance the kind of mental and cultural setting in which it will condescend to speak its message. By the example of its Lord, it is impelled to relate itself to men precisely where they are—in the midst of their convictions, their passions, their doubts, their despair, their faith. "In the beginning was the Word," says St. John's Gospel, "and the Word was made flesh and dwelt among us, and we beheld his glory, the glory as of the only begotten of the Father, full of grace and truth." But the Divine Word takes form in human words, and these human words exist in a rich context of meaning in which men believe and by which they live. Those who bear responsibility for proclaiming the Word made flesh must be attuned to the words which, in the situation to which they speak, move and persuade and convince. Even a suspicious Tertullian who asks scornfully, "What has Athens to do with Jerusalem?" will recognize that at the very least Athens provides the structure of the enemy's attack and for that reason compels the respectful attention of the soldier of Christ.

From the other side of the dialogue it is increasingly recognized that an expression of cultural creativity is almost inevitably religious in its scope and ambition. That is to say, the artist seeks to delineate a broad and inclusive meaning in human experience, to open up panoramic perspectives by which to discriminate and to understand it. A typical expression of this ambition is to be found, for example, in a statement by Jean-Paul Sartre, in which he recorded his purpose—and that of other new playwrights of France—"to explore the

[1] Kenneth Cragg, *Sandals at the Mosque, Christian Presence amid Islam* (London: SCM Press, 1959), p. 94.

state of man in its entirety and to present to the modern man a portrait of himself, his problems, his hopes and his struggles. . . . If that theatre is to address the masses, it must speak in terms of their most general preoccupations, dispelling their anxieties in the form of myths which anyone can understand and feel deeply." [2] It is for this reason that men are prone to make more sweeping claims for their artistic creativity than they make, for example, for their technology or their politics. "Art for art's sake" is a plausible proposition—at least in Western ears—in a way that "automation for automation's sake" or "civil rights for civil rights' sake" is not. Cultural creativity seeks to encompass the totality of the human situation in a way that the physical or the behavioral sciences do not. There is an inwardness about the artist which affiliates him more closely with the theologian than with the scientist or politician. Whatever his conception of theological truth, the artist is at least prepared to concede the relevance of religious questions for an understanding of the human situation. The artist is potentially either the theologian's closest collaborator or his most dangerous antagonist, since like the theologian he stakes out a broad and deep claim for concern and for relevance. Because both are moving with lofty ambition in what is in many ways the same territory, they seem destined to meet and to meet frequently. This book is intended to sketch out the sort of exchanges that seem likely to take place on such occasions.

One point at which Christian faith and literary creativity converge is a sensitivity to the problem of language. Biblical religion knows a God who speaks, whose word comes to his prophets and accomplishes that for which it is spoken. Biblical religion, in other words, is not so ineffable that it cannot be expressed. A word is a legitimate and inevitable expression of divine purpose. The prophet is bidden to speak and to write, and by these means men are sufficiently warned, re-

[2] Cited by Henri Peyre, in Preface to Jean-Paul Sartre, *The Condemned of Altona*, trans. by Sylvia and George Leeson (New York: Knopf, 1961), p. xii.

buked, directed, assured. The experience of Isaiah in the Temple in the year King Uzziah died is characteristic of Biblical religion. The vision of God is a soul-shaking and awesome one. "His train filled the Temple. . . . The posts of the door moved . . . and the house was filled with smoke." God is transcendent, holy, inexpressible in glory and majesty and power. But as Biblical religion understands the divine purpose, this is not the end of the matter. The overwhelming sense of God's magnificence is not the goal of the encounter. From the blazing center of the vision come a voice, intelligible words, a reassurance that though human lips are unclean and quite incapable of expressing the full meaning of the vision, nevertheless by the divine cleansing and burning they may become vehicles of the infinite and ultimate message of God. At the end of his vision Isaiah receives a commission to speak on God's behalf—even though the consequences of the speaking will be a closing of ears and eyes and mind by those who are addressed.

The account of Isaiah's call expresses two things clearly: the power of words and their inadequacy. This power and inadequacy are also known to literary creativity. The word can evoke and point to great realities which transcend ordinary experience. It has power to draw men into participation in aspects of life that would otherwise have remained closed to them. Words can capture loyalty, fire imagination, kindle devotion, sear the conscience. Yet words on occasion are snares; they take the place of action; they make a pretense but no reality lurks within them. They can lie inert and lifeless on a page. They stumble where they should flow. They sound hollow where they should vibrate with life. At the climax of the drama of divine revelation in the Apocalypse, when the seventh seal has been broken, the writer, resourceful though he was in language, records that there was silence in heaven for the space of a half-hour (cf. Rev. 8:1). In the same way, all great theologians and masters of the spiritual life have extolled the virtue of the *via negativa,* the way of renunciation of language and symbol, as a way of recognizing the inadequacy of words. "Our safest eloquence concerning Him," says Richard Hooker, "is our silence." Much theological language is in effect a renunciation of language. "Infinite" rejects the word "limit" as applicable to the Deity. "Immense" repudiates the idea of "measurement" in respect to him. Words are powerful, inevitable, necessary. Words are also earthbound, often powerless, and lifeless.

Biblical religion does not conclude from this awareness of the misleading character of words that they must be eschewed, but that they must be employed with a recognition of the gulf which separates them from the reality to which they point. The principle of theological epistemology, which is called "analogy," acknowledges frankly and fully both the inadequacy and the inevitability of language, and in so doing frees the theologian to join the literary artist in the most luxurious employment of vivid and concrete imagery. Unless one grasps the principle of analogy, such imagery will always be subject to the condemnation of irreverence and blasphemy. Fear of such condemnation leads the theologian who has not grasped the meaning of analogy to the employment of only the most abstract and sterilized words for the communication of religious meaning. However clarifying such language may be, however comprehensible it may render the truth it seeks to express—by its generalizing and classifying—it notoriously lacks the passion and power which evoke responses of devotion and commitment. The language of "infinity" and "immensity" and "impassability" has its place in technical theology; it does not usually feed the souls of spiritually hungry men. The theologian who uses it is quite properly aware of the transcendence of God and the inadequacy of ordinary human words to convey his reality and holiness and power. But unless the theologian can link this insight to descriptive words that relate God to the tangible and palpable world, his theology will evaporate into the rarefied air from which it came. By the principle of analogy the theologian is led to see that he who is inexpressible, high, and lifted up and whose thoughts are not our thoughts, is nevertheless not wholly misrepresented in human similes such as Father, Bridegroom, King, Rescuer, Teacher, and the like.

Cultural creativity and Christian faith find common cause also in a rejection of the adequacy of what has come to be called "scientific" descriptions of reality. Basil Willey in the *Seventeenth Century Background* has shown how the determination of science at that time to deal with what is measurable and verifiable by experimentation was a declaration of war upon the claims of poetry to convey "profound intuitions and glimpses of 'truth.'" Willey quotes Thomas Sprat's *History of the Royal Society*, in which the aim of the society's founders is stated thus: "They have endeavored to separate the knowledge of Nature from the colours of Rhetorick, the devices of Fancy, or the delightful deceit of Fables." The seventeenth-century assumption that all really important things can be discovered and known without recourse to what we should now call—without any derogatory implication—mythological truth is an assumption that would be widely challenged today by Christian theologians; also by poets, novelists, and dramatists; and by an influential school of modern philosophy which acknowledges the penetrating and illuminating power of symbols. The Biblical understanding of nature as sacramental in principle opens up a whole new dimension in nature which is never taken into account in scientific analysis and description. This Biblical sacramentalism appears in modern literature but oftentimes it borders on a kind of pantheistic naturalism. In his volume *Last Poems*, D. H. Lawrence writes:

> There is no god
> apart from poppies and the flying fish,
> men singing songs, and women brushing their hair in the sun.
> The lovely things are god that has come to pass.[3]

[3] Quoted by Dean Peerman, "D. H. Lawrence, Devout Heretic," *Christian Century*, LXXVIII (February 22, 1961), 237-41. This perceptive article is an example of the careful discrimination that is necessary in pursuing the relationships of contemporary literature and Christian faith.

Whatever its shortcomings as a statement of Christian orthodoxy about creation, such a view of nature at least stands in protest against the attempt of a one-dimensional scientism to comprehend reality in experimentally verifiable propositions. Faith and contemporary cultural creativity stand together in a recognition of the ultimate mystery of things and in their determination to evoke and celebrate the awe and reverence which such a mystery calls forth. As natural allies, they confront an ambitious science which, insofar as it is true to the hopes of its seventeenth-century founders, aims to achieve control over the environment—as Bacon said, "to extend more widely the limits of the power and greatness of man." Much contemporary literature shares the suspicion of Biblical faith as to the adequacy of such an ambition to do justice to the full range of human potentiality.

Such are some of the common assumptions and intuitions which contemporary cultural creativity and Biblical faith find themselves able to communicate to one another. But such an area of common interest does not by any means imply a consistent pattern of collaboration between the two. The variations of relationship are as numerous as the artists involved. Some few are seriously and deeply involved in responsible Christian—even in some cases Church-centered—discipleship. At another extreme stand some, like the late Albert Camus, who felt that honesty impelled an admission: "I shall not . . . try to pass myself off as a Christian. . . . I share with you the same revulsion from evil. But I do not share your hope." [4] Camus added, however, in the same famous address to a group of French Dominicans, "The world needs real dialogue . . . and . . . the only possible dialogue is the kind between people who remain what they are and speak their minds." [5] Not a few Christian readers of Camus can testify to the profound marks of such a dialogue in his own work. But despite the profusion of types of relationship

[4] Albert Camus, *Resistance, Rebellion, and Death,* trans. by Justin O'Brien (New York: Alfred A. Knopf, Inc., 1961), pp. 70-71.

[5] *Ibid.*, p. 70.

between contemporary literary artists and the Christian faith, we shall attempt some rough categorization of patterns. The subjective element in such an undertaking looms very large, but the confession of an awareness of this fact may do something to disarm outraged criticism.

Perhaps it will be considered proper to begin with the clearest and closest collaboration of all—that in which the literary artist appears to be consciously endeavoring to render a Christian theme or a Biblical insight in new and compelling imagery within the limits of his literary medium. One might name T. S. Eliot, W. H. Auden, and Christopher Fry as examples of this kind of literary purpose. Eliot's *The Cocktail Party* seems clearly intended to illuminate and make vivid the Christian understanding of the vocation of being human. The fierce struggle of the seventh chapter of Romans echoes in these lines:

> I see that my life was determined long ago
> And that the struggle to escape from it
> Is only a make-believe, a pretence
> That what is, is not, or could be changed.
> The self that can say 'I want this—or want that'—
> The self that wills—he is a feeble creature;
> He has to come to terms in the end
> With the obstinate, the tougher self; who does not speak,
> Who never talks, who cannot argue;
> And who in some men may be the *guardian*—
> But in men like me, the dull, the implacable,
> The indomitable spirit of mediocrity.
> The willing self can contrive the disaster
> Of this unwilling partnership—but can only flourish
> In submission to the rule of the stronger partner.[6]

Eliot is describing "the law in my members" of St. Paul not as the wild, anarchistic, rebellious self of the epistle to the Romans but as the dull, plodding, unheroic self of twentieth-century man. The nature of the conflicts which characterize and dominate the inner citadels of the self is

[6] T. S. Eliot, *The Cocktail Party* (New York: Harcourt, Brace & World, Inc., 1959), p. 66.

nevertheless essentially that of St. Paul. Appropriately enough the literary quality of the Eliot passage is in a much lower key of intensity and passion than the seventh chapter of Romans.

A searching and memorable treatment of the theme of Christian love is the burden of Christopher Fry's play *The Dark Is Light Enough*. The all-embracing and indiscriminate *agape*-love of the New Testament is depicted in the acceptance which the Countess Rosmarin offers to the crude and brutal Richard Gettner, who has brought so much misery into her life. One of the characters early in the play describes the remarkable influence which the Countess exercises despite her lack of officiousness and domination.

> You know the Countess has the qualities of true divinity.
> For instance, how apparently undemandingly
> She moves among us; and yet
> Lives make and unmake themselves in her neighbourhood
> As nowhere else. There are many names I could name
> Who would have been remarkably otherwise
> Except for her divine non-interference.[7]

The play traces the ways in which this "divine non-interference" exercises its influence in the rebellious, unstable, willful life of the outcast Gettner. The Countess gives voice early in the play to a fundamental conviction about human relationships.

> . . . Let us say
> We are all confused, incomprehensible,
> Dangerous, contemptible, corrupt,
> And in that condition pass the evening
> Thankfully and well. In our plain defects
> We already know the brotherhood of man.
> Who said that?
> BELMANN: You, Countess.
> COUNTESS: How interesting.
> I thought it was a quotation.[8]

[7] Christopher Fry, *The Dark Is Light Enough* (New York: Oxford University Press, 1954), pp. 4-5.

[8] *Ibid.*, pp. 20-21.

Even when Gettner in an argument with the Countess's son accidentally—as he claims—shoots and wounds him, Rosmarin is able to guess at the fright and fear that led to the act and quietly forbids that Gettner be punished. Speaking for her injured son, she says:

> . . . I ask you
> Not to make him the cause of punishment,
> Not to make his wound a death,
> Not to turn his challenge into a judgment.
> . . . Pray for him,
> Not because I love him, but because
> You are the life you pray for. And because
> Richard Gettner is the life you pray for.
> And because there is nothing on the earth
> Which doesn't happen in your own hearts.[9]

Gettner, drawn back to the Countess's side by news of her grave illness, misinterprets his own feelings and Rosmarin's and asks her to marry him. But Fry must make clear that his theme is the distinctive love of the New Testament and not *eros*, and so the Countess replies quite simply,

> But truth leaps in me, and I have to confess
> I haven't loved you.

Gettner in bewilderment, still misunderstanding, says:

> I imagine it's more than ever satisfactory
> To have done so much for a mere liking.

But the Countess replies,

> It would have been
> Easier to love you than to like you, Richard.
> GETTNER: Will you tell me, then, what I meant to you?
> A penance you gave yourself? Was I
> An exercise in charity
> Which is proving unfortunately fatal?
> Isn't it a sort of insolence

[9] *Ibid.*, p. 74.

To do for me what you care so little about?
What in God's name was it I meant to you?
COUNTESS: Simply what any life may mean.[10]

The play moves swiftly to its conclusion. Pounding is heard at the door. It is soldiers seeking a Hungarian revolutionist to whom the Countess has given shelter. Gettner starts to leave by a window to escape involvement since he himself was once enlisted in the revolutionist cause, but as he turns to go he realizes that the Countess has died quietly in her great chair.

You're dead, Rosmarin. Understand that.
What is there to stay for? You never showed
Any expectations of me when you were alive,
Why should you now?

He hesitates on the window sill. Rosmarin's "divine non-interference" is summoning him to the single act of courage and heroism in his life.

This isn't how I meant that you should love me.

He comes back and stands beside the chair, ready to meet the soldiers and protect the refugee hiding out upstairs.

Very well, Very well
Be with me.[11]

The pounding grows louder as the curtain falls.

An even more triumphant and successful example of the avowedly Christian writer, seeking to elucidate a distinctively Christian theme, is the widely known "For the Time Being, A Christmas Oratorio" by W. H. Auden. The richness and intricacy of the argument and of the imagery defy summary or selective quotation. Auden's purpose is clear from the outset, for on the title page stands the text from St. Paul's epistle to the Romans: "What shall we say then? Shall we

[10] *Ibid.*, pp. 99-100.
[11] *Ibid.*, p. 102.

continue in sin that grace may abound? God forbid." The essential "offense" of the Christian proclamation of justification by faith and the implications of this offense in the Christian approach to life are memorably set forth in a brilliant and dramatic poem. The encounter between the Christian Gospel and its message of forgiveness and indiscriminate love on the one hand, and the humanistic civilized ambition of contemporary man to make life secure, antiseptic, and thoroughly rational on the other, is unforgettably depicted in Herod's famous speech, "The Massacre of the Innocents." Auden sees clearly how much the Christian Gospel may encourage the weakness and the foolishness in human nature. So Herod says in despair:

> Legislation is helpless against the wild prayer of longing that rises, day in, day out, from all these households under my protection: "O, God, put away justice and truth for we cannot understand them and do not want them. Eternity would bore us dreadfully. Leave thy heavens and come down to our earth of waterclocks and hedges. Become our uncle. Look after Baby, amuse Grandfather, escort Madam to the opera, help Willy with his homework, introduce Muriel to a handsome naval officer. Be interesting and weak like us, and we will love you as we love ourselves." [12]

The elimination of the Christian message is the only alternative to a sentimentalized deterioration of moral fiber and civic will.

> Justice will be replaced by Pity as the cardinal human virtue, and all fear of retribution will vanish. Every corner-boy will congratulate himself: "I'm such a sinner that God had to come down in person to save me. I must be a devil of a fellow." Every crook will argue: "I like committing sins. God likes forgiving them. Really the world is admirably arranged." [13]

So to avoid moral anarchy, Herod is obliged to call for the soldiers and wipe out this Gospel and the Child who represents it once and for all.

[12] W. H. Auden, "For the Time Being, A Christmas Oratorio," in *The Collected Poetry of W. H. Auden* (New York: Random House, 1945), p. 457.
[13] *Ibid.*, p. 459.

If our analysis is correct, writers like Eliot, Fry, and Auden represent a profound and sensitive comprehension of the Christian faith and of its understanding of the human problem and its resolution in Christ. This does not exhaust the possibilities of the dialogue between Christian faith and cultural creativity. Paul Elmen has described at least two other possible types of relationship: "What we have learned to look for is that the work express man's ultimate longing; when we find such expression, the work has religious importance, even though that ultimate concern is never satisfied, or is satisfied by something less than the peace of God." [14] The first of Elmen's categories is that in which the religious longing is never satisfactorily met or accounted for. Examples abound but two will suffice here, one in poetry and the other in prose. The poem is Robert Penn Warren's *Brother to Dragons,* which is based on a brutal murder of a slave by two nephews of Thomas Jefferson. It is of more than incidental interest that the poet undertakes in a tantalizingly brief foreword to the poem to sketch in his understanding of the relationship of poetry, myth, and history—a relationship that has figured prominently in recent theological discussions.

I am trying to write a poem and not a history, and therefore have no compunction about tampering with facts. But poetry is more than fantasy and is committed to the obligation of trying to say something about the human condition. Therefore a poem dealing with history is no more at liberty to violate what the writer takes to be the spirit of his history than it is at liberty to violate what the writer takes to be the nature of the human heart. What he takes these things to be is, of course, his ultimate gamble. This is another way of saying that I have tried to make my poem make, in a thematic way, historical sense along with whatever other kind of sense it may be happy enough to make. Historical sense and poetic sense should not, in the end, be contradictory, for if poetry is the little myth we make, history is the big myth we live, and in our living, constantly remake.

[14] Paul Elmen, "Holiness and the Literary Mind," *Christian Century,* LXXVIII (February 22, 1961), 233.

Early in the poem Warren pays his tribute to the infinite yearning, strange and uncontrollable, which leaps up within the human soul and to which he gives the name "glory."

. . . And that lesson is that the only
Thing in life is glory. That's a hard
Thing to learn and a hard fact to face,
For it knocks society's values to a cocked hat,
Or seems to, for the one thing that man fears
Is the terror of salvation and the face
Of glory. But that face is all. Therefore,
Remember now your seeding and the world's magnificence,
To which the heart would answer if it could,
And sometimes can, and if it can't you'd better
Set your affairs in order and sit down
To the careful cultivation of cirrhosis,
For drink's a kind of glory too, and man
Can't live without some glory after all,
Even a poor kind.[15]

At the end of his poem, the author again returns to this early theme:

We have yearned in the heart for some identification
With the glory of the human effort, and have yearned
For an adequate definition of that glory.
To make that definition would be, in itself,
Of the nature of glory. This is not paradox.
It is not paradox, but the best hope.
It is the best hope, because we have,
Each, experienced what it is to be men.
We have lain on the bed and devised evil in the heart.
We have stood in sunlight and named the bad thing good and the good thing bad.
We have stumbled into the act of virtue and caught only from the tail of the eye
The flicker of joy, like a wing-flash in thicket.[16]

Warren's analysis of the savage butchery of the Negro slave, which is the shocking deed that looms and broods over

[15] Robert Penn Warren, *Brother to Dragons* (New York: Random House, 1953), p. 20.
[16] *Ibid.*, pp. 213-14.

the whole poem, proceeds from this fundamental conviction as to the essential ambiguity of human decisions. He rejects the legendary accretions to the story which describe Lilburn's gleeful invocation of the Devil in the midst of the earthquake which followed the murder.

> No, Lilburn had no truck with the Evil One,
> But knew that all he did was done for good,
> For his mother and the sweetness of the heart,
> And that's the instructive fact of history,
> That evil's done for good, and in good's name—[17]

The misdeed for which the Negro was butchered was only the accidental breaking of a pitcher, but in the ferocity and brutality of the punishment there was some—albeit almost imperceptible—meaning and justification. We are asked to imagine the terror-stricken household after the murder:

> No cups are broken now. No spoons are lost.
> No linen sheet is torn, where Mother lay.
> The foot is set soft to the floor-board, the dish
> Makes contact with the table, but no sound.
> There is order in the house and all the appurtenances
> Of civilization defended. Lilburn was right,
> And the portraits stare from the wall in approbation.
> The house has been set on the headland, on stone, against
> The disorder of the wild land. Lilburn defends it.
> Lilburn would defend civilization and define
> The human mission, bring light to the dark place.
> But what does he defend? Only a pitcher,
> As some poor symbol, not the truth itself.
> He defends the letter while the spirit flees.
> And how define the human? By love of Mother,
> And in affirming love, lifts high the meat-axe.
> How bring the light? He does not bring the light.
> He plunges his heart into the unredeemed dark of the wild land.[18]

Even the mother, Lucy Lewis, Jefferson's sister, feels her complicity in the deed, for it was the passionate devotion of her son to her memory that lay behind the grisly atrocity.

[17] *Ibid.*, p. 143.
[18] *Ibid.*, pp. 151-52.

But even my love had infected my son's heart.
Oh, how can love—after all, dear God, it was love—
Be poison in even the first milk love would offer
To still the raw babe's wail in the world's dark? [19]

But Jefferson resists this argument about all-engulfing guilt which appears to him to be a subverting of straightforward morality. He has put Lilburn forever out of his heart and his thoughts. Lucy suddenly sees why.

Yes, when you learned in that report from Kentucky
What evil was possible even in the familial blood,
Your fear began, the fear you had always denied, the fear
That you—even you—were capable of all.
And so in that consanguinity, still to deny
The possibilities of self,
Even in the moment when you claimed that Lilburn
Had robbed you of your hope of human good,
In vanity and virtue and your fear,
You struck . . .
And as George was to Lilburn, so Lilburn is to you,
And as innocence was all Lilburn wanted, it is all
You yourself want, or have wanted. But, Brother,
If you would assume the burden of innocence—and, dear Brother,
I must say to you now, for it comes now strangely to me to say it,
That the burden of innocence is heavier than the burden of guilt—
But what I mean to say, if you would assume that burden of innocence,
If you would begin now that innocence, you must take
His hand—[20]

So Warren concludes with a reflection upon the paradoxes by which life is accepted and lived despite the cruel dilemmas which beset it.

The recognition of complicity is the beginning of innocence.
The recognition of necessity is the beginning of freedom.
The recognition of the direction of fulfillment is the death of the self,

[19] *Ibid.*, p. 188.
[20] *Ibid.*, pp. 190-91.

And the death of the self is the beginning of selfhood.
All else is surrogate of hope and destitution of spirit.[21]

How close this conclusion comes to a conviction which the psychiatrist expresses in Eliot's *The Cocktail Party:*

> Your business is not to clear your conscience
> But to learn how to bear the burdens on your conscience.[22]

The thin line of difference between Eliot's explicit Christian assurance and Warren's quiet dismay is expressed in other lines from the psychiatrist that occur toward the end of *The Cocktail Party:*

> If we were all judged according to the consequences
> Of all our words and deeds, beyond the intention
> And beyond our limited understanding
> Of ourselves and others, we should all be condemned.

In that "if" is concealed the vision of divine judgment and forgiveness which reverses the judgments of history and of society.

The distinction, however, between the explicitly Christian writer and the writer who does no more than pose the dilemma of the human situation is not a distinction that can be pressed too insistently nor maintained too sharply. The power to raise certain kinds of questions is in itself a fruit of a Christian culture. It has been observed, for example, with respect to the work of Albert Camus—more especially *The Fall*—that the torturing ideal of inner integrity and purity of motive which besets Jean-Baptiste Clamence takes its origin from Christian presuppositions rather than Jewish or, even less, secular ones.[23] Clamence speculates sardonically on the incongruity between one's public image and private self.

[21] *Ibid.*, pp. 214-15.

[22] T. S. Eliot, *The Cocktail Party, op. cit.*, p. 128.

[23] Irving Howe, *New Republic*, March 4, 1957, pp. 16-17. Howe argues that Camus represents "a tradition that is devoted to the torturing of motive. . . . One also sees in *The Fall* that fixation upon motive—it necessarily means a fixation upon impurity—which characterizes Jansenism." Howe contrasts this sharply with "the traditional Jewish morality of the deed."

Besides, if everyone told all, displayed his true profession and identity, we shouldn't know which way to turn! Imagine the visiting cards: Dupont, jittery philosopher, or Christian landowner, or adulterous humanist—indeed there's a wide choice. . . . I know mine in any case: a double face, a charming Janus, and above it the motto of the house: "Don't rely on it." On my cards: "Jean-Baptiste Clamence, play actor." [24]

Does his ability to raise the question of inner purity and integrity qualify Camus as a Christian? What does it mean to say, as he says in one of his "Letters to a German Friend": "I continue to believe that this world has no ultimate meaning. But I know that something in it has a meaning and that is man, because he is the only creature to insist on having one." [25] The theologian or the philosopher of religion would want to raise questions about the viability of that kind of distinction; but it is a clear refusal to make some of the affirmations about creation, providence, and the last judgment, for example, which have traditionally been a part of the Christian creedal confession. And indeed it is just this kind of framework of conviction which would enable a more explicitly Christian thinker to raise Camus' questions about integrity and purity of motive without coming to what Irving Howe has called "the dead end where self-confrontation becomes the destroyer of the self." [26]

The difficulty of drawing neat and precise lines of definition to separate the unbeliever from the Christian is the best testimony to the reality and pervasiveness of the dialogue which we are concerned to understand. It is not surprising, is it, that in a conversation the very exchange itself should exercise an influence on the way questions are stated and the kinds of inquiries that are pursued? Even if one repudiates and rejects the Biblical approach to existence, he will reflect

[24] Albert Camus, *The Fall,* trans. by Justin O'Brien (New York: Alfred A. Knopf, Inc., 1957), pp. 46-47.

[25] Albert Camus, *Resistance, Rebellion, and Death,* trans. by Justin O'Brien (New York: Alfred A. Knopf, Inc., 1961), p. 28.

[26] Howe, *op. cit.*

nevertheless the struggle by which the repudiation and rejection were accomplished. C. S. Lewis has wittily pointed out that the alternative in our time to a Biblical outlook is not that we may be "relapsing into Paganism," however satisfying that may sound rhetorically. "It might be rather fun if we were. It would be pleasant to see some future Prime Minister—say, Mr. Atlee—trying to kill a large and lively milk-white bull in Westminster Hall. But we shan't. . . . A post-Christian man is not a Pagan; you might as well think that a married woman recovers her virginity by divorce." [27] Paganism has been fatally and beyond recovery compromised by two thousand years of contact and conversation with Biblical religion. It is hopelessly and irretrievably involved in looking at problems with some at least of the conviction and slant of the Biblical imagination. No precise lines can disentangle the resulting complexity of insights. Only with the greatest hesitation may one speak about non-Christian writers and, even if one can make such a characterization, it would have to be supplemented by a recognition of the extent to which the Christian cultural tradition has shaped their work.

Two examples are provided among many that might be selected from the current or recent writers. One is the dramatist William Inge. Implicit in all his work is a psychological preoccupation that derives at least in part from a genuine concern for the way personality evolves and a recognition of the perilous and wounding experiences that such development entails. There is authentic compassion in his implied plea for what one critic called "the loving acceptance of defects in one's self and in others." [28] There are many points of contact between this major theme of Inge's and the conviction informing Eliot's *The Cocktail Party* that the question of

[27] *De Descriptione Temporum, An Inaugural Lecture* (Cambridge University Press, 1955), p. 15.

[28] Tom F. Driver in a review of Inge's *The Dark at the Top of the Stairs*, *Christian Century* (January 1, 1958), p. 18. The discussion of Inge in this essay is largely dependent upon Driver's treatment.

human vocation is often a question of human defects and their acceptance.[29] One also remembers Fry's Countess Rosmarin and her unquestioning acceptance of Gettner. What is missing in Inge, however, is a persisting tension and demand which lies concealed in the very acceptance itself. Gettner is summoned by his "acceptance" into an identification with the Countess and with her own instinct for compassion and ministry to suffering and need. Psychological awareness appears to serve Inge as an end and purpose in itself. Tom Driver's criticism of *The Dark at the Top of the Stairs* is rightly directed at this preoccupation and expresses its limitations and indeed its stultifying and anaesthetizing result from the Biblical viewpoint. Psychological orientation in the theater, Driver argues, "changes our attention from the essential *what* or the meaning of an action to the *how* of it." It prevents us from thinking of ultimate concerns or ultimate realities and encourages us to think in terms of cause and effect. The result is the belittling of actions, for when we think we understand an action through knowing its psychological cause, we must perforce feel superior to it, since knowledge is power and the deliverance from fear. The spread of psychology in our drama has gone hand in hand with the disappearance of the hero. The net result of such a preoccupation is a "kind of theatre which under the guise of seriousness actually prevents our asking the most serious questions of all—those questions which have to do, not with what life looks or feels like, but with what it means and what it requires."[30]

One will note by way of contrast that although Eliot concedes the psychological limitations of the characters in

[29] Eliot, *op. cit.*, p. 126.
Edward: Lavinia, we must make the best of a bad job. That's what he means.
Harcourt-Reilly: When you find, Mr. Chamberlayne,
The best of a bad job is all that any of us make of it—
Except, of course, the saints. . . . You will forget this phrase,
And in forgetting it will alter the condition.

[30] Driver, *op. cit.*, p. 18.

The Cocktail Party—and indeed employs the symbol of the psychiatrist, Harcourt-Reilly, as the interpreter of their actions and decisions—the "hero" does not disappear. Celia meets martyrdom on an anthill in Africa, and the selflessness and discipline of the life which leads to that grisly climax is unhesitatingly called by Eliot "sanctity." For all the concessions to the limiting power of factors of a psychological sort, Eliot makes it clear that the vocational path is ultimately one that is chosen, not one that is imposed by psychological or social conditions.[31]

The second example of what we have cautiously called non-Christian is the work of D. H. Lawrence.[32] Critics have not found it difficult to discover welcome evidences of similarity between Lawrence's views, especially on the human condition and on sex more particularly, and those of Biblical religion. His sensitivity to the dehumanizing tendencies of a technological society, with a premium placed on self-conscious manipulation of the forces of life, led Lawrence to denounce often and in a variety of settings the fact that "we have killed the mysteries and devoured the secrets." Peerman cites also his searching criticism of liberal democracy and the atomized individualism which is its inevitable consequence. Included in Lawrence's catalogue of dehumanizing forces at work in contemporary life is, of course, Christianity itself, although he had commendation for some aspects of Catholicism, especially the sacramental and liturgical aspects. Many of Lawrence's criticisms of Christianity have been restated by leading contemporary theologians. How the Lawrence who wrote, "we've got to accept the power motive, accept it in deep re-

[31] Eliot, *The Cocktail Party, op. cit.*, p. 141. "Neither way is better. Both ways are necessary. It is also necessary to make a choice between them." Eliot incidentally echoes here the traditional Catholic estimation of "the way of perfection" as contrasted to the way of the ordinary Christian. The path of sanctity is not the only "good life," but Eliot plainly regards it as better: "the process by which the human is transhumanized" (page 147).

[32] Dean Peerman, "D. H. Lawrence, Devout Heretic," *Christian Century*, LXXVIII (February 22, 1961), 237-41. The discussion here of Lawrence is deeply indebted to Peerman's treatment.

sponsibility," would have rejoiced to read Reinhold Niebuhr's *The Nature and Destiny of Man* or Paul Tillich's *Love, Power and Justice.* Lawrence had many reasons for thinking that Christianity was primarily an ascetical and impractical morality of bloodless abstractions, and his strictures against the devitalizing influence of such ideas sound, as Peerman says, "like an impassioned Niebuhrian."

As we have already noticed, however, in another connection, Lawrence's opposition to Christianity is not just rooted in a caricature of the Biblical faith but rather in a pantheistic affirmation which is fundamentally antithetical to the Christian doctrine of creation. If the Protestantism Lawrence knew was moralistic and not sufficiently aware of the realities of power and life-forces, his alternative proposals, as they emerge in his work, fall into an opposite error of identifying the Deity wholly with the totality of the life-process in the universe. As Peerman asserts, "The problem is one which ultimately concerns transcendence." Too much of the Biblical picture of life expresses the sense of alienation between the "world" and the purpose and kingdom of God to be able to identify Lawrence's rhapsodic celebration of the "magnificence here and now of life in the flesh" with any kind of sacramentalism which could be remotely labeled as Christian. When Lawrence posits an ultimate dichotomy between "a 'good' God" and "a vital and magnificent God," he is expressing precisely the religious attitude against which Hebrew prophetism so resolutely set its face in the ninth century before Christ. Lawrence's quarrel with Christianity is a real one. To understand the reasons for it does not eradicate it.

Whether or not the types of relationship between literary creativity and religious faith sketched here are altogether defensible and whether or not the examples chosen are altogether felicitous, the profundity and pervasiveness of the effect of the encounter have certainly been abundantly demonstrated. Whether the artist is consciously expressing in the fresh and vivid imagery of concrete contemporary experience the perennial Biblical themes or whether he is a kind of John the Baptist who prepares a way in the wilderness of modern life for a serious consideration of the Gospel, baptizing with repentance but not yet knowing whether there be any Holy Ghost, or whether the writer embraces some other religious vision which to the Christian will seem partial and one-sided and incapable of doing justice to the full dimensions of human perplexities and possibilities, the literary artist will receive the greatest respect and interest from the man of Biblical faith. Since God himself makes himself known as present and powerful only by the medium of human words and condescends to be designated by such words, the craftsman of words will inevitably be recognized by the servant of the Word as one with whom conversation can be fruitful and illuminating.

Christianity and the Modern Literary Imagination: A Survey of Allegiances

BY W. MOELWYN MERCHANT

THE WILL to power is not demonstrated solely by dictatorships; behind much of our language in literary conversation there lurk assumptions of force, of willful manipulation of judgment in the direction of propaganda, persuasion, or proselytizing zeal. The phrases which assume "schools" of writers or critics, new or traditional, angry or complacent, imply, in vulgar phrase, a "ganging-up" perhaps inseparable from vigorous literary conversation but nevertheless open to corruption. It is, I suppose, even possible that corrupt expectations will be aroused by the title of this chapter, expectations of false evaluation on my part, of subjecting the modern literary imagination to a propagandist role on behalf of Christianity. Certainly critics who assume that the function of an artist includes being bastion or bulwark to preserve Christian culture are guilty of most unhappy treason. The critic or sociologist who is by personal allegiance a Christian may well find himself, in exercising the critical functions of interpretation and evaluation, more drawn to the non-Christians among contemporary writers than to the Christians; may find himself moreover greatly concerned to claim for the artist and writer the duty of his integrity and the privilege of maintaining unpalatable (including non-Christian) truths. Some of the possibly strange allegiances and relationships which follow from this concern should be explored.

A recent review of Samuel Beckett's latest novel, *Comment C'Est*, concludes:

> Mr. Beckett asks the questions which man is always asking, knowing them to be unanswerable—What am I? What is life?—and though his investigations assume the form of a tragic farce, the quality of his art paradoxically establishes something noble and enduring in the Unnamable and in life "comme c'est." [1]

The novel is in some aspects a bitter expansion of the relations between Pozzo and Lucky in *Waiting for Godot*, a vision of man "flat on his belly, in darkness, in an endless plain of mud." That the reader finds enduring nobility in Beckett's assertion of man's predicament is a measure of the writer's integrity, the fearless clinical isolation in which he examines dereliction. The Christian writer, who recognizes this same predicament and names it "the Fall" and who insists on the same measure of integrity, knows also that there is a conclusion in grace, a final dramatic triumph over the consequences of the Fall, which mitigates the tragedy even in the honest telling. As the audience in the Greek theater knew the conclusion of the dramatic act, could count on the appropriate resolution and denouement, so the Christian writer, reader, and audience know the end in the beginning. One of the most salutary and astringent factors on the literary scene today is the presence of its Samuel Becketts, for whom there is no dogmatic resolution, no triumphant denouement, but for whom (though in other terms) sin and the Fall are the data of existence and for whom the human dilemma has still the nobility of acceptance.

With these comparisons in mind it is of interest here to contrast dramatic statements of man's tragic condition as they are made by Shakespeare in a central Christian tradition, and by Camus, passionately aware of man's solitude, "the

[1] The London *Times Literary Supplement*, April 7, 1961.

cruellest burden this age has laid upon him." Shakespeare's most complex and equivocal statement of the creative power of dereliction is in *King Lear;* before the terrible ambiguity of the final scene, the reconciliation between Lear and Cordelia reaches a radiance which alleviates the suffering, in this passage in Act V, sc. iii:

> We two alone will sing like birds i' the cage;
> When thou dost ask me blessing, I'll kneel down
> And ask of thee forgiveness; so we'll live . . .
> And take upon's the mystery of things
> As if we were God's spies.

Here Lear's hitherto blasphemous denial of the creative order —"Nothing will come of nothing"—is itself creatively denied; his dereliction has brought him personal integrity and the compassionate charity of Cordelia; his "little world of man" is for the moment whole. *Timon of Athens* never achieves the profound complexity of *King Lear,* but in this particular matter of human dereliction, its final statement is more direct than that of the greater play. "Nothing" is for Timon also a positive notion, and at his final renunciation of all wealth, charity, and civic attachment, he cries to the walls of Athens:

> Nothing I'll bear from thee
> But nakedness, thou detestable town.

Through the remaining acts of the play Timon's tragedy is to be worked out in solitary alienation until he reaches the end term of his purgation:

> My long sickness
> Of health and living now begins to mend
> And nothing brings me all things.

In a wholly different dimension from these two tragic statements, Parolles in *All's Well that Ends Well* also has his moment of insight which reflects his conviction that "nothing brings me all things." Few revelations of beggarly spirit reach the point of humiliation which Parolles knows at his unmasking. But the liar, coward, and cheat attempts no swagger nor any resumption of a mask; there is no great contrition, little prospect of even the normal decencies, but there is at least the comic equivalent of the dictum *nosce teipsum:*

> Simply the thing I am
> Shall make me live.

It may be protested that in comedy and tragedy Shakespeare achieves this disenchanted acceptance of the human condition inside a creedal framework, common to his age, which takes account of the grace and the potential nobility of man. This dimension of grace and supernature is absent from many of the greatest creative minds of our day, but the dignity of their affirmations and the clarity with which they accept their responsible roles are unqualified. Four days after receiving the Nobel Prize, Albert Camus gave an interview to Jean Bloch-Michel; he defined the duty of the modern artist as at once "involvement in affairs" and critical detachment from them.

> Like many men to-day, I am weary of criticism, of belittling, of spite, in a word, of nihilism. That which deserves condemnation must be condemned, but briefly as well as firmly. That which still deserves praise must be praised at great length. After all, that is why I am an artist, for even the work of art based on denial still affirms something, and rings the praises of our miserable and magnificent existence.[2]

In an age in which the creedal affirmations of Christendom command the assent only of a minority, this formal statement by Camus, an epitome of the temper which informs his novels, provides part of that climate within which all healthy creativity, Christian and non-Christian, may be pursued.

For there is a temper, a climate of opinion, within which it is difficult to make any creative statements at all. At the same time, since Christendom has no monopoly of sane intellectuality, before we can properly examine the position of the Christian artist within our contemporary culture, it is no

[2] *The Observer*, November 17, 1957.

more than courteous to look more closely at the declarations of non-Christian writers whose beliefs make for health and whose creative works spring from affirmations at least congruous with those of Christians. Camus states one aspect of this congruity: "No great work has ever been founded on hate or contempt. On the contrary, there is not a single genuine work of art which has not in the long run increased the inner liberty of everyone who has known and loved it."

It is not necessary to agree with the principles of historical exploration undertaken by Brecht in *The Life of Galileo* or by Anouilh in *The Lark* to find in these two works statements which make for health, which the Christian artist requires as his intellectual context, his cultural alliance. The first version of *Galileo* was written in the year immediately before World War II and first produced at the Zürich Schauspielhaus in September, 1943. Scene xiii, the moment of Galileo's recantation, has the harshest irony in the play; for Andrea Sarti, Galileo's pupil, and his lense grinder, Federzoni, savor their master's intellectual stand against the Inquisition in the very moments before the crier proclaims his total capitulation. This dramatic irony itself intensifies the nature of their hope:

ANDREA: Well! Force has not prevailed! It cannot do everything! Therefore stupidity is conquered; it is not invulnerable! Therefore, man is not afraid of death!

FEDERZONI: . . . And think, if he had recanted! . . . it would have been as if night had fallen again just after the sun rose . . .

ANDREA: But everything has been changed today! Man, tortured man, lifts up his head and says: I can live. So much is gained when only one man stands up and says 'No.'

Anouilh deploys a different quality of irony in the second part of *The Lark*. The Inquisitor at the trial of St. Joan gradually assumes the status of all willful tyranny. Joan, in her longing for tranquillity, has kept faith both with herself and with her creed: "In what concerns the Faith, I trust myself to the

Church. But what I have done, I shall never wish to undo." This moment of honest assertion is answered by the Inquisitor:

> You hear those words? And you will hear them said on the scaffold, at the stake, in the torture chamber, wherever they come to suffer for the errors they commit. And centuries hence they will be saying it; the hunting down of Man will go on endlessly. However powerful we become one day in one shape or another, however inexorably the Idea shall dominate the world, however rigorous, precise and subtle its organisation and its police, there will always be a man who has escaped, a man to hunt, who will presently be caught, presently be killed: a man who, even so, will humiliate the Idea at the highest point of its Power, simply because he will say "No" without lowering his eyes.

This conviction of the moral power of man's resistance is echoed by Camus in his analysis of the pessimistic nihilism with which the creative mind is most insidiously beset:

> In fact we have no choice. It is [courage] or nihilism. If our societies are going to rush into either totalitarian or bourgeois nihilism, then those people who do not wish to conform will be cut off and have to accept the fact.

This is an important conjunction of statements:

> So much is gained when only one man stands up and says 'No.'

> A man . . . will humiliate the Idea at the highest point of its Power, simply because he will say 'No'. . . .

> Those people who do not wish to conform will be cut off and have to accept the fact.

This is the context, the affirmation of individual integrity by authors who have no sustaining props in the shape of historical creeds, in which the Christian writer accepts his vocation, humbly recognizing the power of his allies, just as he also recognizes the disparity between his creed and theirs.

When this relationship of mutual respect between the

Christian and non-Christian has been established and recognized, it is perhaps more possible to see the particular functions of the Christian writer *as Christian.* In a complex society his first duty will be the reaffirmation of traditional commonplaces. These may be creedal, the interpretation of our human situation, its dignity and its squalor, in terms of creation, sin, grace, and redemption; or they may be derived from the creeds, formal extensions of the Church's teaching on man's place and function in society. Among contemporary English novelists, William Golding has achieved the distinction in *Lord of the Flies* of re-creating the pattern of human sin in a tale which engages and totally disarms the reader by the innocence of its mythology. The story of a large party of schoolboys, isolated on an island by the crash of their transport plane as it takes them from a theater of war, proceeds through a paradisiacal *Coral Island* existence, to the exploration of fear and anger, the establishment of power and dominance in rival groups, the sadistic persecution of the attractive and grotesque little intellectual Piggy, and the anarchy and murder which parody adult conflicts in the world. The writing is direct, concrete, with no mythical allusiveness which obscures other, more complex levels of reference. It requires conscious abstraction from the skillful tale-telling to realize the experimental isolation in which the party of boys has been placed in the working out of their race-history. Yet the structure has a subtle sophistication; one of the central incidents, the deliberate smashing of Piggy's spectacles, raises the story to a pitch of restrained brutality which recalls, in fact and in symbolic power, the blinding of Gloucester in *Lear.* The closing pages of the novel are shocking in the transition to normal life. Ralph, the natural leader, has been savagely hunted by his fellows through the forest fire; the end of the chase is reached at the feet of a naval officer who has landed on the island and whose adult comment places the savage cruelty of the boys' tale into perspective:

"We saw your smoke. What have you been doing? Having a war or something?"
Ralph nodded.
The officer inspected the little scarecrow in front of him. The kid needed a bath, a hair-cut, a nose-wipe and a good deal of ointment.

We may feel that this confrontation of the child's tragedy by the adult world has something of the quality that adult tragedy may have when looked at by divine compassion; but Golding does not blur his tale to allow such speculations. He has been engaged on an exploration which the closing page makes explicit:

For a moment [Ralph] had a fleeting picture of the strange glamour that had once invested the beaches. But the island was scorched up like dead wood—Simon was dead—and Jack had. . . . The tears began to flow and sobs shook him. He gave himself up to them now for the first time on the island; great, shuddering spasms of grief that seemed to wrench his whole body. His voice rose under the black smoke before the burning wreckage of the island; and infected by the emotion, the other little boys began to shake and sob too. And in the middle of them, with filthy body, matted hair, and unwiped nose, Ralph wept for the end of innocence, the darkness of man's heart, and the fall through the air of the true, wise friend called Piggy.

In the clarity of this final sequence of phrases: "end of innocence . . . darkness of heart . . . fall through the air," this paragraph recalls the cold shimmer of Benjamin Britten's music at an analogous moment in the opera based on Henry James's *Turn of the Screw:* "The ceremony of innocence is dead."

The second group of affirmations in the Christian tradition, those which explore the major commonplaces in social, political, and economic theory, do not so completely depend on the personal allegiance of the writer to the liturgy and creeds of the worshiping Church. No more passionate restatement of the medieval doctrine of "the just price" and the role of money in society has been made for our day than in Ezra Pound's *Cantos*, and it is significant that the central term of his statement has been the medieval concept of "usury." [3] The latest extended treatment of his work by G. S. Fraser points to the fidelity of Pound's economic arguments to a central body of traditional thought:

> Pound's hatred of usury, and his distrust of finance capitalism, or of a completely 'free' economy, is not so eccentric as some critics have made out. Distrust of the power of banks is traditional in American politics since Andrew Jackson. . . . And economic ideas with at least a family resemblance to Pound's can be found, for instance, in Cobbett, Carlyle, Ruskin, and R. H. Tawney.

If we push the antecedents of Fraser's exemplars back to their proper origins in patristic and scholastic thinking, this very fair assessment of Pound's ideas finds its fullest source in the prose arguments, *The Money Pamphlets by £*, and others. But this picture is radically if subtly altered if we go to the dominant statement of his position in the Usura passage in "Canto XLV." In place of the abstractions of economic argument, we have now concrete imagery quickened by anger and impatience. For in the realm of usury there is no seemly architecture, no home:

> With usura hath no man a house of good stone
> each block cut smooth and well fitting;

nor, in the usurious society, is there the radiance of images fashioned in belief:

> . . . where virgin receiveth message
> and halo projects from incision;

rather, in the realm of usury, art is an object of mere commerce, created in haste for rapid profit:

> no picture is made to endure nor to live with
> but it is made to sell and sell quickly;

[3] It is still difficult to examine the work of Ezra Pound, especially in an Anglo-American context, without awkward self-consciousness. I think it arguable that one of the unacknowledged reasons for the violent rejection of his writings by some critics is the affront offered by his attack on usury to a culture corrupted by the economics of greed or, in politer terms, "the affluent society."

the very colors, the pure hues of the great illuminators, blue, crimson, and green, are betrayed by usury:

> Azure hath a canker by usura; cramoisi is unbroidered
> Emerald findeth no Memling.

These are the rebellions of an artist against an order he repudiates. But embedded in the poet's malaise there are two statements which a medieval thinker would have found acceptable. The first goes to the simplest, most essential means of subsistence:

> with usura, sin against nature,
> is thy bread ever more of stale rags
> is thy bread dry as paper,
> with no mountain wheat, no strong flour.

For the full resonance of this passage we have to return to "Hugh Selwyn Mauberley":

> Faun's flesh is not to us,
> Nor the saint's vision
> We have the press for wafer;
> Franchise for circumcision.

In the sterile society which Pound has analyzed for half a century, bread, sacrament, vitality, and sustenance have been alike repudiated: "Is thy bread dry as paper"—"We have the press for wafer"; "Mauberley" and the Usura passages comment mordantly on each other. The second passage, with which the canto reaches its closing argument, moves from concern with art and with subsistence to the springs of human life itself:

> Usura slayeth the child in the womb
> It stayeth the young man's courting
> It hath brought palsey to bed, lyeth
> between the young bride and her bridegroom
> CONTRA NATURAM

Usura, which for three centuries we have succeeded in rationalizing under the neutral terms of rent and interest, is for

Pound *contra naturam*, a repudiation of the fundamental law of nature. Pound is an eclectic writer. His concepts, his images, the patterns of his highly allusive verse, depend on a widely ranging sympathy which has made valid contact with Jefferson and Confucius, with Malatesta and John Adams, with Antoninus Pius and Edward Coke. With much of this allusiveness the contemporary reader is impatiently bemused; by some political consequences of Pound's economic arguments he is repelled. But for this central perception in his thinking (as vigorous in the mainstream of "Mauberley" and the *Cantos* as in his prose pleadings), Pound is closely related to the tradition of Christian social thinking, which the Jonson of *Volpone* or the R. H. Tawney of *Religion and the Rise of Capitalism* would recognize as historical commonplace.

At this point a critic who is himself by personal profession of faith a Christian has to face squarely a dilemma of affiliation and allegiance. The literary figures I have cited would seem an incongruous assembly: Beckett, Camus, Anouilh, Brecht, Golding, and Pound from our own day, with Shakespeare from the past. Yet, Christian and non-Christian, in certain crucial analyses of the human predicament, they share common symbols, insights, and presuppositions about the nature of man. In recognizing these fundamental concurrences lies a critical danger; it is tempting for the Christian critic to see in certain of these contemporaries a species of religious fellow traveler, to read and interpret their work as though each were *chrétien malgré lui*. Certain Christian images and symbols, beliefs and attitudes, are recalcitrant and enduring; embedded as fossils in the work of writers who would repudiate the system of belief which is their natural context, they pose a teasing exercise in discrimination for the critic. This is probably the point at which the "Christianity" and "the Modern Literary Imagination" of the title of this chapter make their most puzzling conjunction.

James Joyce is in this respect a relatively easy subject.

His ranging, acquisitive mind accepted the fragments that remained of Christian assent from his earlier education; these fragments assumed their part in his linguistic mosaic, intensifying the emotional texture of the writing while adding one more layer of density to the allusions. The sincerely felt but lighthearted pamphlet *From a Banned Writer to a Banned Singer* illustrates this matter very well.[4] The little work is a piece of advocacy on behalf of a singer who had not in Joyce's opinion received his due and, in the technique of *Finnegans Wake*, it reviews Sullivan's career. With Joyce's usual virtuosity, operatic roles are conflated with national and social references; these reach their most interesting complexity in references to Saint-Saëns's *Samson et Dalila:*

> Who is this that advances in maresblood caftan, like Hiesous in Finisterre, his eyeholes phyllistained, his jewbones of a crossbacked? A little child shall lead him. . . . He upbraces for supremacy to the potence of Mosthigh and calls upon his baiters and their templum: You daggones, be flat!

This carries intensities which seem to go well beyond the professional disappointments of an operatic singer; for, with references to Isaiah 63 and the eschatological passages of Matthew 24, this may in part be paraphrased:

> Who is this that advances in the bloody caftan of the Suffering Servant, like the Jesus of Finisterre [with overtones of the German 'Finster' also], his jewbones on the cross-marked back of an ass? A little child shall lead him. The Most High braces Himself for crucifixion [Fr. 'Potence,' a gallows] calling upon His baiters, and their temple, you Dagon-followers, your temple shall be thrown down.

Though this paraphrase ignores many of the ironic asides (such as the especially Joycean "be flat" in the last line, for

[4] This characteristic squib in support of the Irish singer Sullivan first appeared in 1932 in both *The New Statesman* and *Hound and Horn*. Critical analyses of the work appeared in the *Analyst* (Northwestern University), xiv and xv, and I added brief notes on Biblical overtones in the work in xvi; these were all assembled in *Critical Writings of James Joyce*, edited by Richard Ellman and Ellsworth Mason (New York: The Viking Press, 1959).

Samson's last note in *Samson et Dalila* is B-flat!), it demonstrates the equation, which seems so incongruous, of Samson-Messiah-Christ with the singer whose cause he was championing. While the passion of Joyce's advocacy is intensified by the scriptural references, it would manifestly be absurd to assume any degree of conscious or unconscious assent in this craftsman's assimilation of materials to hand. But Samuel Beckett's *Godot* sets an obscurer problem. The tramps wait for Godot, who is an owner of sheep and goats, and it is their conviction that when he comes, "We'll be saved." Toward the end of Act I, Estragon abandons his shoes with a hint of anonymous compassion:

ESTRAGON: Another will come, just as . . . as . . . as me, but with smaller feet, and they'll make him happy.
VLADIMIR: But you can't go barefoot!
ESTRAGON: Christ did.
VLADIMIR: Christ! What's Christ got to do with it? You're not going to compare yourself to Christ!
ESTRAGON: All my life I've compared myself to him.

For the moment—on the page and in the theater—this is intensely felt, and there are pervasive hints in the work of at least this degree of assent, but it is not dominant in this ambiguous play, and it is rarely present even as a foil in Beckett's later work. The nobility with which squalor, absurdity, brutality are faced has affinities with the enduring dignity of Job, but the pattern of belief which motivates the endurance is very different.

Joyce and Beckett—however deeply they repudiate their intellectual debt to earlier Christian training—maintain a reserved, essentially literary assent to the evocative function of creedal fragments and images. Dylan Thomas' attachment to the emotional religious tradition of his native South Wales was, however, less astringently examined. Two subjects, eucharist and death, recur, frequently in relation to suffering in wartime, to raise expectations of explicit assent which never come to concrete statement. "This bread I break" uses eucharistic references with an ambiguity which allows the utmost freedom of interpretation within a pagan or a Christian scheme:

> This bread I break was once the oat,
> This wine upon a foreign tree
> Plunged in its fruit. . . .

The pattern is traditional, and the intended reference is clear; but the riotous movement of the sap implied in the strong placing of the verb "plunged" in this last line prepares for "sensual" in the penultimate line of the poem:

> This flesh you break, this blood you let
> Make desolation in the vein
> Were oat and grape
> Born of the sensual root and sap.

The syntax of the first two lines in this last stanza permits two opposite meanings: "this blood you let" and "this blood you let/Make desolation . . . ," where blood-letting in the sacrificial sense is counterposed against the emotional devastation of the blood's riot, the "sensual root and sap." A similar conjunction of biblical perception with insights derived from myth and folk tale traverses "And death shall have no dominion." The liturgical framework, each of three stanzas opening and closing with the title-phrase, encloses an intimate amalgam of Christian and pagan reference:

> And death shall have no dominion.
> Dead men naked they shall be one
> With the man in the wind and the west moon; . . .
> They shall have stars at elbow and foot. . . .

The second stanza carries its ambiguity to the point of a conclusion which withdraws from, cancels out the implications of martyrdom in the previous lines:

> Twisting on racks when sinews give way,
> Strapped to a wheel, yet they shall not break;
> Faith in their hands shall snap in two,
> And the unicorn evils run them through;

Split all ends up they shan't crack;
And death shall have no dominion.

If they are isolated from the verse pattern there are dissonant phrases here which work harshly against each other: "sinews give way"—"They shan't break"—"Faith shall snap in two"—"split . . . they shan't crack"—arriving at the statement that "death shall have no dominion" which asserts a conclusion without resolving the dissonances. The ambiguity is intensified by pointing against each other "faith" and "unicorn evils" from their two very disparate realms. Indeed, "unicorn" with its long history of iconography in Christian and pagan art is strongly placed in the pattern. A similar give and take of meaning pervades Thomas' most successful short poem, "Do Not Go Gentle Into That Good Night," from the light syntactical punning in the opening line—"gentle" as noun and adverb—through the calculated incongruity of the vision of the *senex:* "Old age should burn and rave at close of day," to the moving address to his father in the closing stanza, with glancing allusion to the somber relation of Isaac with Jacob and Esau: "Curse, bless, me now with your fierce tears, I pray."

It is possible to recognize these fossil elements in the works of Joyce, Beckett, or Thomas, and to detect the resonances, the increased complexities in their work brought about by the repudiated or unexamined beliefs, without the temptation to annex their work in the name of "Christian creativity." There remains an influential body of contemporary writing produced by men whose private beliefs are explicitly Christian but who write with reserve, the obliqueness of their use of Christian criteria a concession to the cultivated community whose presuppositions are no longer those of western Christendom. T. S. Eliot has pared away the poetry in his language for the theater, "putting it on a very thin diet in order to adapt it to the needs of the stage" in very similar fashion to his abstemious use of theology in exploring the personal relations in plays. But Eliot's concern in this matter has been examined with distinction in his own study *Poetry and Drama* (1957).

Interesting—and less well known in America—is the progressive handling of this problem in the poetry of R. S. Thomas, whose work commands an increasing respect in Great Britain. R. S. Thomas is a Welsh country parson whose five volumes of poetry have all appeared since the war: *The Stones of the Field* (1946), *An Acre of Land* (1952), *The Minister*, a long poem commissioned for broadcasting by the BBC (1953), *Song at the Year's Turning*, and *Poetry for Supper* (1958). The initially impressive fact in Thomas' work is its extreme economy and concentration on a limited theme. Ultimately, though this is rarely explicit, the content of his poetry is the tragic tension between the priest's concern for his people and Thomas' particular sense of frustration at the countryman's dumb rejection of the graces of life, of art, and, perhaps in the final analysis, of sanctity. An early poem, "A Priest to His People," declares that tension with unusual clarity:

> Men of the hills, wantoners, men of Wales. . . .
> How I have hated you for your irreverence, your scorn even
> Of the refinements of art and the mysteries of the Church.

The poem expends its invective against these "men of bone, wrenched from the bitter moorland" until its almost reluctant conclusion, accepting in priestly insight the peasants' toughly admirable life:

> You will continue to unwind your days
> In a crude tapestry under the jealous heavens
> To affront, bewilder, yet compel my gaze.

When the poet is about his own personal devotion, he can achieve the witty simplicity which relaxes in the tradition of meditative symbol:

He kneeled long
And saw love in a dark crown
Of thorns blazing, and a winter tree
Golden with fruit of a man's body

or in the more recent "Pietà":

The tall Cross
Sombre, untenanted
Aches for the Body
That is back in the cradle
Of a maid's arms.

But these moments are comparatively rare; for his more customary expression of the pastoral dilemma Thomas has created his peasant figure of Iago Prytherch, of vacant mind and "soured with years of sweat." Prytherch has grown in stature as the volumes have succeeded each other. When Thomas is emotionally neutral, there is a Wordsworthian quality about this peasant form, more sculptured than human, "enduring like a tree under the curious stars." When the priest and the poet are deeply involved in apparent failure of relation with the peasant, there arises an acid rejection of any community between the graceless countryman and the clerisy:

their skulls
Ripening over so many prayers,
Toppled into the same grave
With oafs and yokels.

The shocking hint of repudiation in the last line is modified to grim irony, which gives way to compassion, in another poem, "Affinity":

Don't be taken in
By stinking garments or an aimless grin;
He also is human, and the same small star,
That lights you homeward, has inflamed his mind
With the old hunger, born of his kind.

The flexible movement of that passage is on other occasions blotted out by anger at the puritan rejection of sacramental realism in the created order. The long poem, *The Minister*, turns upon his bitter understanding of one of the forces which has dimmed perception in contemporary Wales:

> Protestantism—the adroit castrator
> Of Art; the bitter negation
> Of song and dance and the heart's innocent joy—
> You have botched our flesh and left us only the soul's
> Terrible impotence in a warm world.

Few of his poems permit even this degree of generalization. The leitmotiv is always the matter of grace and its operation on recalcitrant men brutalized by labor. One of his most recent poems, "The Survivor,"[5] examines with apparent detachment the eighty-five-year-old "land's thug":

> A slumped bundle of fat and bone,
> Boasting volubly of his feats
> Of strength and skill with the long scythe
> Or gallantry among the blithe
> Servant girls.

The opening of the poem establishes a single allusive overtone:

> What strange grace lends him a brief
> Time for repentance of his theft
> Of health and comeliness from her—

his wife through the dumb years. The strong ending of the second line, "repentance of his theft," relates the peasant to the penitent thief and prepares for the toughly compassionate conclusion of the poem:

> Old and weak he must chew now
> The cud of prayer, and be taught how
> From hard hearts huge tears are wrung.

The spare language and the apparently disenchanted detachment are deceptive; this is sophisticated writing whose passionate motive force is the disparity between the power and sacramental status of the priest and the flaws within his own person and in those to whom he ministers. Though

[5] Published in *The Listener,* March 2, 1961.

other writers—and notably dramatists—have examined the tragic fissure between status and person in king or priest, it is difficult to recall anyone involved in the tension itself writing of it with so much intellectual power and such hurt passion.

As a foil to this powerfully circumscribed and spare art we may place the latest plays of another totally "engaged" writer, Christopher Fry. It would be easy to demonstrate the areas of Christian commitment in his early plays, for many of them were commissioned by the Church: the unpublished play, *The Tower*, was the Tewkesbury Festival play in 1939; *Thor, with Angels* was the Canterbury Festival play in 1948; and *A Sleep of Prisoners* was commissioned by the Religious Drama Society for performance in churches during the Festival of Britain, 1951. But *The Dark Is Light Enough*, first produced in London in 1954, bewildered by its reticent allusiveness those critics who had long spoken of Fry's pyrotechnics, "his restoration of verbal intoxication to the theatre." Closer examination shows that the deft wit of the earlier comedies (always liable to turn to profound gravity—and not solely in the darker plays such as *The Firstborn*) now serves a still profounder purpose. For Fry is here exploring at a distance (the 1848 revolution in Europe) tragedies in human relationships which are at least as intense in our own day. The household of the Countess Rosmarin is torn by conflicting Hungarian and Austrian loyalties. The Countess herself is the dominating figure of the play:

> You know the Countess has the qualities of true divinity.
> For instance: how apparently undemandingly
> She moves among us; and yet
> Lives make and unmake themselves in her neighborhood
> As nowhere else. There are names I could name
> Who would have been remarkably otherwise
> Except for her divine non-interference.

This lightly stressed incarnation of God's respect for man's integrity, while still holding grace in reserve for human demand, brings the Countess into the company of the Duke in *Measure for Measure*, as he moves disguised through his world while lives "make and unmake themselves" among his subjects. So secure is Fry's technique that scriptural references are made with the nonchalance of friendly conversation; they may even depend on occasion on the nice adaptation of theological distinctions—as the Countess speaks of love:

> There we have no free-will.
> At the one place of experience
> Where we're most at mercy, and where
> The decision will alter us to the end of our days,
> Our destination is fixed;
> We're elected into love—

a singularly felicitous adoption of St. Augustine. At a powerful moment in the first act Colonel Janik enters the Countess' home in search of the deserter Gettner:

> I have two thousand men
> Standing in the snow, their lives my trust.
> Peace may go in search of the one soul
> But we are not at peace,

in which war's inversion of all values, even that of the Shepherd, is glanced at in a brief phrase. Later, the Countess, herself exiled to a stable from her cultivated home, with gracious, unemphatic irony recalls another stable:

> You put me under the pain of enmity
> And have driven me out of my possessions,
> And yet this exile, though it is
> No more than a stable yard from home,
> Unites me with you, and with your soldiers.

The motivating assumption of the play—it is central to all Fry's thinking—is the particular integrity of every human person, whether apparently good or bad. Despite all expedience and the pressure of war, the Countess expects that Janik will concede that "One man over another has no kingdom." The spiritual and emotional power behind this assumption is the primacy of compassion, of *caritas* strongly and impartially dispensed. It is revealed most clearly in the scene where Gettner's courage is at the point of total breakdown in fear:

GETTNER: Have a respect for my life
For the sake of your sleep to come, don't betray me.
Go to your imaginations, gentlemen:
Think of death by shooting.
BELMANN: I should more likely weep for stags or partridges.

This contemptuous reduction of Gettner below gamebird or beast is taken up and transmuted by the Countess:

Do, then. Weep for what you can.
It's grateful to our brevity
To weep for what is briefer,

in which it is not unseemly that man's compassion should begin at the thought of a sparrow's fall.

Fry's latest play, *Curtmantle,* handles a theme we have already found potent in Christian thinking, the gap between the aspirations of sanctity or rule and their realization in the facts of daily life. After Eliot and Anouilh it is of fascinating interest to see a play concerned with the reign of Henry II which concentrates on the person of the king rather than on Becket. The shift is made historically significant by moving from the orbit of martyrdom, its theology and motivation, to the realm of law and the irony involved in the king's craving a just order, himself the most anarchic of men. The abstraction of the theme is given dramatic validity in the contrast between Henry's concern for justice, disregarding the values of personal relationships, and his subjects' longing for particular righting of wrongs. When Anesty in the prologue cries:

Where shall I find the King? A law that's just and merciful!
Do I have to walk on forever, looking for that?

he desires not an abstract, kingdom-wide justice but a moment of judgment:

He has only got to lean a moment from his saddle!

Until the last act Henry is sanguine in his direction of the kingdom:

> What isn't well already
> Is getting down on to its knees to be cured.
> God's light, there's no anarchy to come worse
> Than I've already transformed into good government,
> Unless they drive me to a harrowing of hell.

In the play's first production in Holland in March, 1961, the contrast was somewhat muted between this almost demonic force in the person of Henry and the powerful meditative tone of Becket's brooding realization that divergence between king and chancellor was inevitable. This particular mode of the relation between ecclesiastical and state law is essentially an Anglo-Saxon manifestation, and it will certainly have greater immediacy on the English and American stage. It can rarely have been expressed in clearer dramatic terms than in Becket's somber response to Henry in the first act:

> There is a true and living
> Dialectic between the Church and the state
> Which has to be argued for ever in good part.
> It can't be broken off or turned
> Into a clear issue to be lost or won.
> It's the nature of man that argues;
> The deep roots of disputation
> Which dug in the dust, and formed Adam's body.
> So it's very unlikely, because your friend
> Becomes Primate of England, the argument will end.

That speech epitomizes much that has informed Fry's work not only in this play but strongly since the writing of *The Firstborn* and indeed as much in the comedies as in the more tragic works. "The deep roots of disputation" burrow into the texture of all the matters which he has in common with the Christian writers with whom we have been concerned.

I have tried in this survey to establish a relationship between very diverse figures in our current literary scene. Their relation to theological speculation varies from ironic detachment (while recognizing the still potent evocative power of the old symbols) to total involvement in the struggle for worship and its communication. There are manifestly areas of agreement between those clear-sighted writers on the one hand who see man's dereliction in terms of sin and those on the other who see him held in "the absurd" while retaining a vulnerable nobility. Rarely, however, have assent and dissent ranged through so wide a spectrum of distinctions as in our day. At other times of high creativity, in Athens, in Elizabethan England, in eighteenth-century France, there have been profound cleavages of assent and dissidence; but on the whole the cleavages were clean, the allegiances distinct. Today one of the first duties of a discriminating critic is to see the cross-allegiances, the borrowing of tones and attitudes, the acceptance of partially repudiated beliefs, the exploration with humble concern of the very beliefs that divide. Men of integrity on both sides of this dialectic have one particular matter in common; with Keats, each of them, Christian and non-Christian, would reject as "pious fraud" the facile, unexamined acceptance of any dogma. Beliefs, even those grounded centrally in the tradition of Western Christendom, are there for exploration and for validating in experience. Literary creation is one mode of this experience, laying bare for imaginative and critical perception both the common ground for our co-operative occupation and those matters which in our common integrity we agree to regard as questionable. Dialogue can be creative in these circumstances of mutual respect.

The Dark Night of Sisyphus

BY RALPH HARPER

HEROES, CHIEF executives, and priests are by profession lonely men. But lonelier still are all tragic heroes. None are so lonely as the people of the twentieth century who think there is no God but cannot put him out of their minds. Their tragedy is the typical tragedy of modern times: the loneliness of man without God. But this is a new form of tragedy. In the more distant past tragic experience was thought to happen primarily to figures with excessive pride or passion, men and women especially sure of themselves and the world and a deity. We still tend to take Oedipus and Medea as norms for tragedy rather than the warped and weak derelicts of our own time. There is something in-between an Oedipus and a Willy Loman; namely, the man who is responding consciously to the world without God in which all men are to some extent born today. Academic critics widely recognize the necessity to raise the discussion of tragedy above the mere plane of neurosis or congenital weakness, above Arthur Miller's or Tennessee Williams' or William Faulkner's hardly human beings. But the answer is not found by assuming, as European critics have done, that modern tragedy is a coming to life of the myth of Sisyphus. We should not be tempted to read into ancient legends anything more than the strife of man with man. If, for example, the punishment of Sisyphus sometimes seems to be our fate, must we assume that we, like Sisyphus, have rebelled against God or stolen divine secrets? We flatter ourselves too much. For only too many sensitive minds today there is no God to rebel against, and there are no divine secrets.

Also it is misleading to discuss tragedy within the confines of books and journals. Tragedy is not a literary phenomenon at all; literature should be concerned here above all with tragedy as living experience. That is why we would do better to keep in mind the two vastly different assumptions governing life today: that which takes for granted that God is dead and does not care, and that which is not sure about God but does care. Anyone with the first point of view is not so likely to be concerned about the tragedy that befalls mankind when the area of the divine shrinks to a cipher or a question mark. Like Nietzsche he may hail the death of God, so called, as a joyful event, and then like Nietzsche become bewildered when he finds it increasingly difficult to carry on in a world devoid of intrinsic meaning. It is easy to wave one's arms and talk grandiosely of the open seas awaiting adventurers just out of the prisons of religion and hypocrisy. It is not so easy to sail such seas.

To live without God is bad enough, but to live in such a world and to pretend that it is the best of all possible worlds is simply unintelligent. Camus' uncalled-for claim that Sisyphus must be believed happy is an example of this "technique of the exclamation point." But why must we believe that Sisyphus is happy, except to extricate Camus from the disagreeable alternative of having to admit that Sisyphus' fate is unhappy, as Zeus meant it to be? This is a common misunderstanding about modern tragedy and drama, this unwillingness to see that tragedy is not the passage from suffering to noble affirmation and exaltation; we refuse to accept tragedy at face value. And from this misunderstanding arise not only careless analogies to Christianity but also confusion as to the true meaning of tragic experience.

Tragedy does not begin or end with *yes*, and the average person knows this only too well. It begins and ends with *no*. And that is why ordinary people keep on referring to the searing misfortunes they meet as tragedy; why they are impatient of such distinctions as pathos versus tragedy. For them tragedy is not something to be read about but something to be avoided. Any suffering that overwhelms comprehension and staying power reveals the presence of "a secret cause," an imbalance of will and chance, and completely justifies to the unacademic intelligence the title of tragedy. The ordinary man does not expect that suffering will make him feel sublime; that is outside his experience. There may be a surprising peace and acceptance at the end of suffering —if there is an end to suffering—but that is not to say that life is better that way. For one must always maintain the basic distinction between the evil that is part of all tragedy and the pain the evil brings; it is morally improper to accept evil.

Modern tragedy is made possible by the withdrawal from conscience of the divine dimension. To open one's eyes in our world is to be confronted by a blank slate on which one is nevertheless expected to write something meaningful. Nietzsche worked hard to convince himself—and he has been more successful with others than himself—that man could invent meaning since there was no meaning to discover. But the much heralded new truths which were to replace religion have so far proved simply to be exclamations. If there is no Absolute, there are no absolutes; the word means the same whether you capitalize it or not. By the middle of the nineteenth century, people were being born in a world where it was possible to assume that God was dead, and that man was therefore not only on his own but now free to do for himself what formerly God was supposed to have done for him. This was to be a challenge to show up the weaklings and to encourage the strong, this "time of exile," as Camus put it, a time for "nostalgia without aim . . . the endless search for justification." Nietzsche said, "The most painful, the most heartbreaking question is that of the heart which asks itself, 'Where can I feel at home?' " And it is perhaps natural to try to avoid despair by convincing oneself that, since God seems impossible or remote, the very idea of God or home must be an illusion to rid oneself of. This is rather like the Buddhist decision to quell a desire for health and security rather than make the effort needed to cure the sick and feed the hungry. It takes only one step more to pretend that man deliberately got rid of a feeble deity in order to act at last as man. Call this rebellion, call it the murder of God, it is a way of saying that man has everything under control, or will shortly. However, there is little evidence that man does have all things under control or is making a new home for himself better than the kingdom of heaven promised by Christ. To be born in a world in which reason and devotion are not respected, and to know no way to reinstate them and to associate with them only by downgrading them further, is to take a historical situation as final. And if one goes a little further and assumes that life must be believed happy even when it is not happy, that regrets are out of order, the very possibility of the tragic conscience disappears. For the tragic conscience depends first of all on pain and therefore nonacceptance. In fact, wherever the concern about the divine dimension has faded, human beings become subhuman and descriptions of them clinical or criminal.

To be jealous of God is foolish, of course, but it is comparatively healthy. To wish one could bless life as God would is to cling to a spot of affection for some part of creation. Even to say that the sole motive for human behavior is the will to preserve and extend oneself is to hold on to that which is. But freedom without law always leads to self-destruction, and the consistent rebel does not find peace. At the end of his life Camus was able to say, "The only original rule of life today is, in order to be a man one must refuse to be a god." This is the way of humility that Nietzsche was not strong enough to try. It would have meant accepting a world without God and then learning how to live with the tension of emptiness and nostalgia. On the one hand, as Ingmar Bergman says, "How can one believe in God?" On the other, as Dostoevski said, "God has tormented me all my life." This is the tragic tension of our time.

Like Kirillov in *The Possessed,* Nietzsche could only see "that man was the loftiest of all on earth. He was that which gave meaning to life . . . and he was not superhuman, you can take my word for it." He could see the power of the Christ but could only speak slightingly of his love. A small-minded man, this Nietzsche, unable even to rise to that Dostoevskian dilemma of being at heart a Christian while at the same time not believing in God. In the past one hundred years writers and philosophers have been striking theatrical poses instead of wondering or praying. It could be said that they did not pray because there was no one to pray to, or that they thought as much. Rather let it be said that they were dropped into a culture where reason could acknowledge only two sorts of truth with any degree of composure: truth of sense experience and truths of logic and mathematics. Already skeptics were finding it hard to justify moral and metaphysical concepts. The heart kept on having its reasons as before, and even the boldest voices like Nietzsche went on carrying the burdens of honesty and courtesy as scrupulously as the devotees of established morality. But in them we can now see the beginnings of that split in the modern conscience between a rational justification of unselfish ends and an ethic —if it can be called that—of inherited caution. No one has understood this better than Proust, or expressed it more clearly. "We are not provided with wisdom, we must discover it for ourselves, after a journey through the wilderness which no one else can take for us." We are not provided with, and we do not seem to be able to uncover, the truths which earlier generations took for granted, mind and heart together. And yet we go on acting as if they were true. Proust notices, he says, that

> the obligations which have not their sanction in our present life seem to belong to a different world entirely different from this,

which we leave in order to be born into this world, before perhaps returning to the other to live once again beneath the sway of those unknown laws which we have obeyed because we bore their precepts in our hearts, knowing not whose hand had traced them there.

The basic assumption of the modern conscience is Proust's maxim: "We exist alone. . . . Man is the creature that cannot emerge from himself. . . . The bonds that unite another person to ourself exist only in our mind. . . . I saw myself astray in life as upon an endless beach where I was alone." Out of this can come only tragedy, and tragedy of the most radical kind, regardless of the shape it assumes in one person or another. The tragedy of seeming to be born alone in a world "where everything is given and nothing explained" (Camus), takes a man much further into the structure of human possibility than either excessive pride or overweening passion in people who still believe in the gods. For this reason modern tragedy, if understood rightly, will tell us more about the nature of tragedy in general. The more isolated the tragic hero, the more nearly total his inner nihilism, the more likely it is that we can find out whether there is in the end any dignity to man that suffering will not rub out. The naked soul, unsupported by friends, fortune, or reason, is at the moment very much on trial in fiction and in reality. Have we anything to say for ourselves, anything healthy and at the same time reasonable? Or must the tragic alternatives be theatricality or suicide? The answer depends on how one understands the loneliness that is the condition of modern man.

Here again one meets evasion. Instead of starting with the inheritance of estrangement from the divine and accepting this inheritance as the starting point, Nietzsche encouraged himself to believe that he was free to cultivate or not cultivate solitude. (However, it is not solitude that is involved but loneliness.) There was no "good solitude, free, wanton, lightsome," any more than there was the quiet, confident solitude in which religious contemplation can flourish. There was only a man with no belief in a Creator or a Redeemer. And this man could not keep up the pretense for long; soon he was urging himself and the other "free spirits" —were there any? he had not met them—"not to cleave to any person, be it even the dearest; every person is a prison and also a recess." This is the language of one rejected in love or friendship; it is the language of Simone Weil also. "Preserve your solitude—never seek friendship, never permit yourself to dream of friendship . . . I feel that it is necessary and ordained that I should be alone, a stranger and an exile in relation to every human circle without exception." There have always been men and women who are outcasts or maladjusted. What makes the greatness of Simone Weil and Nietzsche significant beyond their maladjustment is their preoccupation with human estrangement from the divine. It is true that, so far as one can tell, Nietzsche had no nostalgia for the divine, while Simone Weil not only loved God but waited in prayer for him to speak (she was, however, confident of what he would not ask of her). But their human—all-too-human—loneliness was not a solitude within which either lyricism or metaphysics flowers, but where the reader's heart is moved solely by the poignancy of abandoned souls.

There are people, so Mauriac said of his Thérèse, "fated to carry loneliness about as a leper carries his scabs." These hearts are "fated to bear an infinite frustration" like Sisyphus. Nothing of this would be guessed from a reading of the main volumes of the Nietzsche canon, the source book of so much of the twentieth-century creed of unbelief. Only in letters to friends and notes to himself did this man dare to admit the truth. "I will not conceal it from you; things are going badly with me. Night more and more surrounds me. It is as if there had been just a flash of lightning, and now it is over." What was over was the pretense on which his critique of the illusions of conventional morality was based, the pretense that his strength and honesty came from his ability to look nothingness in the face and then want to dance for joy.

> Alone I confront a tremendous problem, it is a forest in which I lose myself, a virgin forest. I need help. I need disciples, I need a master. To obey would be sweet. If I had lost myself on a mountain, I would obey the man who knew the mountain; sick, I would obey a doctor; and if I should meet a man capable of enlightening me on moral ideas, I would listen to him, I would follow him, but I find no one, no disciples and fewer masters . . . I am alone.

Unable to listen to God, doubly unable to listen to men, this tragic figure finally tires of his own voice and lapses into a pathetic silence.

> Where are they, those old friends, with whom I formerly felt so closely bound? We inhabit different worlds, we no longer speak the same tongue; as a stranger, a proscribed man, I wander among them; never a word, never a look now reaches me . . . it is terrible to be condemned to silence, when one has so many things to say. Am I created for solitude, never to find anyone with whom I may make myself understood? Incommunicability is in truth the most awful of solitudes. . . . A profound man needs friends, unless indeed he has a God. And I have neither God nor friend.

What had he to say except that others were not sincere when they said they believed in God? What had he to say except that others could not face the turbulence and disorder of life —and that he could—without the opiate of faith in God? Even he could not sustain this loneliness. "Oh, grant madness, you heavenly powers. Madness that at last I may believe in myself. I am consumed by doubts, for I have killed the Law. If I am not more than the Law, then I am the most abject of all." God protect us from our own prayers. Nietzsche's prayer was answered; madness followed. He was not up to his own tragedy, and God spared him further questioning which he could not answer.

With Simone Weil the story is different. She had met God. "He entered my room and said: 'Poor creature, you who understand nothing, who know nothing, come with me and I will teach you things which you do not suspect.' I followed him." And he took her to a church and made her kneel. He brought her to a garret and spoke to her. They ate bread and drank wine together. "This bread really had the taste of bread. I have never found that taste again." And then one day he said, "Now go," and he threw her out on the stairs. She wandered in the streets and lost her way and could not get back. The rest of her life was lived on this memory. "I know well that he does not love me. How could he love me? And yet deep down within me something, a particle of myself, cannot help thinking, with fear and trembling, that perhaps, in spite of all, he loves me." Say what you will, this was her salvation—the light that Nietzsche missed, the light that can light every man that comes into the world.

There are ways of avoiding the extremity of faith or the extremity of madness. There is crime. Had not Dostoevski concluded that once belief in God and immortality had disappeared "all things are lawful"? Was not this Nietzsche's reasoning too? No future life and no God: these two assumptions run through the writings of the late nineteenth and early twentieth centuries. There is no continuity of persons, no punishment either; there is no supernatural; no one who listens or answers. We talk to ourselves. Truly, if there is no God, then everything is lawful, if one can get away with it. Dostoevski's overwrought and comical descriptions of the desperation and tiredness of men without God, who turned to crime to justify freedom, are unexcelled. For he was not interested in the sensualist as such or the moral cretin, but rather in people who turn to crime deliberately because they know they have lost any rational way of justifying self-control or affection. Let these speak—little Lise, Dmitri, Stavrogin, Svidrigailov—they say much the same thing. They are "in love with disorder"; they "want to do evil," for "sin is sweet," and "sometimes it is very pleasant to smash things"; "there are moments when people love crime." They are vicious, of course; they mean to be. This is the difference between them and the run-of-the-mill vicious or neurotic characters of an American play or novel. Dostoevski's people seek disorder and vice as a way of keeping the intellect alive in a world which they did not make and yet are not intelligent or humble enough to transform. They know they are alone, without props; therefore, they act according to their disbelief, freely, which means vilely. For if they acted in any other way, they would be acting like the mimics of another civilization, without a good reason. How can one test one's freedom better than by living dangerously? "Our deepest insights must appear as follies and in certain circumstances as crime," said Nietzsche. Nothing more specious has been said, and yet it has become a genuine alternative for a mind that mistrusts reason and knows no God.

The tragedy of a mind that is tormented by the idea of a God it assumes is dead, is a most interesting tragedy indeed. Dostoevski's image of this doubleness is best contained in Dmitri's claim that he revered the ideal of the Madonna at the same time that he followed the ideal of Sodom. "All contradictions exist side by side." To be in love with vileness and at the same time to be disgusted by it is the double sign of a man who has not yet resigned himself to Nietzsche's fate. In the end Svidrigailov and Stavrogin commit suicide, and the fate of the others is indefinite. Their tension is hardly bearable; they make the gesture of vice and then give up. But their vice is not simply a gesture; it is real, it has malice, hatred, and resentment. No one is more resentful than a man of no beliefs who has little to do and no interest in anyone but himself.

The modern world often seems to be a bored world, as in Bernanos' picture of a French country parish, "bored stiff . . . such is the true condition of man." Boredom is safe only so long as it is inert; but if restlessness is added, and desire, and lust, then beware an outbreak of sadism. Boredom may, on the other hand, turn in on itself, and the world outside may provoke nausea. Then nausea will have become the normal state, as Sartre thought. The bored man, the superfluous city man, the anonymous city man, afraid of existence, and with no clear reason for living, staring at the world around him, living alone, receiving nothing, giving nothing, purging himself in sex "of a certain nostalgia the cause of which I know too well" (Sartre). But what a choice facing the disinherited mind: inertia, madness, crime! Can there be no warmth, no affection in this world? Not according to Sartre. To love is to try to capture someone else. Not according to Proust. To love is to torment and be tormented. This mind "doesn't care about anything because it's completely cold" (Bergman). "Each of us is indeed alone," said Proust. "It is the tragedy of other people that they are to us merely showcases for the very perishable collections of our own mind." It is the tragedy of our own minds that we do not emerge out of ourselves. Nietzsche thought that it might be possible, but his personal failure speaks more loudly than his hope.

Dostoevski treated this possibility more ironically. Many of his characters proclaim the coming of "the new men," the titans. "Everything will begin anew. Men will unite to take from life all it can give, but only for joy and happiness in the present world. . . ." And the Devil retorts, "That's all very charming, but if you want to swindle, why do you want a moral sanction for doing it?" We meet a similar exaggeration, a similar pretense in Camus' justification of his character Meursault. This mollusk, indifferent to all save his physical needs and urges, is said, before his execution, to "lay his heart open to the benign indifference of the universe," whatever that means. And Camus obstinately insisted that he "had tried to symbolize the only Christ of which we are worthy." Fifteen years after making him, Camus discovered that Meursault had "a passion for the absolute and the truth . . . willing to die for the truth." What truth? No truth at all.

Simply the refusal to say he loved his mother when he did not, that he was sorry he had killed an Arab when he was not, and so on. By this time we have left the world of tragedy and are back in a world where nothing matters very much one way or another. This is a real enough world, but it is not tragic or serious. True loneliness cares that it is lonely; tragic loneliness is marked by an awareness of the absence of the divine. Such awareness can take different forms, from nostalgia to resentment to torment to obsessive acceptance. But without some awareness of this, a man is not wholly lonely. Either he has a divine dimension of some sort or he lives an unexamined life, barely human.

Finally we meet the tragedy of the innocent. This is a definite vein in both American and British fiction. Conrad's heroes are essentially inexperienced and therefore innocent. They blunder; they get hurt. But they endure; they learn courage. And Fitzgerald's Gatsby and Dick Diver do not know the world well enough to pass through unhurt by rich and beautiful—and corrupt—American girls. They have a naïveté that cannot stand up to prolonged exposure to money, boredom, and obtuseness. Henry James saw much the same conflict between the innocence of the new world and the cynicism of Europe. There is, to be sure, a certain poignancy in these presentations, but they are traps for our sympathy. In the real world innocence is not always innocent. The innocent get hurt all the time but "their victims lie strewn all round" (Bowen). As "strangers to the world . . . they exist alone," and act with a selfishness that makes one gasp. We would do well to regard innocence as an intermediate stage in the tragic journey, even a forecourt of the palace in which God is being mourned. Besides, as Camus has said, "We cannot assert the innocence of anyone, whereas we can state with certainty the guilt of all." Very well, but what about genocide and slavery? Buber said:

How is life with God still possible in a time in which there is an Oświecim? The estrangement has become too cruel, the hiddenness too deep. One can still believe in the God who allowed these things to happen, but can one still speak to him? Can one still hear his word? Dare we recommend to the Job of the gas chambers: "Call to Him, for He is kind, for His mercy endureth forever?"

Many cannot, either because they do not believe or because they no longer believe God will reply. Ivan Karamazov said, "I can accept God, but not his world." An unjust world presupposes, he implied, an indifferent God. "If there is a God," said Epicurus, "he does not care for us." Or again Buber: "He is, but he is not present."

An unjust world presupposes evil men also. It is easy to shift blame to a hidden or absent God. What torments man more than anything is God's silence. Unable to comprehend it, man protests his innocence. "My case is exceptional. I am innocent" (Camus). "I'm not guilty, it's a misunderstanding. And if it comes to that, how can any man be called guilty? We are all simply men here, one as much as the other. . . . [yes,] that's how all guilty men talk" (Kafka). Innocence, however real or relative, is a position to be reckoned with when one is forced to think of all the forms of desolation in the modern world. And yet if some people hurt and get hurt, just because they are innocent, many more get hurt for reasons which have nothing to do with their innocence. As individuals they are no more, no less, innocent than other men. But when they suffer from the malice of others and do not hear God's comforting word, they too have reached the extremity of tragic suffering. They have passed "through door after door, opened and then locked behind them, through room after room . . . and arrived at the central part of the soul" (Weil). And that last room shall be called humiliation. In it man is insulted and injured not only by men but by God's silence as well. And he would say with Job of God, "If I had called and he had answered me, yet would I not believe that he had hearkened unto my voice." The inhabitant of the chamber of humiliation will feel totally abandoned. This was where the incorruptible genius of Kafka lay, in sketching with the simplest of outlines the last hours of tragedy.

A man is arrested who does not know there has been a crime, who never learns what he is supposed to have done, who asserts his innocence regardless, who seeks help at every turn and rejects help. Called to account and yet too lazy or too frightened to approach God boldly—whether God be the law or the owner of the village—he is condemned from a distance and executed in the open air. Such is life, Kafka suggests, in the age of the eclipse of God. It is now normal to say, "I don't know this law." And it would be obvious that the answer is, "All the worse for you. It is not necessary to accept anything as true, one must only accept it as necessary." This modern passion for truth on the part of a reason which is—so we think—not equipped for any but the most limited kind of truth, is a symptom of the intellectual paralysis that hastens the tragic downfall.

And so with no God to seek or obey or adore, the self is left alone with itself and its case. "I heard once of a young man who thought of nothing but the Castle day and night, he neglected everything else, and people feared for his reason, his mind was so wholly absorbed by the Castle. . . . The thought of his case never left him. 'I have a difficult task ahead of me,' he said, 'and I have dedicated my whole life to it.' " What could this be, this solemn undertaking? The last illusion of all: he wants his rights! As if there could be any rights in a world where everything is given and nothing explained, where innocence is an illusion and God is silent. No, the stripping of the soul must proceed one step more. "You are not from the Castle, you are not from the village, you aren't anything—a stranger, a man who isn't wanted." Utterly crushed by this, does the soul die? Not at all, at least not for some time. But when death comes, the stranger says with quiet persistence, "Maybe not yet, but . . ." What drives the exile on, the one who is, as Camus says, "deprived of the memory of a lost home or the hope of a promised land"? Sheer grit perhaps? What can that be? Although it would be consoling to agree with Camus that "nostalgia is the mark of the human," what can this mean if "the only true paradise is the paradise we have lost" (Proust)? Here we touch on something in human nature that eludes definition. And it may be the vanishing point of the human. But if the individual survives, then it is by being transfigured into another dimension of reality, still within the realm of suffering but beyond its rationale. All that remains that is common to both tragedy and that other world, recognizable in both, is perseverance. And if the next to the last cry was "Recognize me," the last cry is "Take me anyway." The next to the last cry on the Cross was "Why hast thou forsaken me?" and the last "Into thy hands I commend my spirit." It will then be finished, the journey ended.

Whoever loses all and hangs on through pain and emptiness knows tragedy. There should be no argument as to what took him there, whether accident, war, exile, pride, passion, loss of work, death of a loved one. It is the extremity of deprivation, not the means or even the size, that marks off tragic pain from any other. And in this extremity the touchstone of tragic strength is the final endurance from some secret source, even though the loss and waste threaten to blot out all that matters. As Chestov said, "The only true solution is precisely where human judgment sees no solution." All that seems to be left is human persistence. But this is precisely how the presence of the divine can be sensed. When a man is tormented, when comfort, explanation, prospect of restoration and relief are withheld, when even so he will not surrender, then we on the outside know that he has entered the dark night of the soul.

Even Sisyphus lives in that night. Nowhere else in human experience is it so obvious that man has met and is being sustained by God than in tragedy, the same modern tragedy that the saints call the dark night of the soul. The road most commonly taken by the saints to reach this night is that of purification and prayer. The road of tragedy by way of suffering and a passion for the real, the finite. They are much the same. And both are marked by perseverance. This is the secret of tragedy, of its cause, its waste, the secret of its record of endurance and nobility and peace. Whoever says that there is no tragedy for a Christian because he has a future life to look forward to, understands neither Christianity nor tragedy. So long as human nature remains the same, there will be experiences which are hopeless. It makes little difference whether asceticism or suffering has preceded the blackout of the spirit; what matters is that darkness has fallen without killing the spirit. No writers in the past one hundred years have written as faithfully of the dark night of the soul as have Kafka and Dostoevski, not Nietzsche or Proust. And so far no one has noticed the similarity between the tragic experience which they describe and "the dark night of the soul" of the religious life. Tragic experience is religious experience; only the circumstances differ.

From different starting points people can reach the same end. For the saints the ascetic life begins with a determination to purify the self of all that is natural but not essential. Deliberately the ascetic sets out to reduce his life to the barest minimum so that he is left with the one thing that matters: the image of God. Purification is painful, and most men give up. But if one perseveres and holds fast to God and accepts his will, darkness falls, such darkness as one is never really prepared for. Then the ascetic life becomes comfortless and painful (the night of the senses), and after a time the soul feels that God has withdrawn and left him to flounder (the night of the spirit). If at this stage the ascetic loses heart, his loss of faith may so diminish him that he passes the rest of life in bitterness and insecurity. If, on the other hand, he continues to want God, even the God who has apparently abandoned him, he can be given assurance that in just this way does God give power to those who love him greatly.

"God is teaching us that we must live as men who can get along very well without him. The God who is with us is the God who forsakes us. The God who makes us live in this world without him as a working hypothesis is the God before whom we are ever standing." This description of the ways of "the God of the gas-chambers," written by Dietrich Bonhoeffer while awaiting his own execution by the Nazis, can apply as easily to the ascetical "dark night" as to tragic experience. And when St. John of the Cross describes the "cruel spiritual death" of the ascetic by saying that "it thinks that God has abandoned it," that "it is unable to raise its affection or its mind to God, neither can it pray to him—thinking that God has set a cloud before it through which its prayer cannot pass," he could have been speaking of the experience common to thousands of longing hearts in the past one hundred years who were born into a world from which God has apparently fled.

It is no use mourning, "I was not ever thus. . . . I loved to choose and see my path" (Newman). The fact remains that "the night is dark and I am far from home." This experience is common to tragedy and the dark night—so far from home, that home itself seems only a dream. Man has entered the "desert of godhead where no one is at home" (Eckhart). The boredom that precedes profound suffering is the equivalent of the dryness of the night of prayer. The desolation of the night of the spirit is the equivalent of the tragic waste and terror. In either case life is reduced to the point where feeling and reason seem to be paralyzed, and the spirit stumbles along by itself. Blindly and perhaps plaintively, as St. Thérèse of Lisieux:

> I get tired of the darkness all around me and try to refresh my jaded spirits with the thoughts of that bright country where my hopes lie; and what happens? It is worse torment than ever. It's all a dream, this talk of a heavenly country, and of a God who made it all . . . and death will make nonsense of your hopes; it will only mean a night darker than ever, the night of mere non-

existence. . . . You might imagine that my soul was as full of consolations as it could hold, that for me the veil which hides the unseen scarcely existed. And all the time it isn't a veil, it's a great wall which reaches up to the sky and blots out the stars. When I write poems about the happiness of heaven, I'm simply talking about what I'd determined to believe.

It is this determination that indicates the presence of the divine precisely when the spirit feels most abandoned and the darkness thickest. Simone Weil, who knew affliction also, adds, "It is when from the uttermost depths of our being we need a sound which does mean something—when we cry out for an answer and it is not granted—it is then that we touch the silence of God." And this silence is, she concludes, the Word on the Cross.

No tragic experience is more lonely than the dark night of the man of prayer, and no human darkness is thicker and more oppressive than that from the sixth to the ninth hour. "My humanity is the road which all must tread who would come to that which thou seekest," (Suso). God in Christ having identified himself with man by becoming man, in tragedy and in the dark night, we are therefore at one with the Man on the Cross. If, as Bonhoeffer put it, "God allows himself to be edged out of the world and onto the cross," it is because God knows that life is tragic, and that only when the light of the divine in us seems to be extinguished, are we ready to see him. The final perseverance of Sisyphus or The Little Flower of Jesus indicates the same reality, the flame of God's love for us, the flame that keeps us alive even when we can no longer see by its light. No wonder that at the very time that the soul is being tormented by doubt and loss, spectators sometimes observe tranquillity. And yet in the extremity of deprivation and despair the spirit continues to complain, as Bergman says, "What is going to happen to those of us who want to believe but aren't able to? Why can't I kill God within me? Why in spite of everything is he a baffling reality that I can't shake off? I call out to him in the dark, but no one seems to be there. . . . Life is an outrageous horror." This agony is an act of love. "Simply to thy cross I cling." Thomas a Kempis was right when he said, "You see, the cross is at the root of everything." The way of tragedy, the dark night of the soul, is the royal road of the Cross. The darker the night the nearer to the Man on the Cross, the man on the paradise tree.

This has always been so. The difference now is that for a hundred years or so mankind in the West has had to experience tragedy refined to its simplest elements. To be born into a world in which God's absence is noticed and felt is to be hurried unceremoniously down the tragic passage to an abyss. In so many ways, the world has now grown up, especially in its exposure of hypocrisies and illusions. "Now that it has come of age, the world is more godless, and perhaps it is for that very reason nearer God than ever before" (Bonhoeffer). For the first time in history tragic victim and saintly ascetic can meet as friends at Golgotha, the hill of Sisyphus. The God who is Man awaits them with open arms. Saint and hero are nourished by the eucharistic strength they did not know the world had, the strength of the Christ who endured their shame. They will be given his peace that passeth all their understanding.

Twice-Blessed Enamel Flowers: Reality in Contemporary Fiction

BY PAUL ELMEN

J. D. SALINGER'S short story, "De Daumier-Smith's Blue Period," tells about the experiences of a youthful instructor in Les Amis Des Vieux Maîtres, Canadian art school. Among the students who take this correspondence course is a nun, Sister Irma; and though he has never met her, Daumier-Smith finds himself falling in love with his pious and talented student. When the nun's superior, Father Zimmerman, learns that Sister Irma's work is being criticized with more affection than one normally finds in a correspondence course, he withdraws the nun from the school. Daumier-Smith enters his blue period. On the day that the news breaks, he eats a solitary and mournful meal and then walks listlessly back to his room. On the way he passes an orthopedic shop and stops to watch a young lady who, unaware of his presence, is adjusting a truss on a model. When she notices that she is being watched, she blushes, steps back in confusion, and falls over a pile of irrigation basins. Were it not for the pane of glass, Daumier-Smith would have tried to break her fall.

This is Daumier-Smith's moment of truth. "Suddenly," he wrote in his diary, "the sun came up and sped toward the bridge of my nose at the rate of ninety-three million miles a second. Blinded and very frightened—I had to put my hand on the glass to keep my balance. The thing lasted for no more than a few seconds. When I got my sight back, the girl had gone from the window, leaving behind her a shimmering field of exquisite, twice-blessed enamel flowers." [1]

It is clear that we do not have before us an immortal story; but it does have a representative value and raises an important question: What is the sense of reality in contemporary fiction? In this story we can examine the dynamics which move beneath the surface in a great many modern stories. Sister Irma, like the Church she serves, has great attraction for an artist: she is different, colorful, and impossible to attain. When Daumier-Smith discovers that he cannot have even the Platonic friendship he has in mind, he falls into a despair from which he is rescued only when he discovers the commonplace world of trusses and bedpans and people. Sister Irma disappears like a wraith, leaving behind her an ordinary world which for the first time has begun to seem enchanting. This Daumier who is also a Smith has had a vision not unlike that of St. Paul's on the Damascus Road, except that now it is the real sun which blinds him and gives him a feeling of vertigo. He falls in love with the world in its full banality of people and things and events. We find ourselves remembering a remark from *Finnegans Wake,* which occurs when the hero comes across the intriguing idea that the cricketeer Hosty by taking a wafer on his tongue can be united with the body of Christ: "How culious an epiphany!"

Salinger has described what has always been the classically comic situation: the incongruity of placing the mundane world into juxtaposition with the unearthly, so that the disproportion is suddenly obvious. Like many an artist before him, Daumier-Smith then chooses the world, and is able happily to write in his diary, "Everybody is a nun." Whatever the charms of Sister Irma, the girl lying flat on her back in the window is palpably human; and by taking comfort in her unpretentious nearness, Salinger finds his place in the tradition of nineteenth-century realism—somewhere rather far down

[1] J. D. Salinger, "De Daumier-Smith's Blue Period," in *Nine Stories* (New York: Signet Books, 1954), p. 121.

the line behind Stendhal, Balzac, the Goncourts, and Zola. For his literary ancestry turn to the scene in *Madame Bovary* in which, shortly after Emma's death, the Curé Bournisien sprinkles the room with holy water, while the druggist Homais follows him with disinfectant chlorine water. Or turn to the conversation between Ibsen's Solness and Hilda, in which the Master Builder says that he builds no more church towers, but only homes for human beings.

The mood has been sustained in our own century under the label of naturalism—an intense and affectionate interest in the scientifically real, often coupled with an explicit denial that reality has any supernatural significance whatever. The road from Zola and de Maupassant leads to Virginia Woolf, Proust, Dreiser, and Dos Passos, and comes to a kind of destination in James Joyce. In *A Portrait of the Artist as a Young Man,* Stephen Dedalus feels an attraction for the Church which is comparable to Daumier-Smith's interest in the nun. When a priest asks Stephen if he had ever felt that he had a vocation, Stephen admits that he had. "He had seen himself, a young and silent-mannered priest, entering a confessional swiftly, ascending the altar steps, incensing, genuflecting, accomplishing the vague acts of the priesthood which pleased him by reason of their semblance of reality and of their distance from it." [2] But, at the moment of decision, it is reality which asserts its claim. As he is shaking the priest's hand, a quartette of young men come striding down the street with arms linked, prancing in tune to their leader's concertina; and Stephen knows at that moment that he must reject the "grave and ordered and passionless life" of the priest in favor of the actualities of the Dublin streets.

This vocation to the priesthood of banality appears as a leitmotiv in all of Joyce's work. For example, in *Ulysses* Leopold Bloom, after attending mass at All Hallows, went

[2] James Joyce, *A Portrait of the Artist as a Young Man* (New York: The Viking Press, 1956), p. 158.

into a chemist's shop to buy a cake of soap, and then put it in his pocket. The weather seemed not in the least apocalyptic but instead good cricket weather: "Heatwave. Won't last. Always passing, the stream of life, which in the stream of life we trace is dearer than them all. Enjoy a bath now: clean trough of water, cool enamel, the gentle tepid stream. This is my body." [3] The man of letters is interested in what happens at All Hallows—interested, even absorbed, in the whole religious world, such goings-on delighting the connoisseur of the unusual. But he sees only men doing strange things, the sign and not the symbol, the credulity of men, the priest playing a part in Aristotle's spectacle; and so he misses the strangest thing of all. However, he is shrewd enough to know that something more may be hidden behind the surface, something secret and strange, not manageable in terms of his plot structures, and so vaguely threatening. Therefore he turns with relief to the commonplace world, which seems so fathomable, so available to the creative imagination, so ready to be described, to be changed, or even to be destroyed. This is why, as Wallace Stevens said (in "An Ordinary Evening in New Haven"),

> We keep coming back and coming back
> To the real: to the hotel instead of the hymns
> That fall upon it out of the wind.

Acceptance of this creedal statement is part of an artist's orthodoxy, and examples of its authority may be chosen almost at random. The old waiter in Hemingway's story "A Clean, Well-Lighted Place" decides that a Spanish café with its tables and chairs and dangling light bulb is much to be preferred over the surrounding night and its dim forms. "It was all a nothing and a man was nothing too. It was only that and light was all it needed and a certain cleanness and order. . . . Hail nothing full of nothing, nothing is with

[3] James Joyce, *Ulysses* (New York: Random House, Inc., 1946), p. 85.

thee. He smiled and stood before a bar with a shiny steam pressure coffee machine." [4]

Dr. Rieux in Camus' *The Plague* rejects all suggestion of supernatural dimension, concluding that it is better that we spend our lives fighting what we know is bad, namely, sickness; we should, he thinks, attack death and suffering "without raising our eyes toward heaven where He sits in silence." Faulkner's *A Fable* turns on the scene in which the old general pleads with the idealistic private to circumvent the proposed execution by abandoning his dreams and finding his life in a world which may be pure or impure, but is at any event real: "I champion of this mundane earth which, whether I like it or not, is, and to which I did not ask to come . . . ; you champion of an esoteric realm of man's baseless hopes and his infinite capacity—no: passion—for unfact. . . . So once more: take the earth." [5] Each of these examples illustrates what Sartre calls *la littérature engagée*.

What many of the modern storytellers seem agreed in saying is that earth is enough. They think that the matter of a story should be concrete human experience and not the kind of cloudy abstraction which gives worship its numinous symmetry. Happily they have followed Pope's iambic injunction:

> Know then thyself, presume not God to scan;
> The proper study of mankind is man.

They feel that there is more actuality in an engineer running a train than in a man swinging a thurible; and if they had to choose, they would prefer to be abandoned on an island with Lolita rather than with Joan of Arc, with Alexander King rather than with Billy Graham. To the protest of the Christian critic that the visionaries, too, are part of human ex-

[4] Ernest Hemingway, "A Clean, Well-Lighted Place," in *The Hemingway Reader*, edited by Charles Poore (New York: Charles Scribner's Sons, 1953), p. 421.

[5] William Faulkner, *A Fable* (New York: Random House, Inc., 1954), p. 348.

perience, and that they have simply made one metaphysical decision, as the lover of the commonplace has made another, the worldling writer replies that the visionary decision insults life. Even if the dreamer is sincere, believing the nonsense he preaches, he is to be regarded as an enemy, since he is engaged in time and space only as an agent of judgment and redemption, interested in history only to the degree that he can save it or damn it to hell.

The literary artist, like all artists, feels himself to be in love with the coarse texture of the visible world and with the tumult of its events, which he accepts gratefully without for a moment wishing it were something else. He finds the Christian full of pride, manipulating the real world as grossly as a Rain Maker, and he spends his strength exposing the *trahison des clérics*. The minister in the local church seems to him no more sensible than Mme. Blavatsky with her pineal eye and her seven chakras of yoga. Fortunately, he thinks, the real world survives such pious ministrations, even as Falstaff survives the thin-lipped Puritan and his brandished finger. "Dost thou think," he asks, "because thou art virtuous there shall be no more Vat 69?"

II

Salinger's story of the rejection of a fanciful romance with a nun, and his glad acceptance of the enameled flowers, expresses succinctly the kind of choice which the intellectual climate of our time has best prepared us to make. There is everywhere an enthusiasm for empirical reality. What used to be thought of as a *Bürgerlich* motif—the simple pleasures of the hearth, the consolation of acquiring and hoarding things—has become a *Künstler* motif as well. Of course, Daumier-Smith's discovery had been fitfully anticipated by Flaubert's wistful affection for a normal family, and by Emerson's turn to the falling snow rather than to the sermon in the Concord church; but when Kafka expresses his envy of a postman, and when Mann's Tonio Kröger writes to Lisabeta about "the bliss of the commonplace," they speak for a whole ethos.

Philosophic theory, in rebellion against idealism, supplies a solid beat to the orchestration in the form of pragmatism, realism, naturalism, phenomenology, and existentialism. Related obscurely but no less certainly is the faith of Beard, Veblen, and Dewey in the ordinary man living in an ordinary world rather than in any moral or relational construction. It would be surprising if the novelist who looks for his matter in experience did not reflect the factual style of his time. And this has seemed to some critics to throw the artist into a war against the churches. According to Allen Tate: "The subject of the imaginative writer is necessarily men as they are behaving, not as they ought to behave. For this reason, there is a standing quarrel between the imaginative writer and the church. It will continue forever." [6]

This would seem a singularly misleading remark, since the literary artist is demonstrably interested in men as they ought to behave; and the Church must necessarily be aware of men as they are behaving in order to make a sensible suggestion about how men ought to behave; and if Tate had hit on the truth, his remark would point to the manner in which the quarrel could be resolved. But it is probably true that many novelists think they have a quarrel with the Church. What follows from such a critical theory is that the novelist can no longer roam heaven and earth in search of themes but is restricted to a much narrower area: the area of factual reference without any perspective into the Beyond. In France,

[6] "Orthodoxy and the Standard of Literature," *New Republic* (January 5, 1953), 24. According to Aristotle, "It is not the function of the poet to relate what has happened, but what may happen—what is possible according to the law of probability or necessity. . . . Poetry, therefore, is more philosophical and a higher thing than history." Samuel H. Butcher, *Aristotle's Theory of Poetry and Fine Art* (New York, 1902), p. 35. According to Eliseo Vivas, "What literature gives us is a symbolic construct of what life ought to be like in order to answer the demands of an aesthetic apprehension of it." "Literature and Knowledge," *Sewanee Review*, LX (1952), 590.

birthplace of so much literary theory, a new school called the *chosistes* have tried to break out from this impoverishment of theme by paying clinical attention to the *thisness* of objects and doing for literature what the cubists did for the fine arts. The argument is that, by separating people from things, the radical isolation and strangeness of things will become apparent in unending variety. Nathalie Saurraute, Muchel Butor, Claude Simon, Marguerite Durras, and Claude Mauriac are exponents of this newest naturalism but Alain Robbe-Grillet is the *chef d'école.*

According to Robbe-Grillet, a pure realism is most difficult to achieve. "Even the least conditioned observer," he writes, "is unable to look at the world which surrounds him with entirely unprejudiced eyes." Total impersonality, the cool objectivity sought by Flaubert and Joyce, is impossible; it is even impossible to observe freely. "At every instant, a continuous fringe of culture (psychology, ethics, metaphysics, etc.) is being added to things, disguising their real strangeness, making them more comprehensible, more reassuring." The literary vision protects itself from this strangeness by dividing the world in two parts—the few assimilable things which are said to have significance, and everything else in the world, which is said to be absurd. "But the world is neither significant nor absurd," says Robbe-Grillet. "It *is.*" [7]

Chosisme is a forlorn effort to find interest in creation after the Creator has died and man is moribund. Not since Ruskin's criticism of "the pathetic fallacy" in *Modern Painters* has a meddling anthropomorphism been so carefully identified. The intention is that a fastidious description will reveal the presence of alien objects which have their ontological dignity whether men grant them this or not, the tree standing stubbornly in the quad without a by-your-leave from God or

[7] Robbe-Grillet outlined his critical theory in the *Nouvelle Revue Française*, July, 1956. It was translated and published by Richard Howard as "A Fresh Start for Fiction," *Evergreen Review*, I (1937), 97-104. See also J. Robert Loy, "'Things' in Recent French Literature," *PMLA*, LXXI (1956), 27-41.

from men, the fire burning on in the grate long after the don has gone to bed. The writer now can exhaust his reader, but not his subject matter. "Il y a autre chose à dire des escargots," wrote Francis Ponge. "D'abord leur propre humidité. Leur sang froid. Leur extensibilité." [8] One tries to imagine an *Odyssey* which contained nothing but a catalogue of ships. Surprisingly, other arts have been influenced by chosism. Though painting seems to have resisted the trend, a more powerful impressionism having dissipated an interest in visual perception, drama has given us a parallel phenomenon. Samuel Beckett, Eugène Ionesco, Jean Genet, and the theorists of the American Mime Theater have all tried to give the ordinary scene in its full, shapeless banality, without dependence on myth or ritual or dramatic convention. We are invited to be present at a pure encounter, the assertion being that the world need not be trimmed and shaped to fit an artistic need, but is sufficiently engrossing when the last bit of conventional understanding has been prised from it.

While chosism may be dismissed as a kind of left-bank avant-gardism, marked from the beginning as a kind of speculation which could only seem plausible around a table at the Café de Fleurs, there has been a wider acceptance of a very different development in the modern novel: the motif of compassion, rather than of detached chronicle. Modern storytellers have turned with relief to the theme of sympathy for fellow mortals who are in trouble. When Daumier-Smith saw the girl in the shop window fall, he reached out to catch her, hitting the tips of his fingers on the pane of glass. For the first time, the young artist had felt a rush of pity for another human being, and in a flood of sympathy he drew upon the religious word hoard and called even the enameled flowers "twice blessed." They were blessed, not because they were evidences of God's handiwork as in *The Little Flowers of St. Francis*, but because they were artifacts upon which some

[8] *Le Parti Pris des Choses* (Paris, 1942), p. 29.

human hand had labored. They served as symbols of human identity, and so as emblems blessing Daumier-Smith with his vision of identity with suffering humanity. He may have thought about Portia's remark:

> The quality of mercy is not strain'd;
> It droppeth as the gentle rain from heaven
> Upon the place beneath. It is twice-blest—
> It blesseth him that gives, and him that takes.

Daumier-Smith's impulsive effort to break the girl's fall was motivated by the same compassion which gives dignity to Holden Caulfield in Salinger's better-known story, *The Catcher in the Rye*. Holden is an appalling adolescent whose major redeeming feature is his desire to stand guard at the edge of a field of rye and catch children who are in danger of falling over the cliff.

One could do worse than call the literary age in which we live "the age of mercy." R. W. B. Lewis has pointed out that an earlier generation of moderns—men like Kafka and Joyce—worked on a much broader canvas and were capable of metaphysical audacities; but the second generation of moderns have refrained from such elevated speculation in favor of a quieter brand of humanism. According to Lewis, the novelists of our time (the Faulkner of "The Bear," the Camus of *The Plague*, the Silone of *Bread and Wine*, the Malraux of *Man's Fate*) have had nothing to do with an arcane God dwelling in distant splendor, and have turned instead to a God who is present in the midst of life. He thinks that the only transcendence our age is capable of is a concern for others, and that the modern man thinks he is saved when out of the fullness of his humanity he reaches out a helping hand to his fellow in need. It is noteworthy that the fall suffered by Clamence in Camus' novel is not that he failed to heed God's voice, but that he failed to answer the cry of a drowning woman. "Companionship," says Lewis, "is the matrix of humanity in the representative fiction of the second generation."[9]

We have now to examine the implications of this dilemma between naturalism and theism, in order to ask whether the choice for naturalism has borne fruit, and also whether the choice need have been made at all.

III

The clinical attitude towards things which the *chosistes* and their imitators have struck does not seem a promising critical posture. Despite their protests against literary distortion, when they themselves set out to illustrate their theories, they do not give us things but only a literary description of things. It seems odd that this must be said, but a literary principle has helped them decide what things will be described. Again, a literary principle helps them decide what aspect of the thing will be described and what will be left out. The truth is, as Aristotle and Thomas Aquinas pointed out, that particular things are not intelligible as such: an active intellect must abstract genera and species. Both the acceptance of things and the rejection of things can be accomplished only by the abstraction, and try as he will to avoid the pathetic fallacy, the mountains began tiptoeing to the sea as soon as Robbe-Grillet began writing *Le Voyeur*.

Whether every storyteller admits it in his critical theory or not, he craves generality, and his working hours are spent searching for unifying patterns and structures. Raw, unclassified experience offends him unless he can find a place for it in his story; the raggle-taggle of objects and actions and artifacts everywhere around him gives him precisely the kind of vertigo which Daumier-Smith experienced outside the orthopedic shop. Sartre called it "nausea"—the curious bardic qualm which overwhelms an author when impressions tumble in on him faster than he can digest. Not only are there too

[9] R. W. B. Lewis, *The Picaresque Saint* (Philadelphia: J. B. Lippincott Co., 1959), p. 218.

many shops, there are too many objects in the window, and there is neither life enough nor time. When the *tranche de vie* is honestly made, banality and significance run together in an accidental fashion which the artistic conscience is the first to reject. "The realism of modern realism," says Francis Fergusson, "ends with the literal. Beyond that is not the ordered world of tradition, but *Unendlichkeit*, and the anomalous 'freedom' of undefined and uninformed aspiration." [10]

For all its urbanity, the new naturalism seems more and more like a return to the nursery, the only place where colored blocks can be manipulated without embarrassment. If one could sense in the movement the familiar acquisitive instinct—the mood of Hearst assembling *objets d'art* for San Simeon—things would still be held in some kind of setting: they would be instruments of prestige, symbols of a style of life, specimens of the beautiful. Hoarding them for these reasons might still be sin (St. Augustine's *cupiditas*); but one can only pity a collector who lavishes his love on objects because he does not know his Lord. *Chosisme* separates objects from their context, bursting the universe asunder like an intellectual atom bomb. Denis Donoghue has pointed out this tendency in James Joyce:

> It is a mistake to think that modern literature is 'naturalistic,' if the meaning of naturalism includes a devoted engrossment with the finite order. An innocent might assume that if there is nothing left but the sensible object, that object must be the recipient of our piety, our reverence, yes our love. But this is not so. With the decline in specific religious commitment, with the abandonment of the supernatural, there has been a decline in our commitment toward what remains, the thing, the natural object, the sensible event.[11]

We are now in position to venture a guess concerning the reason so much modern fiction turns on the theme of

[10] Francis Fergusson, *The Idea of a Theater* (Garden City: Doubleday & Co., Inc., 1949), pp. 173-4.

[11] Denis Donoghue, "Joyce and the Finite Order," *Sewanee Review*, XVIII (Spring, 1960), 270.

compassion. If, in the absence of God, men turn toward the palpable existents around them, they prove for themselves the discovery Adam made: that these things are not finally interesting. They turn then toward their fellow human beings, as Adam turned to Eve and, since for two thousand years the Church has spoken of charity, they single out their fellows who are most in need. Is not then the theme of benevolence one which the theological critic should applaud? There is hatred enough in the world; if the novelists have rediscovered pity, perhaps the churchman should be grateful and should return to his attack on more obvious enemies such as pornography and advertising and mileage indicators showing zero in the used car lots. The awkward fact is that the Christian critic is not satisfied with a literary compassion which does not go beyond Matthew Arnold's cry on the darkling plain ("Dover Beach"),

> Ah, love, let us be true
> To one another.

There is, of course, no incompatibility between religious impulse and human sympathy; on the contrary, in the New Testament love of neighbor is the note of redemption. But the proper order must be maintained, as in our Lord's summary of the law: love of God first, and then love of neighbor. The difficulty which the Christian feels with all humanitarian proposals of love is that the motive is weak and vague (I do not know why I should love), and the object seems unworthy (my neighbor is not lovable). The sentimentality of pity which has no proper context is demonstrated by the troubles of Scobie in Graham Greene's *The Heart of the Matter.* What supplies the motive power in the orthodox Christian dialectic of man and neighbor is the awareness of a need which all men share and of a forgiveness freely offered to all. Since my need is other than his, though just as great, I can offer him my help without arrogance or pity. However grateful we may be that we have escaped from Robbe-Grillet's surrealistic landscape, we are not better off with the current humanitarianism which parodies the older humanism and which is radically unlike the Christian *caritas* out of which both were born.

The orthodox Christian deals with the sensible world in terms of what Paul Tillich has called "belief-ful realism." He feels like the *chosistes* a passionate concern for banality, and he shares with Camus and Faulkner a sense of terror and sympathy before suffering humanity. But his motive is different. He understands his neighbor as half-angel and half-beast, and also as that fragile splendor for which Christ died. He asks his storytellers for a more thoroughgoing realism which takes account of the figural quality in all particularity, and which does not make the futile attempt to deal with men and things and events apart from the ground of all being. The least otherworldly of men, he confronts the commonplace with utter solemnity, knowing that every least thing—a hair on a head, a fledgling falling to the ground—has its part in the master plot, the synopsis of which has been revealed to us.

The libel of the alleged incompatibility between Christianity and concretion was exposed in Erich Auerbach's *Mimesis: The Representation of Reality in Western Literature* (1946). Despite such exceptions as Eurycleia's discovery of Odysseus' scar, the literature of antiquity found itself unable to deal with banality except in comic terms. It was the contribution of Christianity to Western literature that tragic depth was for the first time embodied in empirical concreteness. The Bible treasures its banalities because God moves through history transfiguring every commonplace. One need not choose between God and the world if the inner, tragic, and problematic event is embedded in concrete reality.

What Auerbach demonstrated by using the techniques of *Stilforschung*, Father William J. Lynch discovered by using the methods of *Motivforschung*. In his book *Christ and Apollo*, Father Lynch comes to this conclusion: "What we need is the restoration of a confidence in the fundamental power of the finite and limited concretions of our human life. But not a cheap confidence."[12] The proper Godward motion is through "the generative finitude," penetrating historical reality in order to come at last before the transcendence of God. In such a progression the literary imagination is just as enthralled with the palpable as Dame Julian was with her hazelnut. What we need fear is, on the one hand, an Apollonian dream which touches finitude gingerly before escaping to infinity, or, on the other, a worldliness which descends so deeply into finitude that it no longer looks for redemption. A Christian novelist sees angels ascending and descending on Main Street.

The Christian reader searches for this dialectical concern as wistfully as Kierkegaard sought for his Knight of Faith. What he insists upon is the theoretical possibility of a genuinely Christic imagination, capable of confronting reality in the manner of Chesterton, marveling at a shadow cast by a garden post, and feeling unworthy of a dandelion; or in the manner of Gerard Manley Hopkins, discovering Christ in clay and coal, in the ooze of oil, in shaking tin foil, in the hurl and glide of a windhover. Such an imagination, when it appears on the literary scene, changes the spiritual climate of its time. "An age of faith," says R. P. Blackmur, "comes about when religious convictions are part of—incarnate in—secular experience."[13]

It should be apparent that great narrative power is freed when a method is used which sets historical event in a matrix of infinite implication. Banality finds a shocking splendor when it is seen against a cosmic plot in which the angels have already rebelled, in which Adam and Eve have already eaten the forbidden fruit, in which God himself has entered time

[12] William F. Lynch, S.J., *Christ and Apollo: The Dimensions of the Literary Imagination* (New York: Sheed & Ward, 1960), p. xv.

[13] "Religion and the Intellectuals," *Partisan Review*, XVII (1950), 227. In the statement immediately preceding Blackmur's, A. J. Ayer makes the familiar error: "Religion," he writes, "by disparaging life in this world . . . has discouraged people from finding the satisfaction that it can provide" (p. 220).

without being overcome. Is there not in this archetypal narrative a richness far beyond that with which Huysmans and Rémy de Gourmont confronted the realism of their contemporaries?

There is of course the possibility that the divine may lose its luminous strangeness in the encounter with banality; when man stages an incarnation, the darkness may overwhelm the light. André Malraux's *The Metamorphosis of the Gods* (1960) is an account of how artists throughout history have humanized the divine, not to show the relevance of the supernatural, but to express man's faulty appetite for irrelevance. The veins on a prophet's hands are carefully painted, because the artist cannot comprehend the prophet's message; in the Autun "Stephen Stoned," the process looks innocent, because the stones are painted like snowballs; in the eighth-century "Christ and St. Mennos," Christ has a friendly arm around the saint's shoulder, as though they were chums. One may observe the same metamorphosis when the Passion story is translated into contemporary terms, as though Calvary happens whenever a good man gives up his life for a cause; Mauriac's *The Lamb*, Kazantzakis' *Christ Recrucified*, Faulkner's *A Fable*, and Silone's *The Seed beneath the Snow* all struggle against the sullen fact that a historical concretion cannot possibly bear any weight of meaning.

Though the possibility of symbolic extension is not unlimited, the fact that banality can hold within itself a dimension of sublimity gives aesthetic theory a metaphysical elevation. In his classic essay "On the Knocking at the Gate in Macbeth," DeQuincey speculated on the reason why the simple sound of knocking which follows the murder of Duncan has an effect of peculiar awfulness and depth of solemnity. He concluded that the power of suggestiveness in this commonplace sound depended on the fact that it marked the boundary of the preternatural. Macbeth and his wife had been in a demonic grip; after the murder they must make their way back into the human condition. The knocking marks the point where "the pulses of life are beginning to beat again; and the re-establishment of the goings-on of the world in which we live, first makes us profoundly sensible of the awful parenthesis that suspended them." The very homeliness of the detail marks with precision the separation between the demonic and the human; and the commonplace can serve exactly the same function, particularly when it avoids the comic by being seen in what Herbert Spencer called "ascending incongruity."

That Daumier-Smith had a valid experience in front of the orthopedic shop is beyond dispute; but his understanding of the experience involved a philosophic error. When he responded gratefully to the enameled flowers, he did not encounter the whole reality of the enamelware, but only those visible accidents which were abstracted from the things in themselves. The possibility of being true to life implies more than a faithfulness to accidental qualities, and involves a recognition of sources and destiny without which the factual world remains absurd. The Church has enshrined the necessity of concretion in its sacramental theology, recognizing for example in its eucharistic doctrine the banality of bread and wine transfigured by its explicit relation to the Ground of Being. When the Church is guilty of the charge of otherworldliness, it must be regarded as unfaithful to its ancient realism.

So far from being betrayed by particularity, God encounters man only in the structures of time and place; he seems particularly to choose such *kairoi* as men would call trivial or even humiliating. For this reason the Christian imagination must confront the actual world in a more complex manner than Daumier-Smith's rude dichotomy suggests. The artist as believer refuses to deny reality to concretion or to ascribe independence to it. The Bible puts on record the fact that he regards history with astonishment, marveling at the parade of mountebanks, procurers, saints, and buffoons.

The Christian writer can never be so engrossed in the

furniture and events of the world—in the enamel basins and in the girls who trip over them—that he forgets the original Fall by which everything was marred. His attitude is rather that of St. Augustine, whose confidence in the peace of God did not prevent his admiration for the peace and beauty of the earthly city. The Christian novelist recognizes not only the plots in which human affairs are so desperately mixed but also the denouements by which a temporary peace may be achieved. If he cannot add at the end, "and they lived happily ever after," neither can his secular counterpart. He knows that the human story winds from complication to complication, and will do so until the end of time. However charming he may find painted flowers, he cannot find in them the consolation of Israel, and his final prayer will be that of John Donne in "La Corona":

> What thy thorny crowne gain'd, that give mee,
> A crowne of Glory, which doth flower alwayes.

So his attitude toward what the critics call "reality" is a kind of frightened attention—*en gémissant,* as Pascal said. He looks at actuality with the interest of an alchemist who stares at his boiling brew of frog's skin, snake bones, and feathers from a molting screech owl, hoping that when the boiling stops there will be left a precipitant which will turn anything to gold. The Christian has this interest in banality, but with the difference that he has grounds for his hope: once, he believes, in a stable on a very ordinary day, very God became very man. Nothing now can seem safely trivial. So he holds character and event and setting in his wistful affection, like a child who for a little while has a butterfly englobed in his hands.

Being and Faith in the Contemporary Theater

BY KAY BAXTER

THROUGH A study of contemporary drama, men can gain fresh understanding of the Christian faith and new insights into the nature of being. This is a bold claim; yet it is one the artist has always made for his chosen medium, for his vocation is to apprehend and reveal truth. William Temple pointed out that the artist's mode of apprehension differs from that of the scientist. The artist does not argue from premises to conclusions. "Rather he puts together the constituent parts of truth and contemplates them in their relation to each other." The record of St. John, ever the chosen Evangel of the artist, persuades not by argument but by delineation of deed and motive; through pondering the record, hearts are touched, minds illuminated, and the divine Word uttered to the soul.

While the Western world drowns in torrents of verbiage, the dramatist (whose medium must always be that of action and reaction) is committed to making his record of experience through precisely this delineation of deed and motive. "Judged by their words," says Molière, "all men are the same. It is their deeds that unmask their differences." For Christians, the one Deed that sums up the "constituent parts of truth," the Deed which unmasks all our differences, is the eternal Deed of the Incarnation, that fact in whose shade all our lives are lived. Any serious artist, developing in a culture shot through as ours is with Christian symbolism, based however remotely upon Christian assumptions about the nature of man, must sooner or later decide what he is going to do, as an artist, about the doctrine of the Incarnation. Perhaps the most unfortunate result of the Puritan ban upon the theater has been that the dramatist, more than any other artist, has been cut off from the traditional source of understanding of man's nature and destiny because he has angrily rejected the Church which angrily rejected him.

Faith and Drama have thus alike been impoverished, the one by the loss to its fellowship of those artists most deeply concerned with the image of Transcendence reflected in human action, the other by the loss of those deep sanctions of the spirit out of which grow the enduring symbolic language of religious art. Today a tenuous bridge is being built between Faith and Drama which will in time, perhaps, join Church and theater. For our serious dramatists are now asking with urgency the true religious questions: Who are we? Where do we find the courage to be? What are we called to become? Is there indeed One who calls?

There is no space in the present essay even to summarize the way in which the religious theme has returned to the theater. A knowledge of the contributions made by Goethe, Ibsen, Shaw, Pirandello, Claudel, must be assumed in the reader, as must an awareness of the effect upon popular thought of the work of Frazer and Freud, and of the developing sciences of anthropology and psychology. Relevant to the subject is the work of the expressionist theater after World War I, with its attempt to identify spectator with spectacle and its aim of releasing, in Max Reinhardt's words, "emotions simple and primitive but great and powerful as befits the human race," a work which reached its hideous apotheosis in the mob response to mob stimuli of the Nuremberg rallies. Relevant too, and of cleansing quality, is the work in the English-speaking theater of the poet-dramatists led by W. B. Yeats, who insisted that audiences bring their minds as well as their emotions to the theater and who maintained a line, though thin and brittle, of plays concerned with compassion, supernatural courage, faith in God, and other traditionally religious enquiries.

Unquestionably, however, the return to the contemporary theater of religious themes is due chiefly to one man, the late and beloved Bishop G. K. A. Bell, who in 1928 reopened the doors of the Church to the drama by commissioning the poet John Masefield to write *The Coming of Christ* and by following this first play with plays from Eliot, Sayers, Fry, and others. Bell saw as no one else had seen that, owing to its exile, the drama was without a language in which to speak of religious matters; and, from that moment, in spite of setbacks and mistakes and wrong turnings, the men and women who worked under his inspiration began the essential task of forging a language adequate for a drama once more preparing to contemplate the Incarnation. Eliot himself has written unforgettably of the cost of this "raid on the inarticulate."

It began before World War II and, in England, to a certain extent was in abeyance through the war, though the work of the Martin Brownes' company, the Pilgrim Players, took drama of quality to many places where serious plays had not previously been performed and though the London theater contributed much, by the performance of light classical dramas, to the continuing development of an audience for serious theater, so that there were always audiences capable of following rich, complex, and involved language.

Yet the dereliction and distress consequent upon World War II, the destruction of trust between man and man which was of all the Nazi crimes probably the most disastrous, and the realization of the meaning of human commitment—all this took some years to make its impact in the plays which were presented for postwar production. Thornton Wilder's *The Skin of Our Teeth* reminded us that Cain never dies; he only slumbers by the hearth from time to time; and, if man does escape, it is by the skin of his teeth. Martin Browne's production at the Mercury Theater of Ronald Duncan's *This*

Way to the Tomb stated with wit and poignancy the fact that the history of sinners, and of penitence for sin, does not alter in essence, though it may change its external manifestations. Eliot's *The Family Reunion* showed the family link between the Greek legend of the Furies (pursuing till they are faced, understood, and accepted, when they become Friendly Ones) and the Christian insight that we are members one of another, so that one soul's full acceptance of suffering may free another from doom and release atoning power. It seemed, from the evidence of such plays, as though men wished to assure themselves that in the ruins of their world they could yet trace a historic continuity with their shattered past.

The different course taken by war in France and the prolonged period of occupation and resistance produced different dramatic reactions. In France, as Harold Hobson has pointed out, the theater was one of the focal points of the Resistance Movement, and the playwright could count upon an audience capable of giving him that participation in shared assumptions which "religious" playwrights today often long for in vain. Anouilh's play *Antigone,* with its stress on the cost of loyalty and the need for total commitment, makes salutary reading for those of us who have never had to ask ourselves what the faith *is* for which we would, in Anouilh's words, "say 'No' and die." It is this dauntlessness for an absolute that gives universal importance to the Antigone story. Yet it is not, of course, Christian. Though there are Christian overtones in the play as retold by Anouilh, it speaks of no future. The story of the Passion of Christ shows that all responsibility is Godward, God himself being both agent and victim, yet demanding of Christ's manhood total assent to total surrender of everything that constitutes manhood in order to effect (as we believe) the "taking of the Manhood into God." No such tremendous weight of responsibility lies upon little Antigone. Her action is purely political, and the only effect it can have (beyond the momentary glory of being herself) is that the idea of the *polis* may be cleansed from the taint of the expedient government of Creon and that the citizens may see by example what it is to be wholly committed. Antigone's task is to be herself—a task beyond the reach of most of us. But the task of the Lord is other: it is to draw all men to him. The commitment in the two cases is equal; the penalty, humanly speaking, the same. But the stakes are not comparable. Antigone's death will not turn the world upside down.

We owe much to the achievement of the French theater in the immediate postwar period. Yet England was not without its experimental work. This experimental theater began with verse plays.

We have mentioned Martin Browne's season of religious productions at the Mercury Theatre in London in 1945-46, a season which saw the performance of T. S. Eliot's *The Family Reunion* and Ronald Duncan's *This Way to the Tomb*. This Mercury season was the logical climax of the Brownes' effort with the Pilgrim Players, who, during the war had taken drama of quality all over England to the most improbable places, thereby giving to people starved by war circumstances the chance of seeing worth-while plays. Quite apart from the intrinsic merit of the individual plays put on at the Mercury, the remarkable fact was that the plays were staged at all and that they were attended by eager audiences in spite of the crippling limitations of space, money, and personnel caused by war-time impoverishment. The success of the venture proved that, given worthy scripts, a public existed for serious plays on religious themes.

Yet, refreshing though the audiences found them, there was something remote from real life about these plays—none of them dealt in realistic terms with the theme which had above all others concerned the men and women who had lived through World War II. It seemed as though the fundamental problem lodged too deep in the spirit to come to consciousness very quickly. When it began to surface, it produced a further series of explorations of that very question of commitment into which the play of Antigone had probed.

There have followed a number of interesting plays on this theme, set in widely differing situations. Graham Greene in *The Living Room* poses the question of marital fidelity, viewed from the standpoint of a Roman Catholic family. The play has moments of truth such as that when the child Rose, desperately and hopelessly in love, sees her lover and his wife together and cries out, "Oh, they are *married!*" In that one poignant cry is expressed more of the doctrine of marriage as an irreversible state, a total commitment, than Greene was able to express in all the subsequent discussion on the relationship. Though the play's claustrophobic effect precludes any sense of the possibility of life abundant, yet it did and does stir the mind to question: What *is* worth dying for?

Two outstanding American plays on the same theme should be noted. Arthur Miller's *The Crucible*, set in Massachusetts in the days of the early settlers but really referring to the McCarthy "witch hunts" against supposed Communists, also asks: What is it a man will die for? Miller shows a society dominated by the narrowest kind of piety, far removed from the "glorious liberty" of the sons of God, but, as in the Antigone story, redeemed to a certain degree by total loyalty to the truth as the protagonist sees it. William Faulkner's *Requiem for a Nun* deals with the same question, attempting to estimate the limits to which disinterested love will carry an ignorant human being. A Negro woman murders a child in its cradle. Why? What was the total commitment which led here to this dedicated act? Has such commitment any validity?

In England, John Whiting's *Marching Song* presents, with the greatest sensitiveness and insight, the problem of a soldier who, at the peak of his military career, is brought violently and tragically to realize that the whole willed direction of his life has been based on error and that his ambition (to "achieve a triumph of arms") must be abandoned utterly in face of his suddenly won knowledge of what it is to be a man.

In each of these plays, the death of the leading figures releases at least the hope of amendment of life in those who remain. Each death in some sense brings vicarious atonement. In all, it is possible to find underlying Christian assumptions, tacit, perhaps unconscious, but nevertheless shaping the plays and making their impact not a purely tragic impact.

Even the dramatist Jean-Paul Sartre in *No Exit* (*Huis Clos*) does not totally exclude the possibility of hope; in *No Exit* the door in fact is not *locked*. "Hell," says Sartre, "is other people"—while self is central, an impeccably Christian statement! Hell, for Sartre, is in the mind of man, wherefore hope remains, for no man knows the limits of growth set for the human mind or for the human spirit. All these plays and others of this period examine, with varying profundity and subtlety, the motives which give, or fail to give, the Courage to *Be*—and this, some years before Paul Tillich published his book under that title.

It was not, however, until 1952 that the staging of Beckett's *Waiting for Godot* changed permanently the tone of the modern theater and did this with a play of profound religious significance. Not for the first time in the history of the drama was the religious aspect of a play almost wholly ignored by dramatic critics. The play was written and first performed in French, where the word *Godot* brings inevitably a suggestion of uncomeliness; in England the name was at once interpreted as meaning "God"; yet the play was variously supposed to be about capitalism and communism, frustration and escapism, about anything in fact except the book of Isaiah and the Apostles' Creed.

In view of its tremendous influence, I shall discuss this play in some detail. It begins under a dead tree outside a city wall, where two tramps are discussing the Crucifixion of

Christ. The tramps are called Vladimir (the name of the Russian Orthodox saint who sent messengers all over the world to find the "best religion") and Estragon (or Tarragon, which is a plant of the family Cruciferae or cross-bearer). The tramps wait for Mr. Godot, a mysterious personage who, if he comes as they believe he has promised to come, will put everything right in their futile and unsatisfactory lives. But Godot doesn't come.

Instead, blustering and overdressed, comes Pozzo (whose name means fool) and with him his servant Lucky (a reasonably modern equivalent of *Beatus* or Blessed One). Lucky is loaded with Pozzo's gear; he does not react when hit or yelled at, and is indifferent to the sore on his neck caused by the cord which tethers him to his "master." Pozzo converses with the tramps, gives them the bones from his picnic, confides that he is taking his "menial" to the market to see what he can get for him, boasts of the capabilities of the menial, and urges the tramps to make Lucky dance and think aloud for them. Under threat the servant obeys, dances, and makes a speech. To what seems a string of incoherencies the tramps react violently and attack the servant, who falls and appears to die, but is eventually revived and lugged off to market by Pozzo, who loses his watch in the melee. To the tramps, left alone again, a messenger comes to say that Godot will not come that evening. This concludes Part One.

Part Two opens with the same scene as Part One, except that the tree which was dead has now put on leaves. Estragon has escaped from his uncomfortable boots which are left in the center of the stage with Lucky's hat, and Vladimir is on stage alone, anxious for his companion's return. When Estragon returns, they quarrel and make up as before and unsuccessfully try to imitate Lucky's last dance. Failing and frustrated by failure, Estragon cries out, "God have pity on me!" "On *me!*" cries Vladimir, and at the cry Pozzo and Lucky appear. Pozzo is now blind. He stumbles and falls. The tramps think of helping him up but call to find out what his name is.

They call him first Abel, then Cain; he replies to both names; they identify him: "He's All Mankind." Pozzo, the fool, is All Mankind. After further interchanges, Lucky, who has been sleeping at the foot of the newly leaved tree, *rises,* and leads Pozzo off toward the city whence they both came. A messenger comes to say that Mr. Godot won't come. The play peters out. "Nothing happens; no one comes, no one goes; it's awful."

Maybe. Yet the play's synopsis is in fact adequately covered by the words "Came down; suffered; was crucified, dead and buried, descended into hell, rose, and ascended." Beckett has written a version of the Passion story, set indeed in a strange land, but of quite startling doctrinal orthodoxy. In the composite Vladimir-Estragon, he shows us the soul spasmodically attentive to and expectant of its Saviour, whom it fails to recognize when he appears, because he is without form or comeliness, in the guise of a servant, bearing the burdens of all mankind, wounded, afflicted, yet dumb . . . dividing the spoils, yes, even chicken bones. There could hardly be a more precise description of the Suffering Servant of Isaiah than is presented in Lucky, the servant on whom the fool, All Mankind, is in fact utterly dependent; and it is a wry comment on the state of religious awareness in official circles that a play so clearly presenting the figure of the Saviour on a public stage, contrary to the law of the land in England, should have aroused not one ripple of protest nor one critical line of understanding.

It may be thought that such an interpretation strains the text. Yet it is solely through attention to the text that the meaning emerges. Take, for example, the great death speech of Lucky, so often dismissed as balderdash. Underline the major statements and the result is roughly this: "Given the existence of a personal God who loves us and suffers, and considering that, as a result of labors left unfinished, man wastes and pines, I resume, in a Word, the skull."

Is this not wholly consonant with the sentence: "Who

for us men and for our salvation came down . . . and was incarnate. . . "? Or, to take another example: Pozzo, the fool, gains nothing at the market except the knowledge of his blindness. Is there a better symbol for redemption than to know our blindness and to accept our total dependence on the Suffering Servant?

These are but two examples; every page of the text produces more like these. To work through the play thinking along these lines reveals, not indeed a word-for-word parallel with the Scriptures, but nevertheless a Crucifixion, Deposition, Descent into Hell, Resurrection and Ascension, deeply pondered on and perfectly scaled to modern theatrical convention. It is of course worlds apart from a "modern version" of the Gospel story; to compare it with Dorothy Sayers' *The Man Born to be King* is like comparing a children's colored cutout with an El Greco; they exist in totally different spheres of being. Certainly this play calls into question the impassibility of the Deity; but certainly also we know that one of the names of God is Emmanuel, God with us, and in an age of desolation and grief this presentation of the Suffering Servant is one which grips an audience with extraordinary power. And if it is true that in meditating on the Passion all that enlightens and enlarges the understanding is to be welcomed, then to think as this play forces us to think, is to think with depth and truth at a point where thought often breaks down into mere emotion.

Jean Anouilh said that the first night of Beckett's *Godot* was as important an event in the theater as was a first night of Pirandello put on by the Pitoëffs in the 1920's. For religious drama it is an event equal in importance to the first performance of Eliot's *Murder in the Cathedral* in the 1930's. For a language has been evolved in this play which is capable of bearing, upon the very slightest of phrases, the greatest possible weight of meaning. *Que voulez vous?* means not only the characteristic French shrugging off of a difficult question, but also in the most precise sense, "What do you will in this matter? For understand that it is all a question of will." The effect of success in evolving such a language is that it is now possible to refer, under the guise of a simple daily expression, to the deep sources of our spiritual anxieties and certainties without the acute embarrassment which we experience when some earnest propagandist attempts, in the older dramatic conventions, to reveal us to ourselves. The intellectual excitement of this kind of play is also intense; you can't take your ears off the words for a moment or you are lost; it demands an attention similar to that required by metaphysical poetry, for the writer is using words in a similarly condensed and loaded way.

In this necessarily limited space it is possible only to indicate some of the questions which have engaged this new kind of serious playwright during the past decade. He asks: *Is* God's will made clear to those who meditate on the mystery of suffering? *Is* salvation a matter of the will? *Is* God's name Emmanuel, or is he indeed the great absentee? Who are the messengers of God—Graham Greene's priest, or Beckett's dumb servant, or the Negro murderess? Does the Church any longer mediate salvation to sinners? What *is* sin? *Is* Hell other people? Are we to understand that all this trail of suffering could be avoided if people acted according to the light they have? The tramps could have eased Lucky's pains; Pozzo could have shared his food; *The Living Room*'s inhabitants could have loved the two erring lovers and the neurotic wife back into spiritual health. Is all this what the authors are saying? Or are they in fact as much in the dark as the characters they portray?

These are fundamental questions, and we are forced to try to think our way through them once we start attending to what our serious playwrights struggle to express. There is, in most of the serious plays of this period, great tension and little lightness. At best the humor is wry; at worst the writing is both heavy and inflated. One is often forced to conclude that, for purposes of the drama, sincerity is not enough.

Of course, it is far more difficult today to write comedy than to write satire or tragedy. A great deal of modern writing never escapes from the downward curve of the pessimist and is rather to be categorized as "puzzled" than even as "tragic"; for to achieve tragedy the playwright must assume that man has dignity to lose, and this is an assumption very much on the wane.

Into this category of puzzlement falls much of the best dramatic writing of our puzzled age. Arthur Miller, Ray Lawler, Tennessee Williams, Eugène Ionesco, Eugene O'Neill, and John Osborne, to name only a few, are all concerned with the great underlying preoccupations of men today—the question of identity and the question of communication. Till now drama has been concerned far more with doing than with being, and it is only in this decade that playwrights (Beckett and Ionesco especially) have invited audiences to attend, without any seduction of rhetoric or beauty of décor—utterly without any of the "embellishment" Aristotle speaks of—a naked inquiry into the being of man and the possibility of his having any relationship whatever with his neighbor.

It is perhaps right at this point to recall what the Christian definition of human identity is. Unregenerate man is "naturally prone to sin." In the words of the Anglican Catechism, the baptized child is made a "member of Christ, a child of God, and an inheritor of the kingdom of heaven." St. Paul describes Christians as "heirs through hope of everlasting life." Man, whether baptized or not, is, we are assured, created in the image of God, born for God's glory and for union with the Creator, and these splendid phrases have no doubt heartened many generations of Christians to shoulder burdens which would otherwise have crushed them.

But what of today? What is modern man's own view of his nature today? What of Eugene O'Neill's Larry at the end of *The Iceman Cometh?* He says: "Begod, there's no hope. I'll never be a success . . . life is too much for me." What of Jean in John Osborne's *The Entertainer?* She says:

"There is no God; it seems that it all began with something as simple as sunlight striking on a piece of rock. And here we are. We've only got ourselves. . . . Somehow we've just got to make a go of it." What of the murderous gangs of teenagers in *West Side Story?*

If we attend at all to what is going on outside the circle of instructed Christians, do we not have to agree with Rudolph Bultmann in *Kerygma and Myth* that the language of Bible and Church is without meaning to the mid-twentieth century? To quote from Ronald Gregor Smith's *The New Man:* "The Knight of Faith . . . can no longer come prancing into the tournament in the panoply of absolute assurance. Absolute solicitude, yes, and absolute resignation. . . . Man is made by his free acceptance, in unlimited openness, of what comes to him out of the surrounding darkness." Anouilh's Antigone, John Whiting's Rupert Forster, and Dido Morgen in *Marching Song* are examples: the one of a heroine in the panoply of absolute assurance (and the end of the play is static), the others of human beings made by their free acceptance of what comes to them out of the surrounding darkness, an acceptance which releases in others a life that can flow once more toward the future.

In recent plays by these dramatists, the problems of personal identity and of communication between individuals are treated in different modes and with very different characterization.

Miller, in *A View from the Bridge,* shows us a "hero," Eddie Carbone, who in the limits of his own society fulfills the Aristotelian requirements for a tragic hero. He is above the average in moral stature, and his fall is due not so much to outside circumstances as to a fatal flaw or weakness in his own character.

Antigone dies rather than betray her own image of herself. Eddie, similarly, courts personal disaster so that his "name" should not be disgraced. As Miller's character, the lawyer Alfieri, puts it: "Most people settle for half, and I like it better that way," but Eddie will not settle for half, and so he dies. Ray Lawler, the Australian author of *Summer of the Seventeenth Doll*, shows us in yet another setting the central figure, Roo, struggling, as he thinks, to assert his own identity in the face of circumstances, but really struggling against accepting manifest destiny.

In France, England, the United States, Australia—is this neurosis universal? The United States, perhaps, is worth another glance, particularly as represented by the playwright Tennessee Williams. Williams, in *Cat on a Hot Tin Roof*, conducts another of his sultry attempts to find out what, if anything, there is in man beyond his sexuality. Yet, in reality, the sexual and homosexual implications of the play are quite secondary. The real interest in the play is in the way Williams exposes the wall of lies built round itself by each shrinking personality as a defense against the rapacity of the rest of the family. He shows brilliantly how this attempted defense achieves in the end only the isolation of each individual within a hard, repellent, outer crust, inhibiting any possibility of true human relationship, the very opposite of the "openness to the future" achieved by Dido Morgen and Rupert Forster in Whiting's *Marching Song*.

Ionesco's influence will probably be felt increasingly in religious dramatic writing, for he makes *things* speak. In a play such as *The Chairs* nothing is said about the supernatural, and everything that happens is real, but all is imbued with an interior reality. People exist. They talk because silence frightens them. Language for them is an escape from reality, and Ionesco himself holds that it is in the deeps which underlie our ripples of conscious communication that we shall discover our oneness. "Each of us," he says, "is, deep down, everyone else." Ionesco believes the theater to be the most compelling medium through which to state this view of the human condition.

Finally, there is John Osborne, whom we have only mentioned in passing. In *Look Back in Anger*, Osborne's

Jimmy Porter wants maturity for himself and his wife, but he does not know where to look for it and is grossly unwilling to pay the price of it if it could be found. He doesn't know who he is or what he is meant to be. His chief complaint is that those who should be the custodians of the secret of the abundant life have nothing to offer to those who seek it. "They all want to escape from the pain of being alive."

Perhaps these brief examples serve to show the preoccupation of the dramatists with questions of identity and of communication. The questions which concern Christians in this context are: What is new in this sense of isolation and anxiety over identity? Has Christianity anything to say about it? Of course, there is nothing new in the problems themselves. Keats and Coleridge both explored the pain of the loss of "my strong identity, my real self," the sense of being "Alone, alone, all all alone, Alone on a wide, wide sea," and indeed both Lawler's Roo and Keats use the same simile of the "sick eagle" to express the pain of this loss. Like Keats, trembling as he apprehends "a sun, a shadow of a Magnitude," Osborne's Jimmy Porter suffers from the fear that he is perhaps mistaken in believing that "there is a kind of burning virility of mind and spirit that looks for something as powerful as itself. . . . I want a warm and thrilling voice to cry out, 'Alleluia, I'm alive!' " It is probable that these expressions relate to no more than the common pain of every young poet or artist who recognizes his own inevitable solitariness, epitomized by A. E. Housman:

> I, a stranger and afraid
> In a world I never made.

But what is perhaps new to this generation is that they have had so little experience of solitude. Moreover, many of them have had the experience of facing the exterior tensions of war in company with comrades, and now must face the interior tensions of civilian life alone. We are often told that this is the age of the non-joiner; what support can Christianity offer in such a situation? Is Osborne right, and is the root cause of this isolation a refusal to face the pain of love, and the fear of what will come to anyone willing to be totally committed?

Surely the Gospel has relevance here as everywhere. On the first Good Friday the disciples deserted their commitment; they could not face the pain of love. Their Leader's conduct was other. He was going uphill, a burden on his back, his face set like a flint, in "absolute solicitude and absolute resignation," in complete openness to whatever was coming to him out of the surrounding darkness, to die with an unanswered question on his lips. I believe that in pondering the reaction of the disciples before and after the Crucifixion and Resurrection we may come to some understanding of the position of our serious dramatists today, and the crucial situation in which they find themselves. They are, I believe, playing for high stakes. They are attempting, in language they are struggling to fashion anew for their purposes, a drama which does really hold the mirror up to this puzzled age. They are, to a large extent, still cut off from most sources of Christian enlightenment, for the Church as it now exists still lacks words of absolution they can understand or accept, or which would reintegrate them into the Christian community. They are prepared, in Arthur Miller's words, to be "wholly known." If *we* (instead of imitating Coleridge's hermit or the nuns in Osborne's *The Entertainer* and crossing *ourselves* for safety) could go out to them in something of the same openness, they might indeed take note that we had been with Jesus. It is very necessary that someone should make clear to playwrights that there is a third alternative to the two they know—tame, meaningless conformity or despairing, nihilistic rebellion. There is the possibility of joining a community of people as committed, as concerned as they are themselves, as naked to contempt, as open to the future, and as much in the dark except that they hold to one fact: the knowledge of the being of One who never settled for half and whose definitive utterance might well, for our day, be expressed in Osborne's words, "Alleluia, I'm alive."

If once this conviction could be shared with our younger writers and artists, we could expect a renaissance of the arts such as we do not at present dream of. In the theater it would assuredly present itself as comedy, and that comedy would be poetic, for it would be the celebration of a triumph, both festival and sacrifice.

In the first chorus of *Murder in the Cathedral,* Eliot wrote these lines:

> Here let us stand, close by the cathedral. Here let us wait.
> Are we drawn by danger? Is it the knowledge of safety that
> draws our feet
> Towards the Cathedral?

And he continued:

> The New Year waits, destiny waits for the coming.

Artists respond to the wind of the Spirit before most of us are aware that it blows at all, certainly before we are aware that it has changed its direction. There have been for us all since 1935 ample causes for a deep desire for the "knowledge of safety." Yet it is Eliot himself who, elsewhere, has warned us that in the corridors of history "neither fear nor courage saves us." Whether we enter the cathedral for safety or don, as many have donned, black shirt or brown shirt because we seek, by wearing some *provided* shirt, to escape from what the later Eliot has called "the intolerable shirt of flame," our efforts have availed us little. Eliot, truly exercising his prophetic vocation, has shown us that this same "intolerable shirt of flame" is the required uniform of the artist. It is the uniform which should be the distinctive garb of the Christian anywhere. "The New Year waits"—it has been twenty years or more, awaiting; and during those twenty years, the Age of Anxiety has attained its majority. What have we learned in the interim, and who have been our leaders in the search for our true nature?

By considering three groups of plays, one may trace a kind of progression in the study of fear and finally discover a hint of possible emergence into a less terror-haunted climate of thought. The first group comprises Miller's *The Crucible,* Anouilh's *Antigone,* Whiting's *Marching Song,* and Sartre's *Dirty Hands.* These are plays which show men facing fear of political pressures. The second group comprises Lawler's *Summer of the Seventeenth Doll,* Osborne's *Look Back in Anger* and *The Entertainer,* Williams' *Cat on a Hot Tin Roof,* and Miller's *A View from the Bridge.* These show man facing fear of the pressures of human relationship. And the third group includes Beckett's *Endgame,* Fry's *The Dark Is Light Enough,* and Bernanos' *Dialogues des Carmelites.* These plays show existential fear pushed to its logical conclusion and bring us, inescapably, face to face with the doctrine of the Atonement.

What does each group tell us about fear and courage? In *The Crucible,* Miller's hero "faces a double fear"—death at the hands of persecutors or condemnation by the interior censor of conscience. He chooses death of the body. Antigone, faced with the same decision, abides by the commitment of conscience, and chooses execution. In *Dirty Hands,* Sartre gives his central character the chance to escape if he will conform, but conforming would mean that the heroic actions of his comrades would be rendered null. He refuses life because to accept it would deprive human action of all sense. Neither Miller, Anouilh, nor Sartre allows the death of the protagonist to ameliorate the human situation. Sartre, in *The Flies,* explicitly rejects vicarious atonement as an ignoble idea. These protagonists have what Paul Tillich, in *The Courage to Be,* calls "the courage to be as an individual." They lack the courage to be as a group. In each play the playwright shows us the effect upon character of a commitment of conscience which in the end proves more important than life itself. The fourth play of the group is rather different. Whiting, consciously or unconsciously, adheres to the theology of Rudolph Bultmann; in the character of Rupert Forster, he takes us beyond the stoic courage to "say no and die" into a new, and Christian, development; namely, the courage to cease trying to stand above human failure and to accept in genuine humility the fact of human fallibility. Accepting his humanness, Forster yet declares his openness to the future—a declaration made not in Henleyesque terms, head bloody but unbowed, but far more in the surrendered attitude of Mary the Virgin when she made her total assent to the total demand of the Annunciation, saying *yes* to whatever new life would be born of that acceptance.

Bultmann, in *Kerygma and Myth,* describes the man of faith as one "open to the future"; he goes so far as to say, "What rose at Easter was Faith." Whiting's play shows, I think, the budding of faith in a man vowed to a closed, death-seeking negation, who turns at last to affirmation and acceptance of the future—and this despite the fact that he takes his own life. Through Forster's decision to die, the people around him are released to take the next step forward in their own spiritual growth.

Tillich's illuminating passage on the interdependence of fear and anxiety has relevance to this play. He writes, "It is the anxiety of not being able to preserve one's own being which underlies every fear and is the frightening element in it." Whiting shows us a man who at the crucial moment of his life faced, and was not destroyed by facing, the fact that he must renounce everything he had previously believed to be his own being. He rediscovered "the courage to be in total resignation."

Neither Miller, nor Anouilh, nor Sartre achieves this movement from the closed to the open; it is because Whiting does achieve it, and does so with no theatrical forcing, that I rank his play so far above the others.

These four plays present man in a setting of political

danger, discovering something of his own identity. The next group deals with man facing failure in his own human relationships.

Lawler's *Seventeenth Doll* shows two tough, lusty cane cutters and their two women up against the decline of human vitality. The men have been, the woman Olive says, "like eagles winging south for the mating season." How will they face the reality, the truth that they are all growing old? Is the doll their fit symbol, or can they summon courage to live humanly? In their struggle to decide lie the play's tensions.

Osborne's two plays show Jimmy Porter and Archie Rice both kicking violently against the necessity of leaving their dream life and coming to terms with reality. Both plays are, at bottom, an inquiry into the nature of compassion, an attempt to discover what movement of human understanding could bring these isolated individuals into meaningful relationship with their world and to explore the fear of never finding an object of devotion really worth following—of never having the courage to face the "pain of love."

Miller, in *A View from the Bridge,* says that in a disordered society the kind of disaster that engulfs Eddie must happen; that in the world as we have made it, a world of law, the help Eddie needs can never be found. In Eddie's circle there is no one who could have endured the pain of love intensely enough to rescue him from the unacknowledged fear of his own guilt. Is this Miller's meaning? If so, he and Paul Tillich are working along the same lines. Tillich, if I understand aright, thinks that guilt feelings arise from a sense of having displeased God; but he believes this tracing of the origins of our feelings is in itself a projection. The laws of God, about breaking which we feel guilt, are in fact the laws we need to observe if we are to be true to our own nature, and Tillich holds that the refusal of our true nature is the root of *all* guilt feelings. Accept this view, and the action of Eddie Carbone at once becomes logical. Marco's love of

Eddie's niece would, if Eddie allowed it to do so, force Eddie to recognize the nature of his own incestuous love for the girl. But, if Eddie is to preserve his own image of himself as a good man, he cannot admit the truth. Therefore the guilt Eddie feels (because, to preserve his self-image he must refuse his own nature) is projected into hatred of Marco, the bearer of revelation. Eddie has to die because to live would mean to live in truth and this is unbearable. Miller is saying that freedom from the anxiety of guilt can only come through resolute acceptance of truth about one's own nature. Perhaps the "certain alarm" with which the lawyer Alfieri views Eddie's death is due to the knowledge that this stripping of the self is beyond the law's cognizance and can only be achieved in the nakedness of love.

The question is put even more pointedly by Tennessee Williams in *Cat on a Hot Tin Roof.* Here the irregular pattern of love, the homosexual tie, is in the past; its shadow falls over the whole play, but I believe that the homosexual relationship is only incidental to the real problem posed by the play. Williams' real subject is the falseness of relationship, the lie in the soul which divides every individual in the play from every other. Anxiety about falseness recurs over and over in Williams' writing, never more horrifyingly than in the two *Garden District* plays which might fittingly be subtitled *Women Eat People.*

The fear of women in their predatory aspect, a frequent theme in contemporary theater, recently terrifyingly exemplified in Duerrenmatt's *The Visit,* is, I believe, due in large measure to this fear of false relationship. Falseness brings loss of identity to the individual enmeshed in its web. A society in disruption imposes falseness on us. The man forced by war or an overcompetitive society into too aggressive a masculinity takes refuge in the homosexual relationship. The woman unsure of her place in a disorganized civilization does the same thing. The sexual side of the story, though it makes "box-office theater," is not the crucial question. And it is only in the third group of our plays that we discover a clue to our present discontents and a mode of behavior helpful in facing them.

The Dark Is Light Enough, Endgame, and *Dialogues des Carmelites,* are three plays remarkably different in texture. If Tillich is right, our best hope of coping with anxiety about existence is to project it into a fear of something tangible which can then be met with courage. Is the threat of personal non-being ("If, dead, we cease to be") a by-product of our global insecurity in an age of nuclear fission? If so, why is so much of the insecurity projected as a fear of women? One suspects it is because woman is the life bearer, and it is life itself which is dreaded because in life resides, logically, the risk of losing life. Had the Blessed Virgin *not* assented. . . .

However, nothing is new under the sun. The Greeks were aware of this necessity for projection and of the terror of the female principle. When Perseus set out to slay Medusa, the Gorgon, he did not look directly at her. He armed himself with a bright shield, and in that mirror regarded, in imagination only, the foe he greatly feared. And he borrowed that shield from Minerva, the goddess of wisdom, thereby calling to his aid, in dealing with the female principle he most dreaded, the female principle he most revered! This is a digression, but one of particular interest in the light of the recent Roman Catholic promulgation of the doctrine of the Bodily Assumption of the Virgin Mary and the discussion of the role of Mary as Co-Redemptress.

In *The Dark Is Light Enough* there is a woman who is dominant indeed but wholly benevolent. The tensions of the play are caused by the question of what limit the Countess Rosmarin is prepared to set to the sacrifices she will make for the salvation of Richard Gettner. She sets no limit; in the end, she gives her own life in order to secure for Richard one moment, before his death, in which he comes to himself and is what he was meant to be—open to the future, prepared to let in the enemy he has fled all his life.

The vicarious atonement is made—and made within the theatrical convention Fry has established. The Christian affirmation that life is won for us by another's sacrificial living is made, and we are shown a situation in which the victim truly dies that faith may truly rise again.

The Bernanos play, *Dialogues des Carmelites,* deals with the problem more directly. One of the characters, a novice of the Carmelite Order, Blanche de la Force, is herself the personification of unreasoning terror; the play's action hinges on the question of what strength can enable Blanche to rise above, or dive under, this fear and emerge on the other side of it. This terror proves in the end to be terror of death, and ultimately it is a twofold movement which rescues her: one mystical, one practical. The Superior of the Convent, on her deathbed, accepts for herself Blanche's terror of death and dies, after a life of courage, in a prolonged agony of fear. "We bear each other's burdens," says a nun commenting on this; "perhaps we can even die each other's deaths." This is the mystic's mode of redemption. The more mundane one is that of another nun in the play who undertakes to forego martyrdom herself (and thereby in her own eyes loses her hopes of glory) in order to be with Blanche, who has been sent away from the community because it is clear that she could never endure the death on the guillotine to which the whole community has been condemned.

These two actions—the willed sacrifice of their own spiritual health by the two nuns—effect for Blanche the release from terror, which enables her to "die into life" with the other members of the community on the scaffold. The theme is the same as that of *The Dark Is Light Enough*; namely, that it is only when someone is found, who is prepared to be with the sufferer right into the abyss, that fear can be conquered. Only perfect love casts out fear.

This is a far more orthodoxly Christian play than Beckett's *Endgame* is, and yet I believe that *Endgame* is making an authentically religious statement. The set is a blank wall, two tiny windows, two dustbins with lids on, a chair like a throne on wheels, a door that leads into a kitchen, another door that leads out, and a ladder. The chair is occupied by one called Hamm, who is covered with a sheet, the face covered with a bloodstained handkerchief. The second human figure, Clov, is occupied in aimless activity, looking out of the window or taking the covers off the two dustbins. Hamm, the seated figure, takes the handkerchief from his face, yawns, holds out the handkerchief at arm's length, and one sees that he wears the dark glasses of the blind. One sees also that the handkerchief is an old one and, very interestingly, that it is a Veronica handkerchief reminding us of the tradition that, when Christ stumbled and fell under the weight of the Cross on the road to Calvary, St. Veronica in pity wiped his face with her kerchief and the linen ever thereafter bore the miraculous imprint of the features of the Lord. This handkerchief is Hamm's. His first audible words are, "Was ever grief like mine?" And he answers himself, "Perhaps long ago—but I mean now?"

The play proceeds. The dustbins hold two remnants of human figures, Nell and Nagg, "cursed progenitors" Hamm calls them. The white ghostly figures of the past are so mutilated that there is no longer any point in changing the sterile sand in their dustbins. Nor is there anything in the world around them off which they can be nourished. Let their light perish and their memory be as if it had never been.

Hamm and Clov alone remain. They represent the part of man that covets and claims godhead, shown in Hamm by his boastfulness, his desire that at least a toy dog shall exist to adore him and so on; while Clov, whose whole function is service, seeks constantly to escape, to "be a beginning." But there is nowhere to go if he goes. Nothing that speaks of the future can enter. Here, within walls, Clov's seed will not germinate. Outside, there is no female principle, no accepting vessel, only a little boy, and he will either die out there in the zero landscape or enter the walled place and die within it.

Hamm still has delusions of grandeur. He still orders Clov about. And in the last scene of the play Hamm wants Clov to wrap him up in the graveclothes again. But Clov refuses—one must not escape from life, however intolerable, into death.

Clov himself tries to make his escape but, in the end, stays. What indeed could he do alone? Of what use is a Clov, a nail, without Hamm, the Hammer? They are parts of a whole, members one of another. Clov's last big speech must be taken with Hamm's. Clov says:

> Sometimes I tell myself, "Clov, you must manage to suffer better—if you want the punishment to stop." Sometimes, I say, "Clov, you must *be* there better, if you want to be allowed to depart"—one day. . . . Words can't tell you about this, but one day it will happen of itself. And then when I fall, I shall weep for joy.

And Hamm, who has earlier told us a story of a man who wanted to be a servant, who has told us that we ought to go out and love each other, and lick each other's wounds, considers at the last moment what it would mean if "it happened—if *He* came down." He questions an absent power: "Are you prepared for him [the man of the story] to increase, while you (O Absent Power) decrease? Yes? Then let us say no more. We are there." What remains? To strip one's self and jettison every last rag of dominance—the whistle, the dog who is a symbol of man's coveted dominion over creation—and at last nothing is left but the "old rag"—the Veronica handkerchief, the sign of human compassion.

Now it seems to me that here Beckett has written far more deeply than MacLeish in *J.B.*, the story of Job's *withstanding* of God to the last desperate moment of stripping of everything that man normally counts as his life. Relentlessly, the playwright has deprived his Hammer-Nail couple of all their possessions except *bare life*. He leaves them with nothing but compassion for each other. In *Act without Words*, Beckett's later play, even that is removed, and man is shown as enduring alone, without response, the remorseless persecution and tormenting of an unseen silent power. What Beckett is repeating to us with ever-increasing intensity is the message of Albert Camus, namely, that the courage required of us is the courage to go right down into despair, not even asking if there is an exit. I think we are wrong if we regard this attitude as un-Christian, for in the story of Calvary we are shown precisely this unshakable compassion.

The only way to change the story, says Hamm, would be to introduce some new characters. The only way to change the story, said the disciples, would be to introduce a legion or two of angels. But this is not now, any more than it was in A.D. 33, the way to Eternal Life.

Perhaps the foregoing pages suffice to show that serious drama today, at least in England, France, and the United States, is concerned with the basic themes of religious thought. It is by no means orthodox; indeed, it calls into question many of the surface assumptions of the ordinary churchgoer. Yet, if we believe that the Christian doctrine of the Incarnation gives the pattern of new life, the doctrine of the Trinity the pattern of relationship of persons, the Atonement the pattern of forgiveness and openness to the future, and Calvary the pattern of the stripping required before man can make the leap into Resurrection—if we believe this and if, so believing, we do our play going with ears attuned to catch undertones, we shall, I think, agree that the divine Word is still uttered to the soul of the creative artist and that dramatists today are indeed grappling, at a far more serious level than for many a long year, with man's deep need for God.

The Christian Presence in the Contemporary Theater

BY E. MARTIN BROWNE

I HAVE asked leave to borrow the title of this essay from an excellent little book by Robert Speaight, *The Christian Theatre,* because it so felicitously expresses the phenomenon with which I am called upon to deal. It is well to begin by recognizing that this phenomenon has occurred in this century for the first time since the Middle Ages. Only now are Christians writing plays as Christians—and for a theater which is fully developed in its own right, not, as the medieval theater was, the outgrowth of worship and ceremony. The "presence" referred to is not yet a very powerful one, perhaps; it goes almost unnoticed by some of the theater's practitioners and by many of its audience. But it has already a considerable influence, and it is unmistakably Christian.

As a practitioner myself rather than a critical analyst, I am concerned with the plays of Christian contemporaries not so much for their literary expression of ideas as for the dramatic experience in which they involve their audiences. This means that form can be as important as content, and that "the Christian presence" is made known not so much by putting Christian ideas into words as by displaying human lives in which the fact of Christianity, and the author's belief in it, make a crucial difference. Drama is action in human relationships; and even when it is religious drama and includes human relationships with forces or beings outside the human sphere, it is still mediated through the human beings in whose fate we become involved. So I would concentrate attention "in the theater" where actors and audience meet, rather than in the study where the drama may be read as literature.

In the earlier years of this century, a silence which had persisted since the Reformation was broken. No dramatist writing in English, and few in other tongues, had dared in the era of religious controversy to take as his subject matter the New Testament or any major event of Christian history. The risks of getting into trouble, both for him and his producer, were too great and, anyway, such material could surely not be entertaining. Those who wanted to be serious in the theater either turned back to Shakespeare or, as the heat of controversy began to cool, followed Ibsen and Shaw into the social and political fields where the nature and destiny of men in civilization were being fought out. To the religious outreach of the aging Scandinavian master in his final plays, no one paid very much attention, especially as he seemed to discover more cloud than clarity on his mountainsides.

With the beginning of the new century, a few dramatists of repute began to write on Biblical themes. Most of these were poets, and the audience they expected to attract was the audience which looked for a return of poetry to the theater rather than for easy entertainment. The latter half of the nineteenth century had seen a progressively wider divorce between the once-close bedfellows, poetry and drama. No theatrical manager would dream of trying to make money out of poetry. The Shakespearean actor-manager—such as Irving, Booth, or Tree—would occasionally stage a new poetic play; but he expected it to be tailored (even by Tennyson) to his own pattern; and its level as poetry was low. The rest of the profession had no part or lot in such things and, with the predominance of naturalism in the following generation, the divorce became complete.

The poets, too, who turned to the Bible for themes were writing for poetry lovers, and chose these subjects largely because of their poetic quality. It is no accident that, in the British theater at least, none of them was a convinced Christian. Theology, having been undermined by liberal humanism and agnosticism, was not at its strongest. Oriental ideas, both religious and theatrical, were exercising a considerable attraction. Romanticism, one might say, was having its final fling; the poet's world still had some of the characteristics of a never-never land. But in the seriousness with which, nevertheless, these poets sought to come to such terms as they could with the Christian revelation there was a steady progress toward a fuller understanding of it.

John Masefield and W. B. Yeats may be the most useful examples of this period. In *Good Friday* (1917), Masefield tells the Passion story with the Christ offstage. (The British Censor of Plays is obliged by law to ban the visible appearance of God or Christ in the theater.) His protagonist is a mad beggar, a romantic projection of suffering humanity. In *The Trial of Jesus* (1923), however, he deliberately restricts his play to private performance by showing the central character. The portrait is of a passive, unresisting mystic with none of the prophetic fire of the Gospel figure. This Jesus is the divine sufferer, who has accepted humanity's evil fate and its cruelties. Moving as it is, the opening Gethsemane dialogue between Jesus and Wisdom derives rather from the apocryphal book of Wisdom than from the New Testament. The nativity play, *The Coming of Christ* (1928), which Masefield wrote for Canterbury Cathedral opens with a similar scene in which the four angelic powers warn the Anima Christi of what he is undertaking. It is very far from the creedal doctrine of the Incarnation. A dogged heroism born of pity is the motive of the final decision to descend to earth. Yet even here the Cross is seen as the outcome of Christmas; the pity is realistic, the price is agreed to.

W. B. Yeats, who, from an Irish Catholic background, reached out into the mythology of his own people and of the East for the satisfaction he did not find in his inherited faith, provides the most illuminating of all plays of this period in his one-act *Resurrection.* In the anteroom of the Upper Room on Easter Sunday evening two young disciples, a Jew and a Greek, are on guard while the Apostles are gathered within "for fear of the Jews." They argue about the Crucifixion. To the Jew, Jesus' death proves that he was only a man—the best of men, but no more than human. The Greek is sure that the death could not physically happen: like other gods, this one only appeared to die. As commentary on their discussion, a procession of Dionysiac worshippers passes and repasses in the street outside. They are singing a chant of the resurrected god. A Syrian enters with the news of the empty tomb. Jesus enters, passing through the room to the Apostles within. The Greek, determined to demonstrate the truth of his thesis, goes up to him and places his hand on Jesus' breast. "The heart of a phantom is beating!" he cries.

In the final speech, after this tremendous moment of drama, Yeats's theme is "Man has begun to die." This is in accord with the trend of Christian thought. Christianity is a religion of realism, facing both life and death as they are. This little play, written in 1931, was in a strange way prophetic of what the next few years would bring—in the world and in Christian drama. For the keynote struck by the Christian dramatists of the thirties and forties was the inescapable reality of the Christian revelation, both of God and of man.

T. S. Eliot comes at this moment upon the scene. Since *Ash Wednesday* (1930), he had wanted to write verse plays rather than lyric poems. The first opportunity came in a roundabout way. Through his collaboration in a pageant play, *The Rock* (1934), which gave him the experience of seeing audiences react to his choral verse, he was invited to write a new play for the Canterbury Festival of 1935. This play was *Murder in the Cathedral.*

The conditions were not of the best, theatrically speaking: an uncomfortable rectangular room with a platform at one end and the only entrance at the other, a professional director and "leads" but an otherwise amateur cast, a run of only eight performances with an audience preconditioned to respectfulness. But this was one of those "given" moments: the sympathy between poet and director, the poet's own condition, the contemporary situation, and the ear of a wider audience were all prepared for the creation of a play which broke new ground. And the fact that the site of Thomas Becket's murder lay not fifty yards from the stage gave a power to the creation which completely outweighed the local disadvantages.

Murder in the Cathedral was startling to its first audiences, both at Canterbury and at London during its long run. It is hard for us now to realize the shock of the Knights' address to the audience or the strangeness of the Chorus, impassioned within a liturgical form, or of the Tempters, cryptically looking sidewise at history. These things have become, like Hamlet's Ghost, parts of a masterpiece. But one thing retains its penetration: the "Christian presence." There is no escaping the absolutes with which the play confronts us.

The Chorus has been called, rightly I think, the true protagonist of this play. The Women of Canterbury travel two spiritual roads: that of the hero, with whom by sympathy they go beyond his death, and that of themselves, the ordinary believers who have been caught up in extraordinary events. It is they who realize the oneness of all men and all nature, in the crisis when good and evil meet head on; it is they who fear for the Archbishop both on earth and beyond the grave; it is they who rejoice in him as their new saint; it is they who at the last confess the failure of us all in face of the love of God.

Forgive us, O Lord, we acknowledge ourselves as type of the common man,
Of the men and women who shut the door and sit by the fire;
Who fear the blessing of God, the loneliness of the night of God, the surrender required, the deprivation inflicted;
Who fear the injustice of men less than the justice of God;

Who fear the hand at the window, the fire in the thatch, the fist
in the tavern, the push into the canal,
Less than we fear the love of God.
We acknowledge our trespass, our weakness, our fault; we acknowledge
That the sin of the world is upon our heads; that the blood of the
martyrs and the agony of the saints
Is upon our heads
Lord, have mercy upon us.
Christ, have mercy upon us.
Lord, have mercy upon us.

The development is conveyed within a dramatic form that recalls the earliest European theater. It has been truly said by Helen Gardner that, though all his other plays are based on the legends used by the Greek dramatists, none of them is so Greek as *Murder in the Cathedral*. In the theater of Dionysus, the Chorus surrounded the altar. In Eliot's play, the Chorus more than once speaks an ode based on a liturgical hymn and, throughout the play, voices the deepest thoughts and feelings of the Christian witnessing the hero's progress to martyrdom.

When that point is reached, the Chorus is again in a classic Greek posture. A Greek tragedy is framed upon a legend which provides the reason for a rite—the worship traditionally offered at a certain site or to a certain god. *Murder in the Cathedral* is shown by its final scene to have the same impulse behind it:

Let our thanks ascend
To God, who has given us another Saint in Canterbury.

The play restores another element common to the Greek and the medieval drama, and since absent from the theater: the direct address to the audience. Eliot's use of it is more medieval than Greek. In the York mystery plays, Jesus on the Cross makes this direct appeal:

Thou man who hast mind to repent,
Look here, and good heed to me take.

> On the rood am I raggèd and rent,
> Thou sinful of soul, for thy sake.

In the Coventry plays, Herod introduces himself thus:

> *Qui status in Jude et rex Israel,*
> And the mightiest conqueror that ever walked on ground.
> For I am even he that made both heaven and hell.
> And of my mighty power holdeth up this world round.

Compare with these the typical instances of a regularly used medieval convention, the Christmas sermon and the "Knights' meeting" in *Murder in the Cathedral.* Becket communicates directly to the audience, as the supposed congregation in Canterbury Cathedral, the spiritual insights he has gained in facing his coming martyrdom. The Knights, annihilating the years between 1170 and 1935, say, "We beg you to give us your attention for a few moments," while they explain in colloquial prose their reasons for murdering the Archbishop. In each case, the audience is being asked to make up its mind about a claim that directly concerns it. Such a demand is not made in the Greek drama; it arises from the Christian doctrine of the Incarnation. God has acted, his love has come right into our sphere of living, and we cannot avoid saying *yes* or *no* to it.

This imperative of choice is constant in all Eliot's plays. The Chorus of *Murder in the Cathedral* fear the love of God more than any disaster that nature or other human beings can bring upon them. (Eliot puts this in the negative form, which has made not a few people miss the point: why does he do this?) Yet they know they cannot escape it. Harry, in *The Family Reunion,* is running from it when the play opens. Celia in *The Cocktail Party* is

> frightened by the fear
> That it is more real than anything I believed in.

"Real" is the key word. Eliot says, in *Poetry and Drama* (1953), that after *Murder in the Cathedral* he turned from past to present because, if the poet is to be effective in the modern theater, he must speak to the contemporary condition and make his audience identify, not only empathize, with his characters. This aim is as relevant for the Christian as for the poet. He wrote recently that he wanted most to see "ordinary plays written by Christians"—to see, in fact, the Christian view of man being exhibited in situations not explicitly related to religion. In the series of plays from *The Family Reunion* onward he steadily moves further and further away from "religious" language. The same movement can be seen in terms of theaters: from the Chapter House of *Murder in the Cathedral*'s original production to the art theater with *The Family Reunion*, and at last on to Broadway and Shaftesbury Avenue with *The Cocktail Party* and its successors. So too the form has changed from the liturgical *Murder in the Cathedral* to the classical *The Family Reunion* and on to the conventional three-act comedy. The verse has been so severely "rationed" of poetry that it is often hardly distinguishable from naturalistic prose, and the stiffness which it imposes is hardly compensated for by the illumination of poetic vision in particular passages. One might rather say that the poetic conception is built into the life of the play and into the creation of its characters. Perhaps this integration can be carried out on a higher level of human understanding than in the earlier comedies, for in *The Elder Statesman* there is a compassion for human frailty and a sudden acceptance of the miracle of human love which have not appeared before. The demand made on human beings throughout the series has been "Know yourself and accept the consequences." Now, with contrition, it is possible to find peace, both in relation to your fellows and to God.

Before passing on to consider the other dramatists of what might almost be called the Canterbury period, we may look backward for a moment and across the Channel to one who was a powerful influence on Eliot, Paul Claudel. Here is the "Christian presence" showing itself in the previous generation and in just as uncompromising a form. Claudel's genius is of the same unyielding kind as Eliot's, but his spirit is harsh and turbulent in its exaltations. The Catholic absolute works sometimes through violent sexual passions as in *Partage de Midi,* sometimes through the compulsions of the soil (Claudel himself came from a bleak countryside), sometimes through fearful sufferings as in the leprosy of Violaine in *L'Annonce Faite à Marie.* Claudel, from a much earlier generation, does not fall behind today's younger writers in the uninhibited expression of emotion; but at the center of this emotion is found the Christian faith, which is the final arbiter of his characters' destinies.

Claudel will stand as a major Christian dramatist. He has no direct followers, but his power was certainly exercised upon some writers in France whose best work was being done as Eliot entered the theater. André Obey, dramatist of that inspired ensemble La Compagnie des Quinze, wrote a mystery play for them, *Noë,* which brought back the ancient form to full life. Henri Ghéon, who, like Claudel, was reborn as a Catholic in a transcendental experience as a young man, devoted his life thenceforth to writing religious plays for popular performance. Maybe a major dramatist was lost in the makeshifts of semiamateur touring companies, but works such as *Le Chemin de la Croix, Noël sur la Place, Le Comédien* are cherished by Christians in many lands. The first-named has been the inspiration of several English writers, who have adopted Ghéon's plan of seeing a scriptural story through the eyes of a group of Christians who express their involvement in it by acting it out. R. H. Ward's *Holy Family,* Philip Lamb's *Go Down, Moses,* and Philip Turner's *Christ in the Concrete City* are well-known examples.

The playwright to follow Eliot at the Canterbury Festival was Charles Williams; the play was *Thomas Cranmer of Canterbury* (1936). Williams was an esoteric writer, who delighted in symbolism and in the idiosyncracies of the human spirit. His thirst for out-of-the-way knowledge led him to write a book on witchcraft, as well as historical biographies and essays in literary criticism. His novels have been called "mystical thrillers," a phrase which well expresses his salient characteristic. The spiritual adventure was to him the most exciting thing in life, and there was no barrier for him between the natural and supernatural worlds. The consequence of this attitude, so profoundly incarnational, has been that, although his writing is "difficult," Williams has, since his too-early death in 1945, been steadily growing in the estimation of Christians concerned with literature. Had he been alive to take part in the recent growth of Christian drama, he might have proved to be its most significant figure.

Cranmer is the best of his larger dramas. It tells, with masterly compression, the story of Cranmer's public life, and treats the historical material with a refreshingly ironic wit. But, at the heart of it, is the struggle within Cranmer's own soul, and Williams' method of dramatizing this illustrates the vigor of his imagination when exercised on religious themes. "*Figura Rerum*, a Skeleton," is the character who stands opposite to Cranmer throughout the play. This creation has a significance far more complex and stimulating than the "Death" in plays such as *Everyman*. He calls himself "Christ's back," the death through which Christ himself and Christians after him must pass to life, the stark truth about oneself and one's world which one cannot escape, the saving grace which one can attain through surrender. The core of this fine play is in the pursuit of Cranmer by this Hound of Heaven up to the point at which, having passed through the despair engendered by his recantation of his beliefs under physical and moral pressure, he finds the courage of complete surrender to God and runs to thrust the hand which wrote "the contrary of God's will" into the fire kindled to consume his body.

This play makes great demands on its audience, and Williams has become better known through his shorter plays written during World War II, notably *The House by the Stable* and its sequel *Grab and Grace*. The first is a nativity-morality; the second is a morality-farce in the true medieval tradition, but theologically of our own century. There is also a more difficult but extremely stimulating nativity play called *Seed of Adam.* It tingles with a life that proves Christianity, for those who face its implications, to be no outworn or moribund religion.

Dorothy L. Sayers followed Williams at Canterbury with *The Zeal of Thy House* (1937). Famous as a writer of detective fiction, she was now to make another reputation as a theologian-playwright. As a poet, she was hardly more than a competent and civilized craftsman using "blank verse." As a dramatist, she was a good organizer but an indifferent delineator of character. But, as a theologian, she combined a firm grasp of the essential tradition with a lively sense of its impact on people. Her best work in drama was done during the war and for broadcasting. *The Man Born To Be King* is a life of Christ in twelve 50-minute plays. The pride that her hero in *The Zeal* takes in his craftsman's skill is justified by Dorothy Sayers' own skill, in the tautness, balance, and sweep attained in this series which, though occasionally flawed by deficiencies in character drawing, certainly deserves to stand as a classic in its medium. It presents the Gospel story, interpreted in the light of the Christian creeds, in a vital and convincing manner.

The other major dramatist of the Canterbury Festival was Christopher Fry. He wrote *Thor, with Angels* in 1949, when he had already attained a West End success with *The Lady's Not for Burning.* Alternating between the theater and the Church, he produced *Venus Observed* in 1950, *A Sleep of Prisoners* for performance in churches during the Festival of Britain, 1951, *The Dark Is Light Enough* for Edith Evans in 1953, and a new play, *Curtmantle,* in 1961. His early play, *The Firstborn,* was on a Biblical subject, the Exodus, but his religious attitude is not fully explicit in this play.

Fry finds God at work in every aspect of life, and though the glow that was upon the world for him ten or twelve years ago has mellowed, it has not faded. The spiritual adventure for him is to match the wonder of God's creation with the daring of one who "has courage to exist in God" and let "lonely flesh be welcome to creation" (as Cymen, the hero of *Thor, with Angels,* says in expression of his new-found faith). The concern of Fry's religion issues directly in the living of the Christian life; and his pacifism is not a negative, antiwar crusade but a reaching out toward his fellows and toward a transforming goodness. His four soldiers in *A Sleep of Prisoners* "can only stay and alter":

> Good is itself, what ever comes.
> It grows, and makes, and bravely
> Persuades, beyond all tilt of wrong:
> Stronger than anger, wiser than strategy,
> Enough to subdue cities and men
> If we believe it with a long courage of truth.

This optimism is rare in our time and may seem overextended, but it is not facile; and for the most part it is not expressed in verbal affirmations such as the above but in dramatic action. The love that grows between the disillusioned soldier Thomas Mendip and the Lady, Jennet, as they both face death; the reward given to Cuthman's dogged faith in *The Boy with a Cart;* the Christlike heroine of *The Dark Is Light Enough* in her dealings with an incorrigible son-in-law: these are some of Fry's exhibitions of good in active form. His affirmative attitude tends to result, perhaps, in a certain unreality about the dangers that beset his chief characters (the witch hunt in *The Lady,* the fire in *Venus Observed*) and about the badness of the bad ones. Fry is not an escapist, however; he is a romantic, whose creative life is made difficult because it is lived at an antiromantic moment in literary history. One is doubly grateful for his existence on this account. That his faith is firmly Christian in basis is everywhere evident; and it is refreshing to find that his ebullient comic phrases spring more often than not from the Bible and the Book of Common Prayer. "Peace on earth and good tall women," says the drunken Skipps in *The Lady,* "and give us our trespassers as trespassers will be prosecuted for us." Nowhere is Fry's felicity in verbal incongruity better illustrated than in this scene.

If Fry sometimes fails to convince us of evil, a Catholic writer who entered the stage door early in the fifties succeeds in this very well. For Graham Greene, grace, it seems, began to operate as the soul reached its nadir. In rebellion against the narrowness and self-righteousness often characteristic of practicing churchfolk, he seems to enclose young Rose in *The Living Room* within the double net of her own true but adulterous love and the bigotry of the relatives who practice the faith she cannot deny. The result is a kind of passion play: the girl commits the mortal sin of suicide but with a prayer (known only to us) on her lips, and her death becomes the means of resurrecting the others by softening their hard hearts. Again, as with Eliot and Williams, no punches are pulled theologically. Greene moved with his second play, *The Potting Shed,* into the difficult realm of miracle; but the real point in this play is in the search for the truth which can only be revealed in terms of love—and only then can redeem. His most recent play, *The Complaisant Lover,* would qualify as Eliot's "ordinary play written by a Christian," and the result of the Christian impact on its story would repay analysis. Greene has certainly contributed to "the Christian presence."

What is to happen to that presence in the future? None of those cited above are young, and no one of comparable stature or promise seems to be following them. In Britain, the theater is dominated by a generation who distrust and who keep aloof from or abuse Christianity in their plays. The new realism of the sordid has the greatest appeal both in Britain and the United States, unless it is being superseded by the new fantasy of Beckett and Ionesco. Neither shows any apparent interest in orthodox Christian theology. Is the day of the "Christian presence" over, then? In the direct sense, maybe it is. But one can discover signs that the uncompromising Christian theater of the older generation has made its mark upon the imagination of the younger, and one may be permitted the guess that what is really happening is a re-formation of the art of the theater in terms analogous to the transformation (as yet hardly at all understood) which has come over our world in the last few years. The artists' intuition may be ahead of their own understanding, as well as of ours. And within that intuition we may well discover a new picture of the face of Christ.

The Voice of the Poet in the Modern City

BY RALPH J. MILLS, JR.

(*For John Nef and Mircea Eliade*)

> Father, O father! what do we here
> In this Land of unbelief and fear?
> —William Blake

EVER SINCE the time of Blake, and more particularly since the middle of the nineteenth century, the poet has found himself confronted with the expanding domination of the modern City. By City I mean the urban world and society with all its desires, values, and aims which is the ever-changing product of our highly developed technical knowledge, scientism, and commercial enterprise, as well as the various ideologies that have sprung up with them. The word *City*, then, I am employing symbolically in this essay to denote a complex of forces and qualities. But I do not wish the City to be conceived simply as an abstraction; we must not forget that it engages the lives of modern men and women who exist under the conditions provided by technological advance and in a common confusion of ideas, standards, and beliefs. The City, as I would like to think of it here, belongs peculiarly to our contemporary experience; it is the mode of existence created by world-wide conflicts and by shifting currents of scientific, industrial, political, and economic forces. Thus the City cannot be identified as London or New York, Berlin or Moscow; it consists rather of the pervasive atmosphere of technological society and the massive state in which all of us have still to live, or try to live, the life of human beings.

In peace or in war, the events of the present century have combined to fashion an inescapable public nightmare. The realities of daily life move increasingly beyond the control of the individual who, amidst greater comfort and mobility, becomes lonelier, more anonymous, more frustrated. Against this victim of the beneficent society, we can set the victim of the totalitarian regime: the persecuted Jew, the displaced person, and the political refugee. Ralph Harper, in the Introduction to *The Sleeping Beauty*, summarizes the paradoxical character of twentieth-century existence:

> This is a century of homelessness and exile, of nervous disorder and persecution, of actual enslavement and barbaric cruelty. It is also a century of the greatest advances in technology and comfort, of the profoundest social and critical sensitiveness. The greater the wisdom and the more widespread the social aspirations, the greater the disillusion with false leaders and false movements. When things go wrong, as they so often do, disillusion then matches expectation.

This statement about the age is equally a statement about the life of the City; within it, ideologies and opportunities call out to the bewildered person, coaxing him further into the labyrinth of dead-end passages, mirrored rooms, and sham treasures of the artificial fun house the City fabricates. The recent complaint of some novelists that the grotesquerie of human events now exceeds the author's imaginative reach, so that he finds it hard to make a fiction authentically representative of contemporary life, frighteningly illustrates the nature of the illogical dream we frequently think we inhabit. While Proust and Joyce, by a feat of imagination, captured the life of their time and place, change and development in society have become so rapid, so constant, that the present-day novelist must choose a much smaller segment of reality as his province because he cannot account for more. Or he may move into the poet's territory and take over some of his methods—think of Joyce's last work, of Virginia Woolf, Henry Green, Djuna Barnes, Samuel Beckett, Philip Toynbee, and John Hawkes.

The City—as the complex of elements by which we have already defined it—is also seen as the result of history and of man's progress toward a conclusion which is grand if unformulated. Science and technology promise utopias that the pure flow of time or history must inevitably bring about. Such ideas are the shared property of the City-dwellers and, in general, go unquestioned. Very often this hazy inspiration of endless progress rushing forward uncontrollably into the splendid, though indistinct, vistas of the future receives a religious sanction in the popular mind or is even confused with religion. We can gather from these inclinations that Western society, as Mircea Eliade has so well said, is obsessed with history to an abnormal and dangerous degree. "Western philosophy," he writes in *Myths, Dreams and Mysteries,* tends "to define man as above all a historical being conditioned, and in the end created, by History." History thus becomes *the* dimension in which man has his being, a temporal dimension into which he is hurled at birth, to use Heidegger's terminology, and out of which he is cast at the moment of death. For the modern mind lacking religious faith, time is man's element; outside of it lie chasms of nothingness, offering to the observer the metaphysical *frisson* of Pascal's gaze into the empty spaces of the universe but unsupported by the French thinker's belief. History, for this skeptical mind, can be a god, one who rules with mindless and impersonal law the destinies of men, civilizations, whole worlds, and who binds all creation to the same temporal wheel, as Dylan Thomas demonstrated in his early poems:

> The force that through the green fuse drives the flower
> Drives my green age; that blasts the roots of trees
> Is my destroyer.
> And I am dumb to tell the crooked rose
> My youth is bent by the same wintry fever.

The force that drives the water through the rocks
Drives my red blood; that dries the mouthing streams
Turns mine to wax.
And I am dumb to mouth unto my veins
How at the mountain spring the same mouth sucks.

The hand that whirls the water in the pool
Stirs the quicksand; that ropes the blowing wind
Hauls my shroud sail.
And I am dumb to tell the hanging man
How of my clay is made the hangman's lime.

("The force that through the green fuse")

So the City identifies itself with the gratuitous processes of history as the City of time and fact alone, and views itself as the succession of its manifestations in time—but in no other dimension. These convictions encourage a certain attitude toward nature. While the City-dweller thinks of himself as sealed in time, with annihilation after death his only release, he wishes to extend his domain to the superhuman: his conquest of nature by science and engineering is a means of asserting superiority over and taking revenge upon the physical-temporal dimension to which he feels tied. If nature and its laws can be subdued and exploited, man will have transcended, in some obscure sense, his bondage to it and might become a limited sort of god himself. Consequently, the City-dweller is divorced more and more each day from the natural world and is situated in a framework of artifice made possible by continuous technical innovation. The mental attitude which initiates with such ruthless energy and zeal this transformation of elements of the natural into something anti-natural has been described trenchantly by Romano Guardini: "The technological mind sees nature as an insensate order, as a cold body of facts, as a mere 'given,' as an object of utility, as raw material to be hammered into useful shape; it views the cosmos similarly as a mere 'space' into which objects can be thrown with complete indifference." [1] Furthermore, Guar-

[1] Romano Guardini, *The End of the Modern World*, trans. by Joseph Theman and Herbert Burke (New York, Sheed & Ward, 1956), p. 74.

dini points out how the impulse motivating the efforts of technology is, plainly, the will to political power—a truth printed in bold type in our daily newspapers. The City, in all its secular and pragmatic devotion to the fact, thrives on man's antagonism toward the material cosmos, on his nationalistic and ideological attempts to conquer the material world more quickly than his rivals; and the City thrives on man's failure to see that creation—however imperfect the arrangements as we presently know them—is the home to which he belongs. But this technical perfection is gained at an "expense of spirit," a cost of inner life no distraction or contrived sedative for the nerves can allay.

THE POET

Inside the gates of the City and amidst the clamorous noises of men and machines, the voice of the poet responds with dogged persistence to the reduction and degradation of human life he finds there. Armed with a single weapon, his speech, the poet confounds the City's false estimate of man and the universe he populates. I say the poet "responds" rather than rebels, because the hysterical rebellion of some younger American writers has not freed them of the City's claims but confirmed them as its victims. Dope addiction, sexual license, and frenzied shouting hardly ruffle the City's self-confidence; and these poetic antagonists at last destroy themselves or are turned into celebrities. Their moral charges against society—and they are real enough—are used as objects of laughter and derision for mass entertainment.

The two important aspects of the poet's response to the City or the modern world we might call rage and mystery. I have borrowed these words from René Char's book of poems, *Fureur et Mystère,* and quite appropriately, I believe, because Char has spent much of his imaginative effort in declaring the poet's role in our time. Rage needs little discussion; it is the poet's anger at hypocrisy and untruth, at violence done to man, nature, or language. In our terms, the City is a repository of these false values and so is accused by the poet's moral passion. A poem, "Pity this busy monster," by E. E. Cummings aids in explanation of both these words.

> pity this busy monster, manunkind,
>
> not. Progress is a comfortable disease:
> your victim (death and life safely beyond)
>
> plays with the bigness of his littleness
> —electrons deify one razorblade
> into a mountainrange; lenses extend
>
> unwish through curving wherewhen till unwish
> returns on its unself.
>
> A world of made
> is not a world of born—pity poor flesh
>
> and trees, poor stars and stones, but never this
> fine specimen of hypermagical
>
> ultraomnipotence. We doctors know
>
> a hopeless case if—listen: there's a hell
> of good universe next door; let's go.

If we are at all familiar with Cummings' free and original use of language, his habit of employing negative prefixes, such as *non-* or *un-*, to connote inhuman or negative qualities, we will understand the range of his satirical invective here. But we ought also to notice that the poem includes, at its center, the values from which Cummings derives his judgment. "A world of made/ is not a world of born—pity poor flesh/ and trees, poor stars and stones . . ." These lines offer, in a compressed but lyrical manner, what the poet holds up for comparison: the world of natural creation, its closeness to man through his physical being, its presence in his life. Cummings' criticism of the "world of made" acquires most of its force from those values and their ramifications.

Through the inclusion of values, he brings us to the other part of the poet's response we need to consider: mystery. The poet's criticism, no matter how true it is, falls short of its intended results if it is not completed by mystery. Mystery is the value the poet reveals to us at the core of experience, but the experience in this case *is* the poem. Thus mystery does not consist of a code of conduct, or a message we can extract from the poem, or a scheme guaranteed to cure what ails us; it remains inseparable from the work of art, a way of seeing, an attitude. While we cannot withdraw it intact, we can, by our encounter with the poem, be altered *in ourselves* through the revelation of meaning and value within the poetic universe. And the pattern of that universe extends by analogy and correspondence to the larger world in which we are born and die. Mystery demands finally that we recognize the inviolability of creatures and things, the depths of communion which may obtain between any combination of them, and their inexhaustibility to meditation. Here I think we could do no better than to recall Philip Wheelwright's definition of "the mysterious" as "the radically enigmatic, not the temporarily puzzling . . . that character or quality or relationship in things which, however much 'explained,' always transcends in its essence any totality of explanations given."[2] In addition, the poem can make present to us the permeation of visible, tangible reality by the invisible and can direct our attention to the sacred. The poet's vision creates, through the words and images and rhythms in which it takes form, the sense of mystery as an essential ingredient in our perception if we give to that vision the concentration it merits. The world is seen in poetry as a living whole where everything participates in everything else; it is no longer the object of exploitation but of reverence and wonder: the earth of our origins, of our destinies.

Another aspect of modern poetry—of most poetry in fact—deserves mention along with the poet's double task of evaluation and revelation, and that is the personal element.

[2] Philip Wheelwright, *The Burning Fountain* (Bloomington: Indiana University Press, 1954), p. 74.

We need scarcely comment upon the feeling of grim impersonality in the life of the City. Isolation, fear, violence, egoism, frustration, and a good number of other human afflictions burgeon in its cold efficiency. Everywhere one is aware of the increasing loss of personal characteristics in the affairs of daily existence. But the poet counters this impersonal tendency with a personal voice.[3] It is in the nature of the personal voice—and the individual value and responsibility that go with it—to dissolve the walls the City raises between us and within us. Kenneth Rexroth says:

> The arts presume to speak directly from person to person, each polarity, the person at each end of the communication fully realized. The speech of poetry is from me to you, transfigured by the overcoming of all thingness—reification—in the relationship. So speech approaches in poetry not only the directness and the impact but the unlimited potential of act.[4]

So the act of writing and the act of reading, though they are separated in time and by space, are joined; reading completes the circle of communion in which poet and audience, self and other meet. "All real living is meeting," Martin Buber writes in *I and Thou*; and we must not allow ourselves to forget that literature is an integral part of our living or it is nothing at all.

Some readers may believe that the personal voice is missing in a great deal of this century's poetry, but this is more of a theoretical illusion than a poetical truth. The notion of the poet's impersonality has come to us from some of the best poets and literary critics of the past fifty years; and yet it does not seem, to me at least, that the notion quite fits the experience of the poetry—through which the author's voice still reaches us. In spite of masks and disguises, we can readily

[3] On this subject see Walter J. Ong, S.J., "Voice as Summons for Belief," in *Literature and Belief, English Institute Essays 1957*, edited by M. H. Abrams (New York: Columbia University Press, 1958), pp. 80-105; and Nathan A. Scott, Jr., *Modern Literature and the Religious Frontier* (New York: Harper and Bros., 1958), Chapter V. I am much indebted to both these authors.

[4] Kenneth Rexroth, *Bird in the Bush: Obvious Essays* (New York: New Directions, 1959), p. 12.

detect the voice of T. S. Eliot within the speech of his fictional narrators and other invented characters; of Ezra Pound among the fragments of lyric and polemic, foreign tongues, and literary ancestors that are pieced together in the *Cantos*; of Edith Sitwell behind the mockery and laughter of her clowns, apes in tail coats, and eccentric country squires. The poet's voice, in any event, is not simply a matter of surface qualities but lies embedded in his arrangements of language and thought.

The poet's voice raises itself from the chaos of the City, and we can hear the voice because it is surrounded with the aura of silence in which it is to be comprehended. The communion of the poet and the reader through the poem brings about a new unity, a reconciliation of man with man in the spirit and before the prospect of existence. For the modern poet encloses in his art, even if we cannot always easily detect it, an image of the ideal, a notion of regeneration that comprises the mysterious and is balanced against the actuality of the City as we normally know it. Poetry tends, at any time, to fashion an image of the unity and perfection we lack on one or another level of our being. What is and what might or ought to be mingle in the experience and vision of the contemporary poem. The poem, once written, is loosed in the impersonal world of the City where, as T. S. Eliot says in *Four Quartets*, "Shrieking voices/ Scolding, mocking, or merely chattering,/ Always assail" it. But there, too, the poem is available to those who will take possession of it. Let us now see, briefly, some of the terrain of the spirit that is uncovered by the modern poet's rage and mystery.

IMAGES OF HELL

In a few minutes the train was running through the disgrace of outspread London. Everybody in the carriage was on the alert, waiting to escape. At last they were under the huge arch of the station, in the tremendous shadow of the town. Birkin shut himself together—he was in now.

The two men went together in a taxi-cab.

"Don't you feel like one of the damned?" asked Birkin as they sat in a little, swiftly-running enclosure, and watched the hideous great street.

"No," laughed Gerald.

"It is real death," said Birkin.

So ends the fifth chapter of D. H. Lawrence's *Women in Love.* Those who know this great novel of our modern predicament will remember that Birkin is a somewhat disguised version of Lawrence himself or, if you will, a Lawrence-type, while Gerald represents industry, will-to-power, the mechanical and unnatural man who has sacrificed his specifically *human* life to the City and its interests. This short passage records Birkin's reactions to his arrival in London, but Lawrence portrays those reactions in terms of a descent into Hell. The regions entered by the two men resemble those of a nether world cut off from all that is beautiful or natural—an inferno constructed from cement and steel by the ingenuity of reason pressing for power and wealth. To Birkin, as to Lawrence, the City is abhorrent, and entrance to it carries fearful associations from classical and Christian literature of the kingdom of the dead or the condemned.

Perhaps it seems digressive to include a portion of a novel in a paper on poetry, but I should like to emphasize the point that what Lawrence does in this passage has innumerable parallels in contemporary writing, and especially in poetry. For I believe it is possible to say that much of the value asserted by the modern poet in his art depends for substance on his having had, prior to the imaginative formation of that value, a full taste of its opposite. It would be difficult for us as readers to accept Dante's divine vision in the *Paradiso* if we had not already witnessed the infernal vision preceding that final glory. The mythical and moral calm of Shakespeare's last plays likewise assumes its grandest proportions in our imagination when the characters and happenings of those dramas stand out against the background of evil, suffering, torment, and loss that is our memory of the great tragedies. In contemporary poetry as well, the experience of evil sears and purges the poetic mind, compels the writer to discover a view beyond the ruling ideas of the City.

The various manifestations of Hell in modern literature arise from the poet's unique sensitivity to the world he inhabits, his beliefs about the different dimensions of reality, and his own aesthetic and moral propensities. Louise Bogan, in her essay "The Secular Hell," notes that the decline of religious faith—and who can doubt this is one of the crucial issues of the times?—frees Hell of religious control as a concept having only supernatural status, while the idea of Heaven "fades out":

> The magic which religion straitens and controls for its own purposes; the "will" that religion tames; the fear and guilt which religious practice resolves and accommodates—all these escape into the "profane." The magician and sorcerer (who "wish to coerce nature, instead of allying themselves with it") take up the priest's power. The individual conscience, meanwhile, is asked to bear the full weight of the individual's transgressions.[5]

"Magician and sorcerer" point to the scientist and technician who run the machinery of the City, though not all of it. But Miss Bogan's implicit supposition is of first importance: with the dwindling faith in the survival and judgment of the soul after death, man makes a Hell out of his earthly existence. His utopias lapse into tyrannies. In his blueprints for perfection according to *his* will, man's imperfection sooner or later shows through, usually with a vengeance. The poet draws on man's latent sense of the diabolical and the infernal by presenting the evil of his society through the imagery of Hell.

The early poetry of T. S. Eliot—that is, the poems through *The Waste Land* (1922) and "The Hollow Men" (1925)—constitutes a journey into the Inferno which is all about us in the streets, at teas, and in restaurant conversa-

[5] Louise Bogan, *Selected Criticism* (New York: Noonday Press, 1955), p. 308.

tions, in the houses of high finance, and the lowest of boarding houses or brothels. Yet this infernal world of outward appearances and events has its counterpart in the more intimate Hell of the individual's relation to himself, to others, to the absence of God, from which results his secret anguish before a universe empty of lasting significance. The situation of Prufrock is a case in point. His perceptions, in the familiar opening lines, create the reality seen from there on. Nevertheless, we must not mistake Prufrock's inner conflicts for the *only* reality, nor should we, in consequence, credit him for living alone in a Hell which is entirely of his own making. The environment he has always inhabited, and now cannot flee, is conducive to the fragmentation of the self; it is a Hell of inanity.

> And would it have been worth it, after all,
> After the cups, the marmalade, the tea,
> Among the porcelain, among some talk of you and me,
> Would it have been worth while,
> To have bitten off the matter with a smile,
> To have squeezed the universe into a ball
> To roll it toward some overwhelming question,
> To say: "I am Lazarus, come from the dead,
> Come back to tell you all, I shall tell you all"—
> If one, settling a pillow by her head,
> Should say: "That is not what I meant at all.
> That is not it, at all."
>
> ("The Love Song of J. Alfred Prufrock")

This form of damnation fascinates Eliot, for we come across it with marked regularity in his poems: spiritual sloth or indifference, the condition of a society from which all evidence of the spiritual has disappeared. Though Prufrock's characterization of himself as Lazarus, raised from the dead by Jesus, is harshly self-deprecatory, it conveys also a rough truth about this society, for whose members the knowledge possessed by Lazarus could not be of less interest. Eliot's poem leaves the impression of an eternal afternoon tea from which Prufrock and his acquaintances are unable to escape—nor do they wish to! But Eliot has lent his protagonist both conscience and self-consciousness. Prufrock's vision of the mermaids is a strong intimation of another, doubtless more profound, level of experience, but his awareness merely sinks him despondently in his present dilemma.

The Hell which Eliot discloses, then, assumes in the individual the form of a living death; and Prufrock and the Hollow Men, the narrator of "Gerontion" and nearly all the inhabitants of the Waste Land are stricken by it, to cite only the most prominent examples. The drama of indifference, or moral torpor, these figures enact is so excruciatingly painful that, one supposes, sheer obliteration would come as a relief:

> Unreal City,
> Under the brown fog of a winter dawn,
> A crowd flowed over London Bridge, so many,
> I had not thought death had undone so many.
> Sighs, short and infrequent, were exhaled,
> And each man fixed his eyes before his feet.
> Flowed up the hill and down King William Street. . . .
> (*The Waste Land*)

The locations here are several: not just London or Baudelaire's Paris, but the City; and also the vestibule of Dante's *Inferno*, where those "whose lives knew neither praise nor infamy," and those others "who against God rebelled not, nor to Him/ Were faithful, but to self alone were true" [6] have their eternal dwelling-place. If the particular quality of Eliot's Hell is the death-in-life of the spiritually indifferent, its usual geography is that of the modern City. Baudelaire was the first magnificent poet to chart the metropolis; and Eliot has followed his direction, blending in his imagery the outer life and the inner man until even the ordinary course of affairs in the City yields up hidden demonic pressures:

[6] Dante, *The Divine Comedy, Hell,* trans. by Dorothy L. Sayers (Harmondsworth, Middlesex: Penguin, 1949), Canto III, p. 86.

His soul stretched tight across the skies
That fade behind a city block,
Or trampled by insistent feet
At four and five and six o'clock;
And short square fingers stuffing pipes,
And evening newspapers, and eyes
Assured of certain certainties,
The conscience of a blackened street
Impatient to assume the world.

("Preludes")

The end which Eliot envisages for this civilization is implicit in its nature and bursts forth at the finish of "Gerontion" and again in "What the Thunder Said" (*The Waste Land*).

What is the city over the mountains
Cracks and reforms and bursts in the violet air
Falling towers
Jerusalem Athens Alexandria
Vienna London
Unreal

In the years after "The Hollow Men," Eliot moves steadily toward the visionary poetry of *Four Quartets*. But even the latter does not leave Hell behind. The third section of "Burnt Norton" opens on a scene in the London underground which returns us to the same spiritual indifference we noticed in the crowd flowing over London Bridge. These commuters in the City's depths again resemble the lost souls of Dante:

Neither plenitude nor vacancy. Only a flicker
Over the strained time-ridden faces
Distracted from distraction by distraction
Filled with fancies and empty of meaning
Tumid apathy with no concentration
Men and bits of paper, whirled by the cold wind
That blows before and after time,
Wind in and out of unwholesome lungs
Time before and time after.
Eructation of unhealthy souls
Into the faded air, the torpid

Driven on the wind that sweeps the gloomy hills of London,
Hampstead and Clerkenwall, Campden and Putney,
Highgate, Primrose and Ludgate. Not here
Not here the darkness, in this twittering world.

The poet's initiation to a contemplative state in *Four Quartets* seems to require of him that he enter once more these infernal regions, though he must, as the last lines above indicate, pass through into a purifying darkness and solitude. The underground train, in Eliot's symbolism, belongs to the linear movement of time and history; those wholly involved in that movement are trapped in the temporal order and have abandoned faith in the divine act of Incarnation by which time and the Timeless are brought together.

Eliot serves as one of the best and most representative poets in whose writings the imagery of Hell is brought to clear, meaningful focus, but he is hardly unusual in this practice. Edith Sitwell, Wilfred Owen, Edwin Muir, W. H. Auden, Stanley Kunitz, Robert Lowell, and Richard Eberhart are chief among the poets who have given us fierce portraits of contemporary life as one of torture, damnation, and spiritual lassitude. And it is not simply the inhuman streamlining of existence by means of technology that provokes the poet's furious retaliation, but the corruption and apathy, the metamorphosis of persons into things or statistics, the sterility of relationships, the substitution of communications for communion. In Stanley Kunitz's poem, "My Surgeons," the doctors of the title are a hellish compound of the evils and vicious ideals of the age whose tactics are reminiscent of concentration camp and secret police:

My surgeons are a savage band,
Surely their patient is ill-fated.
Their tricks are coarse: the small sweet hand
I seized was wax, or amputated.
With the humiliated swollen-footed
And the lost persecuted their traps are baited.

Deftly they opened the brain of a child,
And it was full of flying dreams;
Father was prowling in a field
With speckled tongue and a collar of flame.
They labeled it "Polluted Streams,"
The body floating with the name.

They studied a prostrate fever-chart
With unmitigating eyes; one said,
"Bohemian germs, *Weltschmerz*, bad art
and Spanish fly. Off with his head."
Another, "Fascist. His boot is filled with blood."
They cut me up till I was red.

Lastly they squeezed out of my veins
The bright liquor of sympathy;
I lost the touch of souls, the reins
On white revenge, and I was free
Of pity, a solid man of snow.
But in the night to whom could I go?

Lie down with me, dear girl, before
My butcher-boys begin to rave.
"No hope for persons any more,"
They cry, "on either side of the grave."
Tell them I say the heart forgives
The world. Yes, I believe. In love.

Every action of the "surgeons" is a calculated mutilation of the human self, a deprivation of its living worth; we notice that the poet himself metaphorically undergoes each of the successive operations in all their horror but survives to defy this treatment by performing the act of love, which unites him with the girl in a personal communion of selves. The poem is likewise a personal utterance in the teeth of precise, machinelike evil.

The diabolical elements in Kunitz's poem are quite obvious, though the author draws on the ethical tradition of Christianity rather than its theological assertions. We need to recall Miss Bogan's theory that the notion of Hell, once it has been severed from institutional moorings, floats free but can appear just as frightening and certainly more immediate. It is not uncommon, therefore, to discover demonic and infernal imagery in the work of poets who are without any noticeable religious adherence, for the idea of Hell is inscribed on the Western mind and does not automatically disappear with the advent of skepticism. The City, the gas ovens and hydrogen bombs, the power politics and monolithic states: these productions of twentieth-century man provide inescapable evidence for the poet that Hell, whatever and wherever it may otherwise be, exists here and now before his very eyes.

From her early satirical poems and experiments with the music of verse to her prophetic odes and songs of the 1940s, Dame Edith Sitwell has employed images of Hell in keeping with the changes and preoccupations of her beliefs and her poetic imagination. We see in the rich, ample body of her writing an alteration in the conception of Hell from a secular expression of grotesque mockery at the hollowness of modern English life to a religious view of man's folly in the scheme of the universe. The intentional preciosity of *Façade, Bucolic Comedies, Rustic Elegies,* and so forth, their indebtedness to Baudelaire and Laforgue, Russian ballet and the *commedia dell' arte,* should not lead us to think the poet is evading completely the actualities we have brought together under the symbol of the City. Indeed, the artifice and theatricality of these poems lend devastating strength to the criticism she levels. The world first appears here as some mechanical contraption or occasionally as an enormous puppet stage. "This modern world is but a thin match-board flooring spread over a shallow hell," Dame Edith wrote in an epigraph to *Façade* in 1922. "For Dante's hell has faded, is dead. Hell is no vastness; here are no more devils who laugh or who weep—only the maimed dwarfs of this life, terrible straining mechanisms, crouching in trivial sands, and laughing at the giants' crumbling." The infernal again enters mortal experience. Often enough, this "shallow hell" takes on the revelation of an existential nothingness beneath the tattered face of things. So disturbing is the vision that it must bring the poet herself close to the edge of vertigo and terror:

> Then underneath the veiled eyes
> Of houses, darkness lies, —
> Tall houses; like a hopeless prayer
> They cleave the sly dumb air.
>
> Blind are those houses, paper-thin;
> Old shadows hid therein,
> With sly and crazy movements creep
> Like marionettes, and weep.
>
> Tall windows show Infinity;
> And, hard reality,
> The candles weep and cry and dance
> Like lives mocked at by Chance.
>
> The rooms are vast as Sleep within:
> When once I ventured in,
> Chill Silence, like a surging sea
> Slowly enveloped me.
>
> ("Clowns' Houses")

Dame Edith saw the modern world collapsing the old dimensions of reality: the attributes of the supernatural dropped within the province of the natural; man tried to build his Paradise on earth and made, instead, a Hell. The disparity between those who lust for power and money and those—the poor, the hungry, the outcast, the clowns—who are exploited by them becomes a constant theme with the publication of *Gold Coast Customs* (1929). After that poem, which juxtaposes the frenzied ritual of a cannibal tribe with the behavior of the English Lady Bamburgher and her friends, who represent Western society, Dame Edith lapses into poetic silence for a decade and emerges in *Street Songs* (1942) with a mythical and visionary art unforeseen in her previous writing. *Gold Coast Customs* is her true infernal experience, an introduction to the regions of the demonic that prepares the poet for the visions of cosmic renewal to follow in "Green Song," "An Old Woman," "Holiday," "The Canticle of the Rose," and other later poems. The concluding stanza should convince us that Dame Edith has suffered inwardly the violence and degradation her poem depicts, has endured it as the ordeal of Hell:

> Gomorrah's fires have washed my blood—
> But the fires of God shall wash the mud
> Till the skin drums rolling
> The slum cries sprawling
> And crawling
> And calling
> "Burn thou me!"
> Though Death has taken
> And pig-like shaken
> Rooted and tossed
> The rags of me.
> Yet the time will come
> To the heart's dark slum
> When the rich man's gold and the rich man's wheat
> Will grow in the street, that the starved may eat,—
> And the sea of the rich will give up its dead—
> And the last blood and fire from my side will be shed.
> For the fires of God go marching on.

In this process the poet is initiated, through her art, like a priest or a primitive shaman into a higher life of the spirit.[7] The experience of Hell, as we see, is succeeded by a death of the old self—and a death to the world of the City—and the promise of rebirth in the sacred. Dame Edith's imagination in the ensuing years moves beyond the City as it is—a Hell—to a plane of reality in which evil is absorbed or dissolved or transformed by a larger mythical and religious pattern.

[7] For a discussion of initiation rites, see Mircea Eliade, "Sense-Experience and Mystical Experience among Primitives," in *Myths, Dreams and Mysteries*, trans. by Philip Mairet (New York: Harper & Row, 1961), pp. 73-98; and *Birth and Rebirth*, trans. by W. R. Trask (New York: Harper & Row, 1958), especially the Epilogue, pp. 132-36.

Not all modern poets pursue such an elaborate plan of development, but there are few of any merit in this last half-century who have been able to avoid the imagery of Hell in their work. The City throws up bulwarks, shoddy values, and activities that hinder the deeper apprehension of reality; and the poet knows that he must, if he is to be honest, penetrate, describe, and pass through this living damnation. Richard Eberhart, in his poem "A Testament," insists that prevailing conditions urge the poet to his task of discovery of the real and to his second task of speaking to those who will hear him:

It is what I never quite understood
About my formidable day
Was the truth, the trust, and the good
Where the final values play.

It was the ungraspable part
As events and crises interfered
Was the bold quest of my art,
The blood, the crystal tear.

It was the lack of direct mating
With authority, politics or powers
Gave thrust to loving and hating,
Allowing the purest hours.

It is the world's inability
To nourish my senses whole
Brings on the subtle utility
Of the total strength of soul.

I sing of something so far and deep
Ages will find it clear,
Love that is a grasp, a leap,
And faith, landfall of fear.

Henceforth this testament
Of the struggles of my bone and time
Is made; for those meant
Who cast the spirit, seed the sublime.

MYTHMAKING

So far I have discussed the atmosphere and predilections of the City, as well as the poet's manner of associating his negative responses to the City with the idea of Hell drawn from Christian literature and thought. I remarked also that the personal voice of the poet speaks as man to man in the impersonal context of the City and recalls the individual to a sense of his own being. But I have said nothing of the poet's isolation, a loneliness of the spirit that has led him along unexpected paths. The division between society and artist is, however, an historical phenomenon we recognize generally. It corresponds in many respects with the devaluation of language to a level at which it can only—if we believe the semanticists and language philosophers—rightfully perform the job of indicating ascertainable facts or of expressing inner emotive or psychic states having merely a subjective validity. Language and symbol, after the close of the Middle Ages, as Erich Heller says in *The Hazard of Modern Poetry*, were gradually restricted to a reality which could be gauged by the senses or measured by instruments of science. Man was divorced from the transcendental realities to which he earlier had access through image and word, and the poet began to break with the narrow rational and empirical calculus of the scientific outlook to which his society was attracted. Both Blake and Hölderlin at the end of the eighteenth century withdrew to an interior world of the spirit for the resources necessary to their art but no longer available in the outer environment, where faith was relaxing and the City was beginning to rear up into its present shape. Blake contrived, from his occult reading and his visionary imagination, the complex private religion of his prophetic poems. Hölderlin named the gods anew, called across a widening gulf upon the supernatural:

Near, near and
Difficult to grasp is the Almighty.
Yet where the danger lies, there
Likewise lies the salvation.
In darkness dwell
The eagles; fearless the sons
Of the Alps pass over the abyss
On delicate bridges.
Massed around us arise
The summits of time, and the dearest
Live close, yet exhausted
Among their separate hills:
Give to us guiltless water,
O give us wings for the faithful
Voyage and the return! [8]

But these lofty zones of the spirit demand extraordinary stamina: Hölderlin died in madness; and in the last part of the nineteenth century Nietzsche's mind gave way before the universe he had proclaimed a yawning void empty of God. In the same years, Mallarmé attempted to make of his poetry the sacred rite of a new dispensation that would evoke an absent sphere of essences; and the adolescent Rimbaud stretched poetry to another extreme by the creation of a magical and nearly self-sufficient kingdom in *Les Illuminations*. Poetry became a solitary occupation, a reckless and heroic endeavor to objectify in art a privately constructed set of beliefs supported by the divinely inspired powers of imagination. After Blake, Coleridge, and the German philosophers, the human imagination was felt to be the sole means for attaining to realities not grounded in physical data or in usefulness but belonging to an invisible climate of the spirit that existed in its own right.

The romantic poets began a search for the absolute, for the lost God, that carried on through the symbolist movement into the literature of the present time. So strong has

[8] "Patmos," in *Some Poems of Friedrich Hölderlin*, trans. by Frederic Prokosch (New York: New Directions, 1943).

this motive been that the French critic Marcel Raymond, in *From Baudelaire to Surrealism,* says that poetry for a hundred and fifty years has "tended to become an ethic or some sort of irregular instrument of metaphysical knowledge." The poet, lacking institutional adherence, at odds with the views of his society, has forged his own metaphysics with the tools at hand: personal ideas and perceptions, strength of imagination and artistic skill. As a result, we frequently observe in the poetry from Yeats and Rilke to Dylan Thomas and Hart Crane efforts to supply a mythological system or otherwise to endow a body of metaphors, symbols, and images with consistent, though subjective, spiritual values and, in this way, to preserve the writer's moments of luminous experience or revelation within the form of the work where they can be discovered and shared. The knowledge and insight derived from the poetic enterprise are opposed to the logic and reason, the scientific and technical learning which dominate the City's ideology.

For those poets who are professed Christians the situation is much the same. Each of them has found the meaning of Christianity as if he or she had come upon it for the first time. A profoundly personal rediscovery of religion seems to me a common bond between T. S. Eliot, Edith Sitwell, Allen Tate, Robert Lowell, Brother Antoninus, Edwin Muir, and W. H. Auden.

But just as some poets have suddenly uncovered the spiritual order embodied in Christianity, there are many who do not accept its claims or who find that their spiritual experiences do not fit readily into the categories of organized religion. Among the major writers who use their poetry to gain a comprehensive vision of man and the universe traditionally supplied by religion, I choose two—W. B. Yeats and Wallace Stevens—to demonstrate the literary developments I have been hastily sketching.

Yeats was, from an early age, fascinated by magic, folklore, and the supernatural; these interests are prominent in his poetry at the start. His dabblings in Rosicrucianism, occultism, and various other hermetic practices left their stamp on his evolving thought, for the knowledge of symbolism he acquired from these investigations spurred his imagination as nothing else but Irish politics could. And, true to say, Yeats was capable of genuine visionary experience, as a poem like "The Cold Heaven" from *Responsibilities* (1914) amply shows:

> Suddenly I saw the cold and rook-delighting heaven
> That seemed as though ice burned and was but the more ice,
> And thereupon imagination and heart were driven
> So wild that every casual thought of that and this
> Vanished, and left but memories, that should be out of season
> With the hot blood of youth, of love crossed long ago;
> And I took all the blame out of all sense and reason,
> Until I cried and trembled and rocked to and fro,
> Riddled with light. Ah! when the ghost begins to quicken,
> Confusion of the death-bed over, is it sent
> Out naked on the roads, as the books say, and stricken
> By the injustice of the skies for punishment?

In the following years, Yeats composed *Per Amica Silentia Lunae* (1917), a preliminary essay on his ideas of the soul, the will, the mask and daimon; these ideas were systematized in a full-scale mythology, *A Vision* (1925; revised 1937). This work, a plan of universal history and symbolism as well as a scheme of psychology, explained an entire metaphysical doctrine in which he could ground his attitudes, his metaphors, and symbols.

The Yeatsian mythology locates our own era at the end of a two thousand year cycle of history initiated by the birth of Christ; but since history is destined to move in alternating cycles or "gyres"—each with its governing character—our own days, as this poet sees them, are bound to be days of wrath and violence announcing the death of Christian civilization and the inauguration of a new cycle. Yeats's famous prophetic poem, "The Second Coming," treats in its grim irony and in its vicious, dreamlike imagery the period of dissolution:

Turning and turning in the widening gyre
The falcon cannot hear the falconer;
Things fall apart; the center cannot hold;
Mere anarchy is loosed upon the world,
The blood-dimmed tide is loosed, and everywhere
The ceremony of innocence is drowned;
The best lack all conviction, while the worst
Are full of passionate intensity.

Surely some revelation is at hand;
Surely the Second Coming is at hand.
The Second Coming! Hardly are those words out
When a vast image out of *Spiritus Mundi*
Troubles my sight: somewhere in sands of the desert
A shape with lion body and the head of a man,
A gaze blank and pitiless as the sun,
Is moving its slow thighs, while all about it
Reel shadows of the indignant desert birds.
The darkness drops again; but now I know
That twenty centuries of stony sleep
Were vexed to nightmare by a rocking cradle,
And what rough beast, its hour come round at last,
Slouches towards Bethlehem to be born?

Here, in a kind of trance or revelation from the world soul of the seventeenth-century English Neoplatonists, the poet witnesses the emergence from sleep of the historical cycle that has been dormant throughout the Christian age. In spite of the horrible appearance of the symbolic beast, the cycle, according to Yeats, will not be purely evil; only the time of transition from one cycle to another exhibits turmoil and disorder. Much of Yeats's poetry that takes cultural disaster as its theme has had a frightening relevance to the world events it appeared to predict. But such application ignores the larger strands of the poet's thought with which his work is woven. Within that design, "The Second Coming" is a profoundly anti-Christian poem—and not, as it seems when examined outside the design, a humane cry at a glimpse of oncoming terror—because the hope for Christ's return implies not merely the judgment of men but heralds "a new heaven and a new earth," while in Yeats's system it begins just one more of an infinite number of cycles.

What position does one maintain before the inevitable demise of our civilization and—more important—before the prospect of a history which runs its course in determined spirals? In poems like "The Gyres" and "Lapis Lazuli," Yeats insists that it will do no good to protest or resist; another world will rise happily on the ruins of this one. "We that look on but laugh in tragic joy," he wrote in a Nietzschean posture. Surely we can admit the prophetic truth in many of Yeats's poems, especially in relation to the crises of the last five decades; and his style and music are rich, as is his symbolism. Yet it is a different matter to accept the doctrines, the poses, and some of the politics. Yeats labored to contain within the formal limitations of his art a bulk of spiritual perceptions which would remain beyond the province of churches and orthodoxy—a renegade vision—and still fly its metaphysics in the face of modern positivism, the creed of the City. This poet tried always to be true to his experience, and it was often contradictory; but his sincerity turned him into the legendary example of the writer in search of a myth, a self-made philosophy that would enable him to reconcile the apparent disharmonies of his experience.

Wallace Stevens is a poet burdened with preoccupations, not unlike Yeats's in some respects: mainly in the wish to find a substitute for Christianity.[9] But Stevens devoted his career to sounding, in poetry, the possibilities of the human imagination in a universe where trust in immortality had decreased considerably, and he did not try to propound a complicated mythology. All the same, his thought is subtle and difficult. The recurrent metaphors of Stevens' poems grow naturally out of his sensual delight in the material world, in the variousness of the seasons, in the texture of words, which are things

[9] Nothing is more enlightening on this subject than the "Adagia" from Stevens' notebooks. See Wallace Stevens, *Opus Posthumous*, edited by S. F. Morse (New York: Alfred A. Knopf, 1957), pp. 157-80.

in themselves. Our perception of these earthly goods is not due to their presence alone; man's imagination transfigures the objects of creation in the act of perceiving them. Thus the imagination—and its potential—serves as an agent of union with the blunt fact of the tangible universe—and its potential.

What Stevens means by this union is the acceptance of "the imperfect" as "our paradise." Since "the death of one god is the death of all," as he believes, religion is impossible and life itself should be honored as the supreme value. The emperor of ice cream, in the poem of that title, is the lusty spirit of earthly existence which, like the gift of ice cream he extends to us, is sweet, perishable, and of short duration. The poem is also about funeral preparations for a dead woman, but Stevens upholds the celebration of life, its ordinary routines, even on this occasion. Death is ordinary and natural, too, and ought to be treated as such:

> Call the roller of big cigars,
> The muscular one, and bid him whip
> In kitchen cups concupiscent curds.
> Let the wenches dawdle in such dress
> As they are used to wear, and let the boys
> Bring flowers in the last month's newspapers.
> Let be be finale of seem.
> The only emperor is the emperor of ice cream.

This "realism" displays only one tendency of Stevens' mind; the other spends itself in making up the spiritual deficit left by his naturalism and agnosticism. And it is the imagination which will come to replace whatever man has relinquished in the way of gods and systems of belief. As early as 1915, in "Sunday Morning," this poet set forth the idea of an earthly paradise, of life considered as divine in itself. Stevens repudiates the pangs of conscience of a woman in the poem who has lazily failed to attend church and counters with a lyrical argument which is religious in its own quite different terms:

Why should she give her bounty to the dead?
What is divinity if it can come
Only in silent shadows and in dreams?
Shall she not find in comforts of the sun,
In pungent fruit and bright, green wings, or else
In any balm or beauty of the earth,
Things to be cherished like the thought of heaven?
Divinity must live within herself:

Passions of rain, or moods in falling snow;
Grievings in loneliness, or unsubdued
Elations when the forest blooms; gusty
Emotions on wet roads on autumn nights;
All pleasures and all pains, remembering
The bough of summer and the winter branch.
These are the measures destined for her soul.

We have, in these lines, the problem of belief as Stevens saw it and his desire to render it a wholly human affair. Imagination can adjust man harmoniously to brute creation—which often appears as the image of a rock, "a world unpurged." Only through the interplay of imagination and reality can man and the physical world be made over in a new reality that fulfills the potentialities of both. Furthermore, ideas and beliefs are relative, inventions of a time and place; they should be recognized as convenient fictions and yet be adhered to—because there is nothing else. When a set of fictions is outworn, man must re-create the world in a new image.

Far exceeding Coleridge's expectations for imaginative powers but realizing, in a sense, Matthew Arnold's prediction that poetry should be the modern religion, Stevens elevates this faculty until it is the sign of man's own divinity: "God and the imagination are one," he says in one of the adages from his notebooks; and in another: "God is in me or else is not at all (does not exist)." [10] The image of the rock symbolizes both the boundaries and the possibilities of Stevens'

[10] *Opus Posthumous*, edited by S. F. Morse (New York: Alfred A. Knopf, 1957), pp. 178, 172.

world: it is the origin and goal of life, "the starting point of the human and the end, /That in which space itself is contained. . . ." Man, by his imaginative activity, transforms this given reality and dwells in the midst of the cosmos he has enriched. Little wonder, then, that Stevens grew mystical in his feelings about this divinity he had appointed. He was gifted with a religious sensitivity, for his poems erupt continually in Biblical and theological metaphors and vocabulary, but always in the service of his own endeavor to prove that "the purpose of poetry is to make life complete in itself."

One cannot easily doubt the honesty of effort in Yeats or Stevens, Rilke or Crane; they illustrate the tremendous urgency and dedication of the poet's role when all else appears to be warring ideologies, material advance, and moral decay. Relying only upon their imaginations and sensibilities as sources of knowledge, these poets try to bring to light through their poems a metaphysical order out of the dark calamity of modern experience. Yet one may finally think that there is a certain incompleteness of vision here which is not, to be sure, a failure of form or technique. And each of them deserves the title, "witness to the spiritual," bestowed on Rilke by Gabriel Marcel. But their inability to break through the confines of a private mythology or to break through the recondite subjectivity of their metaphysics and find a dimension of reality which has substance outside of poetry and the imagination prevents an unreserved reception of their spirituality. An exotic and eccentric body of thought like Yeats's may well inspire a number of great lyrics, but we reach a point with this poet beyond which we cannot give our consent, for to do so would be to subscribe to his philosophy —something we are not certain Yeats himself did.[11] Now this is not to say we cannot grant him Coleridge's "willing suspension of disbelief" as we read; that attitude is required

[11] Yvor Winters also takes up the validity of Yeats's thought in *The Poetry of W. B. Yeats* (Denver: Alan Swallow, Swallow Pamphlets #10, 1960).

for the reading of any imaginative literature. There remains, however, a qualitative difference between sharing Yeats's experience with him in a particular poem and accepting to the full the implications to which that poem is committed in the author's scheme of ideas. In the first instance, we are confronted with what I shall call, for lack of a better name, "the aesthetic experience proper"; in the second, we are involved in the aesthetic experience but we are also led past the borders of the poem toward the larger interpretation of reality on which the poem rests and which will demand our agreement or disagreement. We have, at last, to make these judgments about poetry, about the universe a poet calls up in his work; and they are personal judgments because they indicate our part in the communion with a writer through his art—and the ultimate value we attach to that art in our lives.

CONTEMPLATION

In contrast to the poets who give themselves to the creation of private systems and myths, there are those for whom the visionary experience lies, broadly speaking, within the range of Christian faith and its tradition of symbolism and thought. But, as we said before, Christianity strikes a writer of this kind with all the force of a new revelation and compels him or her to a radical choice and assent made in isolation. Sometimes the choices are visible in the poetic work itself, and we have Eliot's *Ash Wednesday* in modern literature to remind us of what can be done artistically with the subject. But in other poets the change may be slow and almost imperceptible, as in the case of Edwin Muir or unexpected and decisive, as it is with Dame Edith Sitwell. The result of the choice, so far as we are concerned with it here, is often a mystical or visionary quality in the poetry.

Contemplation is the word I would select to cover the general experience underlying this religious poetry; and I shall take, by way of explanation, a passage from *New Seeds of*

Contemplation by Thomas Merton dealing with the contemplative attitude and experience:

> Poetry, music and art have something in common with the contemplative experience. But contemplation is beyond aesthetic intuition, beyond art, beyond poetry. Indeed, it is also beyond philosophy, beyond speculative theology. It resumes, transcends and fulfills them all, and yet at the same time it seems, in a certain way, to supersede and deny them all. Contemplation is always beyond our own knowledge, beyond our own light, beyond systems, beyond explanations, beyond discourse, beyond dialogue, beyond our own self. To enter into the realm of contemplation one must in a certain sense die: but this death is in fact the entrance into a higher life.

Merton describes the sort of experience which happens outside of poetic creativity and gets into poetry solely through metaphors, symbols, and parables—the devices by which we try to comprehend the ineffable analogically. Language is, for a poet of this experience, at best a mere approximation of the felt presence of that Otherness. Edwin Muir, who discusses this spiritual awareness in his autobiography, has left another remarkable account in "The Poet":

> And in bewilderment
> My tongue shall tell
> What mind had never meant
> Nor memory stored.
> In such bewilderment
> Love's parable
> Into the world was sent
> To stammer its word.
>
> What I shall never know
> I must make known.
> Where traveler never went
> Is my domain.
> Dear disembodiment
> Through which is shown
> The shapes that come and go
> And turn again.

Heaven-sent perplexity—
If thought should thieve
One word of the mystery
All would be wrong.
Most faithful fantasy
That can believe
Its immortality
And make a song.

For Muir the "parable" and "mystery" consist of what he called the "fable" of human existence, the enactment by the hidden self in each of us of the archetypal stages in man's history: innocence, the fall, life in time, the search for grace and redemption. This drama is lived usually without our knowledge, for we can only seize momentarily in dreams and visions, as Muir did, these cosmic resonances of our seemingly insignificant existence. Now this recognition by the poet is not an aesthetic phenomenon; it occurs prior to the process of literary composition. The difference between the poetry of Yeats, Stevens, or Rilke and that of Eliot, Muir, Kathleen Raine, or Edith Sitwell depends on the two distinct types of poetical and spiritual experience these writers seek to convey. Among the former, the visionary experience takes place *in the poem* as an aesthetic event or in a metaphysics styled to buoy up the poem on a sea of pure imagination. The vision does not arise from a true or objective interpretation of the world and man and being, because there is no longer any truth, but simply revolving truths which appear and disappear. So, as Erich Heller says in his essay on Nietzsche and Rilke in *The Disinherited Mind,* "the 'real order' has to be 'created' where there is no intuitive conviction that it exists"; the poet makes himself "the begetter of new gods." Hence the godlike imagination of Stevens, the mythology of Yeats—these are fabricated systems of reality, products of imagination, to which the poet who creates them also responds aesthetically by writing poems based on such "supreme fictions," to borrow Wallace Stevens' phrase.

The "contemplative poet," if we can use this title to distinguish him from the "mythmakers," finds an order in his spiritual and meditative experience instead of building a private universe of subjective beliefs to nourish his poetry. I do not mean to imply that the contemplative poet discovers an agreed-upon truth, for we are still in the City and still beset by its restrictions and hypocrisy. But, to return to Erich Heller's statement, this poet does intuit a real order, a structure and truth in reality. Kathleen Raine's poem "Ex Nihilo" stems from that kind of intuition and even describes it:

> Out of nothing we are made,
> Our cities rise upon the void,
>
> And in chromium-plated bars,
> Shadows drink their fill of tears,
>
> Women's transient fingers pass
> Over silks and flowers and glass,
>
> Cameras and motor-cars
> Spin on the hub of nothingness
> On which revolve the years and stars.
>
> Beyond the houses and the fields
> Rise the forest-shrouded hills,
> And upon each leaf is traced
> The pattern of the eternal mind
> That summons kingdoms from the dust.
>
> Above the forests lie the clouds,
> White fields where the soaring sight
> Rests on the air's circumference,
>
> And distant constellations move
> About the center of a thought
> By the fiat of that love
>
> Whose being is the breath of life,
> The terra firma that we tread,
> The divine body that we eat,
> The incarnation that we live.

Plainly, the experience on which this poem is founded is a revelation of the order of created things and the Creator who holds all in existence. Miss Raine's vision is not, however, in its beginnings either aesthetic or poetic but contemplative; it is part of her inner life which she attempts to realize as poetry. Her apprehension of a spiritual order is not manufactured for the sake of poetry; it exists independently. The same may be said for Auden, Muir, Frost, Eberhart, Tate, Ruth Pitter, and many more poets. Poetry will frequently clarify such an intuitive understanding, give it body through words and imagery, bring it more sharply before consciousness; but poetry will never be completely responsible for the understanding itself. "The unattended moment" Eliot treats in *Four Quartets* places a similar illumination well in advance of the poems centering about it:

> . . . the moment in and out of time,
> The distraction fit, lost in a shaft of sunlight,
> The wild thyme unseen, or the winter lightning
> Or the waterfall, or music heard so deeply
> That it is not heard at all, but you are the music
> While the music lasts. These are only hints and guesses,
> Hints followed by guesses; and the rest
> Is prayer, observance, discipline, thought and action.

The art of the contemplative poet is predicated on the belief in a universal order external to himself, in a relationship between the material and spiritual realms. In his poetry, he gives speech to what is known first in silence or flashes for an instant and is gone, the "hints and guesses" of which Eliot writes. Above all, he insists upon the objective truth and sacred meaning of the knowledge he has received.

Perhaps it will seem that we have removed ourselves to a pleasant distance from the City under whose threatening shadow we began. That is not, however, the impression which I should like to leave. For the poetry we have discussed is no more and no less than the personal voice of the poet speaking to us inside the City. The poet's rage and criticism judge our man-made environment, censure its ideas. Mystery fills out the vacancy left in the wake of rage by suggesting value, whether it be the way of a new myth, a poetic system complete in itself, or the disclosure of a spiritual pattern, a divine Presence within the cosmos touching our lives if we will be attentive. This paper, then, shows a few prominent ways in which the contemporary poet has assumed moral, metaphysical, even theological responsibilities. The nature of the modern City thrust these labors at him. And the poet has answered with the fully human song: the poetry of his whole being.

*The 491 Pitfalls of the Christian Artist**

BY MARTIN JARRETT-KERR, C.R.

I read yesterday, in Renan's very discerning study of Lammenais (1857): "Nothing is so tiresome as Catholic polemics, for the apologist grants himself many advantages that the disinterested critic must refuse himself." Hence it is better to elude discussion. Many of my friends, and often the best of them, became converted. I kept my affection for them, and it was often very keen, but I ceased talking with them.

This is readily recognizable as coming from André Gide in *So Be It*, the last little work he wrote before his death. Among his friends and acquaintances Gide knew many converts. Paul Claudel, François Jammes, Henri Ghéon, Charles du Bos, Jacques Rivière, Jacques Copeau, and Jacques Maritain are among the most famous; all are either writers or persons connected with letters. And there was François Mauriac, too, not a convert but with something of the convert's fervor after his "reconversion." Gide talks about them again, later in his book:

A certain number of my former friends . . . became converted. Without having exactly broken off with them, I was immediately convinced that conversation with them had become impossible. Any subject that was dear to me had to be cautiously avoided. It didn't seem to me that their conversion notably improved their characters; on the contrary, their worst shortcomings drew encouragement from being henceforth consecrated to God. Copeau, Jammes, Claudel, Ghéon . . . even buttressed their arrogance

* Our Lord said that I must forgive my brother unto seventy times seven: it is the 491st occasion that is the real test.

from that moment forth with a sort of conceit that quickly made them unbearable to me. Backed by the Church, they *couldn't* be wrong. *I* was the arrogant one for refusing to give in, to subordinate my own thought to what had been acknowledged as true, etc. . . . Subsequently I recognized the same collective conceit among the Communists, though on a quite different plane. Both groups taught me something, demonstrating the value of the individual by their irrational claims.[1]

And, earlier, in his *Journals* (March 5, 1929) he had implied that it was precisely the behavior of his Christian friends that had kept him from the Church.

I would not swear that at a certain period of my life I was not very close to being converted. Thank God, a few converts among my friends took care of this, however. Jammes, or Claudel, or Ghéon, or Charlie du Bos will never know how instructive their example was for me.

Gide thus regarded Catholics and Communists as almost identical in certain respects:

It always seems to me that between men of good faith equally concerned with the public welfare there must eventually be agreement. But *they* are not of good faith, as I am reluctantly obliged to admit. . . . It is as true for the one group as it is for the other the moment they believe that *the end justifies the means.* From that specious doctrine have been born, and are born even today, abominable errors.[2]

(This is a well-known polemical accusation, especially against Jesuits, which ignores authoritative condemnations by the Church of this very doctrine. But Gide was not always scrupulous in his references.) He admits that not all Christians, not even all Catholics, are alike. He makes, for instance, a specific exception of one, Paul-Albert Laurens, a convert who had always stood up for him (Gide); and of Claudel he says:

[1] André Gide, *So Be It, or The Chips Are Down,* trans. by Justin O'Brien (New York: Alfred A. Knopf, 1959), pp. 30, 44-45.

[2] *Ibid.,* p. 46.

. . . unbelievers are not the only ones to be annoyed by the triumphant Catholicism he incarnates. Claudel aims to win out on every score. Is it a surprise that a Bernanos, profoundly Christian and open to suffering, should become indignant and wonder if it is possible to reach Paradise in a Pullman car? [3]

Now it will be said that both Claudel and Gide are special cases, and this is true. But this merely means that Claudel exhibits in capital letters the perils that beset every convinced Christian artist. In Gide, of course, he had to deal with a particularly subtle and evasive person. Gide points to the deterioration in character of his friends due to their conversion; but his own relationship with them is not always entirely honest. "I have," he says, "a great regard for integrity." And he claims: "My mind is as little inclined to controversy as a mind can be. Instead of standing up to my opponent, I wear myself out trying to understand him." And finally, with an air of injured innocence, he says: "People insist that I should be Claudel's enemy. That he owes it to himself to be mine is not quite the same thing. I am not at all averse to his taking his stand against me. What an odd state of mind he has!" [4]

When one reads side by side his correspondence with Claudel and his own private journals at the time of writing, one cannot but be aware of a certain disingenuousness on his part. On December 7, 1911, Claudel wrote to Gide and referred to the news that Mme. Gide's sister had recently been converted to Catholicism.

I am very much moved [wrote Claudel] by your news of a conversion in your family. When shall I hear of your own conversion, dear friend? I'm much less shy—if ever I was really shy—of talking about these questions. Religion seems to me such an enormous, monumental affair, like the works of Nature! . . . [Religion] is something as vast as the starry vault, where the ocean itself has room to move, and one can breathe to the limit of one's lungs. It

[3] *Ibid.*, p. 128.
[4] *Ibid.*, pp. 26, 46, 127-28.

is, on the contrary, the unbeliever who lives in a shrivelled and diminished world . . . and who has nothing above him but the smoke-blackened ceiling of his study.[5]

Gide replied, apparently very warmly, on December 10:

. . . I'm almost afraid to tell you how much I was moved by the other part of your letter. I still feel that I haven't the right to tell you of this until I make up my mind to go with you all the way. . . . The secret of my incapacity to believe . . . lies rather in the fidelity which I owe to those people, my relations and my seniors, who lived in such constant, noble, and radiant communion with God, and gave me my noblest images of abnegation.

Claudel wrote again on December 12, and tried to press the point further home:

. . . How moved you must have been by that conversion, by the intervention of Somebody so close to yourself and in such astonishing circumstances! But why do you suppose that you would be unfaithful to those lovely and noble beings who surrounded you in your childhood if you were to go further along the road which was pointed out to you? . . . That closer union with both one and the other which allows of the Real Presence and of obedience to a visible Father is entirely compatible with the examples which you were given in childhood. . . .

Gide did not reply to this for three weeks, but, when he wrote on January 7, 1912, it was as cordial and even submissive as ever.

How could I leave your letter so long unanswered? Was I afraid of being led on to answer you in too confidential a tone? No; but a thousand anxieties withdrew my attention from you. . . . I am waiting for the greatest possible state of calm in which to write to you. . . . Outside of Catholicism only isolation makes sense to me. I am isolated, my dear friend. I'm not at all proud of it . . . but what can I do? For of all those who write and play at politics, there isn't one whose Catholicism doesn't manifest itself to me by the iniquity of its effects. (And it's because you aren't like those others that I have listened to you with such at-

[5] This, and the passages following it, are to be found in *Correspondence between Claudel and Gide,* edited by R. Mallet, trans. by John Russell (London: Secker and Warburg, 1952), pp. 169-78.

tention.) They use the crucifix as if it were a bludgeon; and as soon as they or their writings are called in question they hide behind the holy sacrament. To draw near to Christ for me is to draw away from them.

(Gide pretends to make an exception to Claudel, and yet he uses language about the others which is precisely that which he later uses of Claudel himself.) Claudel will not let him go. He replied on January 9: "Alas, if you mean to delay your conversion till every Catholic or *soi-disant* Catholic behaves like one of the saints, you will wait a long time. . . ." And, not getting an answer, he wrote again on January 15:

It is not with the motes from one's neighbour's eye that the house of God can be built, but with the beams that one takes out of one's own. . . . The decadence of Art is due to its separation from what people so stupidly call Morality, and which I call the Life, the Way and the Truth. That is the urgent question of the hour, on which we must absolutely take sides.

But meanwhile Gide was quietly noting in his diary (January, 1912):

I should like never to have known Claudel. His friendship weighs on my thought, and obligates it, and embarrasses it. . . . I can still not get myself to hurt him, but as my thought affirms itself it gives offense to his. How can I explain myself to him? I should willingly leave the whole field to him, I should give up everything. . . . But I cannot say something different from what I have to say, which cannot be said by anyone else.

Another example of Gide's disingenuousness is connected with Claudel's comments on his novel *La Porte Étroite*. Claudel says of it, in a letter of May 10, 1909:

Your book was an invaluable document on Protestantism. . . . Protestantism has no sacraments, there is no longer any real substance in God's relations with mankind, and no longer any religion in the true sense of the word, where both parties loyally provide their share. . . . God never speaks directly. Whence that strained, quibbling, sorrowful morality which at first sight seems so much at variance with the dogma of predestination. . . . You revive that old quietist blasphemy which was developed *ad nauseam* in the last century, and which says that piety needs no reward, that the noblest love is the most disinterested. How could God's love be more perfect if it were contrary to reason and had no rational origin? For the whole of creation God is the supreme and unique Good: how could he not be the same for us? Shall we love him more purely when we have robbed him of his very essence? . . . God's bounty cannot be separated from Himself. To deny the one is to reject the other. Love that is not nourished by interest would be a poor sort of love. . . .

Gide replied, apparently with gratitude, on June 18:

Your letter was a great source of joy to me, for everything you say about my book—even your reservations, whether psychological or dogmatic—everything shows that the book is a success. You realize that it is animated by pure, religious feelings; and also—what is equally important, you realize that the drama of the book resides entirely in its unorthodoxy. . . .

But his comments on this letter of Claudel's at the end of his life show that even at the time his private reactions were very different from anything he was saying in writing to Claudel himself:

. . . Claudel did well to educate me by the amazing letter he wrote me about my *Porte Étroite* pointing out the Protestant heresy in the fact of loving good independently of the promised reward. He subsequently made clear in a conversation that the Catholic must humbly love and practice virtue *because* . . . and that my Huguenot pride rebelled against, the bargain, the agreement with God, the tit-for-tat. In the beginning I was surprised, almost angry, upon seeing that sort of bookkeeping. Subsequently it greatly helped to open my eyes and show me that the whole system of indulgences and of "assuring one's salvation" depends on it. It was better to break off, and that is what I did.[6]

The reservations in the relationship must have been mutual. For, only a week or two before, Claudel can be found still writing affectionately to Gide: "I think that you now believe in Christ the God, and this makes me infinitely happy. That is enough for your salvation" (letter, December 8, 1912).

[6] Gide, *So Be It, op. cit.*, p. 137.

Gide is already noting in his *Journal* (November 19): "Went to see Paul Claudel yesterday at his sister's. He receives me with great cordiality. . . . [He] is more massive, wider than ever; he looks as if he were seen in a distorting mirror; no neck, no forehead; he looks like a power-hammer."

The controversy becomes a tedious one. But, as we look back on it, even making allowances for Gide's evasiveness, what is most disturbing is that Claudel seems to have had a double standard of judgment. When Gide was younger and still a possible subject for conversion Claudel could not only have warm personal relations with him but could express a high opinion of his writing. Writing (March 3, 1908) to Gide about his *Enfant prodigue,* he says:

It reveals more of your soul, more of your thoughts, than any other book of yours that I know. And what a pleasure it is to savor that noble style of yours—so flexible and so distinguished, above all (I would say) so easy, and so homogeneous that it unrolls the narrative from beginning to end without a moment's loss of continuity! [7]

And in the letter quoted already about *La Porte Étroite,* he says:

I shouldn't like to say that I've understood it perfectly, despite the high quality of an admirable style which insinuates itself into one's being like some warm intoxicating liquor. One seems to be enveloped on every side in that solemn end-of-summer atmosphere. . . . The language is suave and mature—a suavity full of anguish. A Dantesque sweetness, but beneath that is something terribly bitter—I don't like to say despairing.[8]

But when Gide is finally seen to be not only unrepentantly fixed in his homosexuality but firmly resistant to conversion, Claudel sweeps him aside. His final judgment on Gide is made clear in the famous interview in March, 1947, published in Albert Camus' magazine *Combat.* "I don't see that Gide has any talent at all. . . . What I still can't understand is

[7] *Correspondence between Claudel and Gide, op. cit.,* p. 72.
[8] *Ibid.* ("Letter," May 10, 1909), pp. 89-90.

his influence. From the artistic and intellectual point of view Gide is nothing. His influence is one of the mysteries with which I am surrounded. . . ." And the reasons for Gide's non-conversion are straightforward:

> . . . he accepted no guide. He offers an appalling example of cowardice and weakness. . . . I had a lot to do with Gide when I thought he was profoundly Christian . . . and I knew nothing of his abominable failing. . . . Mirrors fascinate Gide. His *Journal* is just a long series of poses in front of himself . . . [it is] a monument of insincerity. . . . For my part I combat his influence with every weapon I have. What would you? It's Yes or No.[9]

Somewhat ingenuously Claudel protected himself against the sort of accusation leveled at him by Gide—and which could be leveled at most converts by any hostile witness. In an earlier letter already quoted (December 12, 1911), he says, "The convert is often like a man whom no woman finds attractive, but who has a wife who is blind." But this is a double-edged defense of the Christian artist: for it seems to imply that if the world, like his wife, comes to appreciate him it is only because dust has been thrown in its eyes.

Gide was not the only person who suffered from Claudel's apostolic arrogance and tactlessness. In 1953 the well-known actor-manager Charles Dullin died at just about the time his friend the playwright Armand Salacrou was writing *Dieu le Savait,* with a part (the octogenarian, Armand) specially designed for him. Dullin had had an operation, but in fact it was only exploratory. He was found, however, to be inoperable and was brought back into his ward where he spent several days of agonized dying. Salacrou was by his bed much of the time Dullin was in the hospital and, after his death, wrote a moving expression of his loss. Dullin had been his best friend, and more than that—"although I am not a Christian and, indeed, refused to make my first communion at the age of ten, it is thanks to him that I understand what a 'spiritual director' means. A spiritual director (*directeur de*

[9] *Ibid.*, pp. 233-35.

conscience), not a theologian." Salacrou follows this up with a furious attack on the notion of providence:

What is this cruel game we call life? If God knows the answer, why doesn't He tell it? . . . When my turn comes I expect nothing but an annihilation (*une effacement*) comparable to the annihilation that preceded my birth. But if I did suddenly wake up and find myself face-to-face with God, I'd be the first to reproach Him for His silences, His absurd game of hide-and-seek; I should ask Him the reason for His abandonment of me, for my blindness and solitude.

When this was published, Claudel wrote a note to Salacrou, saying that he was moved at the account of Dullin's death—but why had no one thought of sending a priest to him? He added that it was nonsense to speak of God's silence "since God has been screaming His head off from the height of the Cross for two thousand years. It's not His fault if so many people plug their ears."

This was quite enough, and Salacrou exploded with a statement *Mes Certitudes et Incertitudes* which he felt worthy of inclusion, along with the rest of the correspondence, in one of the volumes of his plays.[10] First, he said, someone *had* fetched a priest to see Charles Dullin; the sick man had been polite, as always, but had refused any prayers. And anyway, Salacrou continued, the mystery of suffering is enough to put anyone off God.

The existence of a creation without God, without purpose, would seem to me less absurd than the presence of a God existing in His perfection and creating an imperfect man so as to make him run the risk of eternal damnation. And if at this very moment my pen fell from my hand, I should die, as I have lived, without hope. . . . From my childhood I have taken refuge in a Determinist philosophy—a concise one, narrow, rigorous, a total mechanistic determinism.

Salacrou went on to complete his play whose very title, *Dieu le savait*—"God knew it all along," implies determinism.

[10] Armand Salacrou, *Théâtre*, VI (Paris: Gallimard, 1954).

Into the mouth of the chief character, Daniel Doublet, he puts a long speech expounding a determinist, or better, a predestinarian creed. It is, as a matter of fact, Salacrou's most involved, unreal, and least successful play. That is irrelevant to this essay, except insofar as Claudel's blundering intervention may have made things worse.

Thus we see how religious conversion failed seriously (according to those who knew him) to soften the harshness of one poet's character—and indeed, perhaps even gave it an excuse for crusading and domineering. Gide's last interview with Claudel is unforgettable (noted in his diary at the time, May 15, 1925):

> At my ring, Claudel came to meet me, and holds out his hand. He seems to have shrunk. A short, swansdown-lined jacket of coffee-colored silk made him look still thicker. He is enormous and short; he looks like Ubu. We sit down in two arm-chairs. He completely fills his. Mine, a sort of chaise-longue, has such a long back that to be comfortable in it I should have to get too far away from Claudel. I give up and lean forward.
>
> In the presence of Claudel I am aware only of what I lack. He dominates me; he overhangs me; he has more base and surface, more health, money, genius, power, children, faith, etc., than I. I think only of obeying without a word.[11]

But most of this, of course, refers to Claudel's personal attitudes and relationships. Since we must not judge writers by their characters, can we say anything about the perils of Claudel's kind of religious imperialism for his poetry? Generalizations about so massive a dramatist and poet as Claudel are themselves perilous. But I think it is possible to say, first, that one of the dangers he faced is that which faces anyone using his long, free-verse line: the danger of indiscipline, of mere oratory replacing genuine statement or observation. This was certainly true of Charles Péguy, and I think it is true of parts of a play like Claudel's *Le Soulier de Satin*, and of much of *Les Cinq Grandes Odes*. Second, I think we can

[11] *Correspondence between Claudel and Gide, op. cit.*, pp. 227-28.

say that Claudel is at his greatest when he is writing religious drama, like *L'Annonce faite à Marie,* which does not require grand doctrinal statements, or plays, like the fine *Partage de Midi,* in which the passionate human element seems in fact to overthrow the nice theological balance.

II

François Mauriac is much more open, sympathetic, understanding of non-Christian artists than Claudel and most of his friends were. No doubt this is partly because Mauriac was a "born Catholic" whose faith merely underwent crises of deepening, whereas Claudel, the two Maritains, Léon Bloy, and the others were converts. Indeed, Mauriac's formal account of the place of religious belief in the artist's life is unexceptionable and well put.

> . . . Catholicism, even if the practice of it is intermittent . . . more surely than heredity, serves to embank the thick and muddy flood, to direct its course, and . . . to lead it back, at length, into its eternal bed.
>
> But no, that image of embanking is deceptive. The religious life does not curb, rather does it satisfy the poetic craving, not like a fairy-tale which might be true, but like a coherent vision of existence, while, at the same time, leaving a sufficient margin of uncertainty, mystery and darkness to maintain that element of disquiet without which there could be no art, if, as I believe, every great work of art is an attempt to prove an answer to that "What are we? Whence do we come? Whither are we going?" [12]

As a result, Mauriac's judgments on Gide, for instance, are far more conciliatory and charitable than those of most of his fellow Catholics. It is true that Gide quotes him as saying, in reference to his (Gide's) old age, "Henceforth, how can this corpse mean much to us"; but this was probably a casual aside in one of his articles for *Figaro.* Generally he complains of "that sort of blundering busybodying of which

[12] François Mauriac, *Mémoires intérieurs,* trans. by Gerard Hopkins (London: Eyre and Spottiswoode, 1960), p. 37.

André Gide's Catholic friends were guilty during his life," and quite understands how "it sometimes irritated Gide to feel all round him so many Christians on the prowl."

What is more, Mauriac says explicitly: "I do not ask that the novelist should affirm anything. I would go so far as to agree that any positive affirmation on his part is to be shunned and runs the risk of destroying his work." [13] And his criticism of the naturalistic novel, such as Zola's, is surely perfectly just. He has been describing his own childhood:

> The poetic power of childhood to transfigure and to dramatize, has, in my case, been carried to extremes. I have lived at the center of a universe which was at once delicious and formidable. . . . When a "grown-up" told me a story, I had first to be assured that it was "true." . . . For me the land of marvels had to be inhabited and filled with the kind of people I met with, the kind of objects that I knew.

This might seem to lead to a demand on Mauriac's part for naturalism. But it was precisely religion that modified this: he says:

> My young years were saturated in it. It laid siege to me from all sides—from without by means of its liturgy and church-observances . . . from within, by the habit, which I acquired very early, of talking to somebody whom I could not see, though he could see me, and to whom I was answerable for even the least of my thoughts. . . . [So] the practice of religion from earliest childhood bred in me a taste for the dream which would turn out to be true, for an invisible reality. I knew that nature could be imbued with grace, for I had lived with that knowledge long before I had had any idea of what "grace" and "nature" meant.
>
> Much later, my horror of the kind of universe I found in Zola, came, not from what he showed, but from what he did not show. I should have found his books less repellent had the invisible been not only absent from them, but denied. . . . What could be more purely material than Balzac's world, less pervious to Christian Grace than Proust's? But neither author denies this other side (or place) in the human story he is telling. It is just that they are unaware of it. . . . They deny that there is a secret.

[13] *Ibid.*, p. 234.

I do not ask that the novelist should affirm anything. . . . All I ask is that he shall not deny what for me is spirit and life. The naturalist novel died of this denial.[14]

But it will be seen that Mauriac has landed himself here into a patent contradiction: having complained that the naturalists don't deny "the invisible," merely ignore it, he goes on to say that they die because they deny it. The non-Christian critic will surely say that Mauriac is trying to eat his cake and have it too. And this leads to two further objections against Mauriac, one as a literary critic and the other as a novelist; and they both arise from his Christian allegiance. Apropos a rereading of *Wuthering Heights,* he defends the psychological emphasis in literary criticism (which he admits to be old-fashioned):

Perhaps, after all, I have no right to be called an artist—as that word is understood today—I, who find nothing to interest me in a book divorced from its writer, in an autonomous production which is just language and nothing more; I, who try . . . to feel my way back to the primary source of a work of art, to that spirit from which it leapt fully armed, and in which my contemporaries do not believe. . . .

I am setting off again . . . to follow her trail through the creatures of her imagination. . . . I know the precise places in *Wuthering Heights* where it is she who is speaking and making a direct confession. I recognize her voice: a moment more, and I shall be pressing her hot and feverish hand.[15]

The "psychology of invented characters," he says, tells him something about that of a young woman (Emily Brontë) who actually lived. "That is why I feel so far removed from the generation of writers which dates immediately after my own, for which the word 'psychological' has taken on so pejorative a meaning that any work to which it is applied automatically becomes disqualified." How does he defend this old-fashioned point of view? The answer is, strikingly, with a theological apologia:

[14] *Ibid.*, pp. 233-34.
[15] *Ibid.*, pp. 62-63.

> . . . now that I am a writer who is approaching the end of his days, I find myself alone imbued with that saying of Lacordaire which was graven in my mind when I set out: "Sooner or later one reaches the point where one is only interested in souls." I should have preferred him to say "human beings," because it is the heart of flesh and blood that really matters to me. Through the creatures of *Wuthering Heights* it is the heartbeats of Emily Brontë that I count.

Now this is a very honest and remarkable admission. For it shows how what C. S. Lewis long ago called "the personal heresy" in criticism can in fact grow out of a particular theological viewpoint. It is not, fortunately, the only Christian viewpoint: Lacordaire's remark—even with Mauriac's very necessary emendation—has its own obvious limitations. Emily Brontë's "hot and feverish hand" is, mercifully, unrecoverable.

But the admission is also significant for Mauriac's own creative practice. In 1939, Jean-Paul Sartre wrote an article on Mauriac's novel *La Fin de la Nuit* (the sequel to *Thérèse Desqueroux*) in which, analyzing one passage, he shows how Mauriac has himself entered into the narrative and tried to usurp the place of God; Sartre concludes, "God is not an artist: neither is M. Mauriac." [16] In the *Mémoires intérieurs*, from which I have been quoting, Mauriac refers to this. He has been speaking of the critic, Jean Paulhan, of whom he says:

> There is no vice in him. He has never tried to settle accounts with anybody, as did Jean-Paul Sartre with me, on the eve of the war, with a degree of violence which I have never resented. For I happen to be one of those on whom, when they are at death's door, extreme unction has a revivifying effect. To his youthful aggressiveness I owe it that I gave more attention than usual to the novel at which I was then working. Of all my novels, *La Pharisienne* shows the fewest signs of haste.

This novel (in English *The Woman of the Pharisees*) published in 1941 shows indeed some advance on many of his

[16] The text of Sartre's review is given in my study *François Mauriac* (Cambridge: Bowes & Bowes, 1954), pp. 39-40.

previous novels and is among Mauriac's best—some consider it his greatest. But neither it nor the briefer novels, and plays, that followed it succeed altogether in escaping the kind of disabilities which Sartre points to.[17] To acknowledge theoretically what these disabilities are, and to overcome them in practice, are two different things. But to ask that they be overcome in practice is not, in fact, to ask the impossible of a novelist. Though Mauriac himself has seldom managed to overcome them, at least he has recognized that there are those who have managed to do so. One such writer is, for example, Nathaniel Hawthorne, whose novel *The Scarlet Letter* Mauriac rightly admires, and of which he says:

> Some may hold that a novel which interests us mainly because of its theological implications can scarcely claim any very considerable degree of importance from the literary point of view. But the fact that, in spite of an outmoded technique, it still, after a century, has so great a power of suggestion, does, so it seems to me, bear witness to the richness of a literary form on which certain modern practitioners would impose their own narrow code. . . . A novel can express anything and everything, and can achieve, as does *The Scarlet Letter*, the remarkable triumph of turning a cruel caricature of Christianity into an apologia which opens a door upon the mystery of evil.[18]

In this recognition of Hawthorne's distinction there is, I think, a grace which shows that Mauriac, whatever his deficiencies as a creative writer, has that humility which his Christian profession should help to give him.

III

One of Mauriac's defenders in Great Britain has been Graham Greene, who wrote a eulogy of Mauriac's novels in *The Lost Childhood* which appeared at about the same time that Mauriac was writing a congratulatory account of Greene's

[17] There is no space in this essay to illustrate. In my book on Mauriac five passages from *La Pharisienne* are analyzed from this point of view.
[18] Mauriac, *Mémoires intérieurs, op. cit.*, p. 118.

novels in *Mes Grands Hommes*. But in fact when we look around for a test case in England of the dangers facing the Christian artist, it is Greene who stands very much in the middle of the target area. I have already, in a previous work (*Studies in Literature and Belief*), discussed some of Greene's earlier novels; but it may be of interest to see whether there has been any change of emphasis or direction in his later ones, especially since so many literary critics have pointed to the earlier weaknesses.

Since *The End of the Affair*, the last of the "religious" works, Greene has written three plays and a new novel. In his first play, *The Living Room* (1953), the main characters are a young woman, Rose Pemberton, and her uncle, Father James Browne. Rose is a more or less lapsed Catholic, who is in love with a married man, Michael Dennis, a lecturer in psychology. Michael, whose wife is an invalid, does not take seriously his affair with Rose; but she is so deeply attached to him that, when she sees that he has little serious intention of divorcing his wife, she commits suicide. Though Michael says of her that she is a non-practicing Catholic and doesn't believe in prayer, in fact her last words on the stage, after taking an overdose of tablets, are "Bless Mother, Nanny and Sister Marie-Louise, and please God don't let school start again ever. . . ." The theme is hackneyed enough; but Greene tries to save it from cliché by centering attention on Uncle James. He is a cripple and unable to exercise any of his priestly ministry, and lives (with his two elderly sisters) what he complainingly regards as a totally useless life. Even when consulted by Rose and Michael about their problem, he can only repeat the platitudes of the moral theologians. He does at times rebuke his sisters for their lack of charity, and it is suggested that he—and also to a lesser extent his dotty elder sister, Teresa—are forces for goodness, that they somehow cancel out the tragedy of the suicide. Rose, we are to suppose, is saved by his prayers (and her own stammering baby prayer given above); and the old lady, Teresa, at the end of the play conquers a superstition that no one may sleep in a room where somebody has died.

The end is not ineffective; but to get there we have to have the extraordinary caricature of a psychologist in Michael Dennis. He is a university lecturer but behaves so ineptly that one cannot imagine any faculty employing him. And his conversations with Father Browne are on the level of coffee-room discussion about analytic couches. Thus when Rose asks why the old ladies won't let anyone sleep in the Living Room, James replies: "You'll have to ask Dennis. He lectures and writes books and teaches psychology. I expect he'd call it an anxiety neurosis. Or something more difficult. I'm a priest and I've given up psychology." And, after Rose's suicide, Michael, who is its cause, has an anxious discussion with Uncle James, in which he admits he feels a bit guilty about the whole thing.

JAMES: I thought your Freud said there was no such thing as guilt.

MICHAEL: For God's sake, don't talk psychology at me today. Psychology wasn't any use to her. Books, lectures, analysis of dreams. Oh, I knew the hell of a lot, didn't I, about the human mind—She lay on this floor. . . .

JAMES: Psychology may teach you to know a mind. It doesn't teach you to love.

Grace that is shown triumphing over papier-mâché enemies of this kind is not very impressive.

The second play Greene wrote, *The Potting Shed* (1957), is suitably named for it seems to be a potted version of two of his earlier novels, *The Power and the Glory* and *The End of the Affair*. From the former comes the drunken priest; from the latter comes the miracle which startles the atheist family. A priest, the black sheep of the Callifer family because he had been converted to Christianity and later ordained, offered his faith on behalf of his nephew, young James Callifer, when the latter tried to hang himself in the potting shed. As a result, James recovered by what seemed to some a miracle—since the doctor summoned in had said he was dead. But Father William Callifer was taken at his word and lost his faith for thirty years. He had prayed, "Take away everything, even my faith, but let him live"; and now, thirty years later, he says, "I thought I'd lost Him for ever." James, whom Father Callifer had been trying earlier to instruct in the Faith, is now convinced of its truth, simply because of Father Callifer's seediness and drunkenness:

JAMES: Have you ever seen a room from which faith has gone? A room without faith—oh that can be pretty and full of flowers. But a room from which faith has gone is very different.

He could not, as a result, be called an exemplary Christian. He has had a "nervous breakdown" because he doesn't remember what went on in the potting shed, and the secret has been kept from him. But when he does find out and discovers the Christian faith at the same time, he tries to make it clear to his ex-wife, Clara, that she needn't fear it has made much difference to him.

CLARA: I don't belong to your world of God and prayer.
JAMES: Oh prayer. I don't want to pray. Something happened to me, that's all, like a street accident. I don't want God. I don't love God. But He's there—it's no good pretending. He's in my lungs like air.

However, the play ends with Clara returning to him.

Again, the atmosphere is oppressively forced. The free thinkers are guyed—the play opens, for instance, with a very obvious caricature of a funeral oration, being practiced for old H. C. Callifer (who is dying upstairs) by Dr. Frederick Baston, his best pupil. And the result is merely to make one more aware of Greene as a sarcastic Catholic (sneering at unbelieving simpletons) than of the characters on the stage. And the "miracle" in the potting shed has about the same depth and seriousness as an Indian rope trick.

I pass over his third play, *The Complaisant Lover,* since priests, and even God, are pleasantly not among the *dramatis personae* (it is a competent West End comedy about an apparently non-terminable adultery). But his last published novel, *A Burnt-Out Case* (1961), has so many of the old ingredients that it is worth looking at, if only to see how impossible it is for Greene to escape from the playpen he has built round himself.

The novel is essentially an extended metaphor. A leper who has had most of his limbs eaten away before the disease is brought to a halt is a "burnt-out case." Querry, a famous architect, comes (largely by chance, as to the most inaccessible place he can find) to a *Leproserie* in the Congo, because he has nothing more he can create; he has had considerable success in his life but now finds it dry powder in the mouth. Dr. Colin, the leper doctor who befriends him, says of him after his death: "He had been cured of all but his success; but you can't cure success, any more than I can give my *mutilés* back their fingers and toes."

In order to make Querry's character as a cynical but essentially honest and humble man stand out clearly, Greene sets him off (once more) against three impossible caricatures. First there is Rycker, the Catholic sensualist, an ex-seminarian now married to a silly wife and working as a planter; he is the least unconvincing of the three except for the melodramatic end when he shoots Querry. Then there is Parkinson, the agnostic, unpleasant, wholly egotistical journalist, who tries to build up Querry into a saint, i.e., into a good story for his paper. And finally there is Father Thomas, the sententious and unbelievably stupid religious who, like Rycker, is convinced that Querry really is a saint—at least until the end, when he accepts the suspicions about Querry's adultery with Marie Rycker and turns to equally absurd condemnation.

The atmosphere of the novel—Congolese heat and humidity—pervades the thinking and the imagery. Given that *ambiance* it is, of course, right; yet it seems somehow appropriate that Greene should have chosen that *ambiance*. Here is a description of a scene in the hospital:

The air in the hospital lay heavily and sweetly upon them; it was never moved by a fan or a breeze. Querry was conscious of the squalor of the bedding—cleanliness was not important to the leper, only to the healthy. The patients brought their own mattresses which they had probably possessed for a lifetime—rough sacking from which the straw had escaped. The bandaged feet lay in the straw like ill-wrapped packages of meat.

We are inevitably reminded of Scobie coming into his bedroom in *The Heart of the Matter*—"His wife was sitting up under the mosquito-net, and for a moment he had the impression of a joint under a meatcover." Or, as Mrs. Rycker (Marie) looks out of her house at the shed: "In the yard a lorry backed towards the shed. It was piled high with nuts for the presses and the ovens; they were like dried and withered heads, the product of a savage massacre."

Parkinson is a fat dummy, but it is hardly to be fair to him for the author to step into the novel and comment:

There is a strong allurement in corruption and there was no doubt of Parkinson's; he carried it on the surface of his skin like phosphorus, impossible to mistake. Virtue had died long ago within that mountain of flesh for lack of air. A priest might not be shocked by human failings, but he could be hurt or disappointed; Parkinson would welcome them. Nothing would ever hurt Parkinson save failure or disappoint him but the size of a cheque.

The Superior is faint, intelligent, composed, always ready with the oh-so-wise answer—indistinguishable from Greene's other professionally sage and liberal priests or confessors. Father Thomas is quite unbelievable. Here he is quoting the newspaper article that Parkinson has written about Querry and the religious community working among the lepers:

" 'To the heart of Africa. Near the spot where Stanley once pitched his camp among the savage tribes, I at last came on Querry. . . .' " Father Thomas looked up. He said, "It is here that he writes a great many gracious things about our work. 'Selfless . . . devoted . . . in the white robes of their blameless lives.' Really, you know, he does have a certain sense of style."

And, unfortunately, much of the time Querry himself, on whose veracity the whole novel depends, is a figure made to theory. There is an extraordinarily stilted conversation between him and Parkinson in which Querry makes sententious epigrams that only Graham Greene could have thought up for him. In answer to Parkinson's question as to why he should have come out to the Congo at all—"If you are so bored, why not be bored in comfort?"—Querry says: "Boredom is worse in comfort. I thought perhaps out here there would be enough pain and enough fear to distract. . . ." And when Parkinson asks him if he thinks he could easily seduce Rycker's wife, he replies, "It's an awful thing when experience and not vanity makes one say yes." The novel ends with a supreme piece of cynicism that does not ring true except to Greene's rather twisted desire to avoid serenity at all costs. After Querry's funeral the agnostic Dr. Colin is talking to the Superior in the dispensary about future plans for the hospital. A boy of three is brought in and the doctor examines him.

> "He's infected all right," Doctor Colin said. "Feel the patches here and here. But you needn't worry," he added in a tone of suppressed rage, "we shall be able to cure him in a year or two, and I can promise you that there will be no mutilations."

The "suppressed rage" seems to be that of Greene, at odds with both sides: with the Christians, because they won't take the unique opportunity their religion gives them for getting the thrill of damning themselves; with the unbelievers, because they won't disbelieve fiercely enough to deserve damnation.

IV

Let us turn from these Christian novelists to two Christian poets. W. H. Auden is of course in quite a different category from the last two writers we have been considering. He is one of the most impressive poets of our time, and yet also one of the most puzzling. Not puzzling in the sense of obscure and allusive—this could be said of many of his contemporaries and followers—but puzzling in the sense that it is hard sometimes to see what he would be at. This can only be a brief note on one section of a wide topic: a note about the problem of tone.

It is true that the difficulty of the right tone faces every poet writing at a time when

> No civil style survived
> That pandemonium
> But the wry, the sotto-voce,
> Ironic and monochrome.
>
> (Dedication, *Nones*, 1952)

But one feels that this wry, sotto-voce, ironic, and sometimes, alas, even monochrome style has too often infected his own writings. For the element in his poetry which has most often given critics pause is the kind of slang and vulgarity that are present, for example, in this speech of Joseph in *For the Time Being*:

> My shoes were shined, my pants were cleaned and pressed,
> And I was hurrying to meet
> My own true love;
> But a great crowd grew and grew
> Till I could not push my way through,
> Because
> A star had fallen down the street;
> When they saw who I was,
> The police tried to do their best.

Or, again, in "Quant's Song" in *The Age of Anxiety*:

> Let me sell you a song, the most side-splitting tale
> Since old Chaos caught young Cosmos bending
> With his back bare and his braces down,
> Homo Vulgaris, the Asterisk Man.

Auden is trying to do two things when he writes like this: first, to escape the vapid, lukewarm language of traditional piety; and second, by the use of contemporary and studiously chatty language, to shock us into awareness that the eternal significance of particular revelation belongs to now—or conversely, that to keep it at an archaic and hieratic distance is to drain it of life. So when in the "Flight into Egypt" in *For the Time Being* the Voices of the Desert cry to Joseph and Mary:

> Come to our well-run desert
> Where anguish arrives by cable,
>   And the deadly sins
>   May be bought in tins
> With instructions on the label—

we are doubtless meant not only to laugh—which we do—but to see the temptations as a permanent structure of life. The risk, however, is that the severely contemporary may become the severely limited, especially when it finds its expression in teenage language.

In *The Age of Anxiety*, Quant reminisces about the first of the seven ages of life, the age of the schoolboy:

>   In a vacant lot
> We built a bonfire and burned alive
> Some stolen tyres. How strong and good one
> Felt at first, how fagged coming home through
> The urban evening.

"Fagged": yes, appropriate schoolboy word; but doesn't it also put a schoolboy brake on the wheel of poetry? A little later Quant switches to a different style:

>   For Long-Ago has been
> Ever-After since Ur-Papa gave
> The Primal Yawn that expressed all things
> (In His Boredom their beings) and brought forth
> The wit of this world. One-Eye's mistake
> Is sorry He spoke.

This seems to me merely aphoristic cleverness, especially when we compare it with passages that do come off, such as this soon after:

He pines for some
Nameless Eden where he never was
But where in his wishes once again
Over hallowed acres, without a stitch
Of achievement on, the children play
Nor care how comely they couldn't be
Since they needn't know they're not happy.

Too often we find Auden leaning back upon the great psychological abstractions, trying to make them sound up to date by putting them into slang language about "our great mum," or

I've made their magic but their Momma Earth
Is His stone still . . . I shan't be at peace
Till I really take your restless hands,
My poor fat father. How appalling was
Your taste in ties.

When we compare these things with some of Auden's successes, we are driven to ponder what has happened. By his successes I mean such things (to cull only from his last three volumes) as the secular poem "In Schrafft's" (*Nones*); almost the whole of the fine "devotional" sequence "Horae Canonicae" (*Shield of Achilles*), which contains some of the most moving poetry Auden has written; or from the latest (and mostly disappointing) volume *Homage to Clio*, the elegant "Reflections in a Forest," the neat and profound "Objects," and the witty "An Island Cemetery." But perhaps "Friday's Child" is a useful test case, for here, though the meter is skittish, the theme is utterly serious, dedicated as it is to the German Lutheran pastor Dietrich Bonhoeffer, martyred in 1945. If the poet does splits like this, even if he brings it off, shan't we be in danger of saying merely "how clever, how athletic"? I think the answer is: the poem is a success but only just. We breathe again at the end and, alas, part of our enjoyment has been deflected by the constant fear of a spill.

He (God) told us we were free to choose
But, children as we were, we thought—
'Paternal Love will only use
  Force in the last resort

On those too bumptious to repent.'—
Accustomed to religious dread,
It never crossed our minds He meant
  Exactly what he said.

. . . .

Since the analogies are rot
Our senses based belief upon,
We have no means of learning what
  Is really going on,

And must put up with having learned
All proofs or disproofs that we tender
Of His existence are returned
  Unopened to the sender.

. . . .

Meanwhile, a silence on the cross,
As dead as we shall ever be,
Speaks of some total gain or loss
  And you and I are free

To guess from the insulted face
Just what Appearances He saves
By suffering in a public place
  A death reserved for slaves.

It is brilliant, and profound, but it is immensely risky. The risk is the risk not of laughing in church—no harm in that—but of giggling at the altar. Or to put it another way, the temptation is to be so afraid of being taken too seriously that one develops a nervous snigger—or even, at more dangerous moments, the temptation to apologize for belief by pretending to join in the laughter at it. Perhaps in the end Auden succeeds best where he is least self-conscious about how his tone will be taken, and where his wit is worn lightly enough to capture attention, but based solidly enough to drive in the serious lessons of humility which he can sometimes authoritatively offer us. As in the neat, effective poem "The Sabbath" in *Homage to Clio,* the animals walk round Eden on the seventh day, after the expulsion of Man, relieved to be without Man:

> Waking on the Seventh Day of Creation,
> They cautiously sniffed the air:
> The most fastidious nostril among them admitted
> That fellow was no longer there.
>
> . . . .
>
> Ruins and metallic rubbish in plenty
> Were all that was left of him
> Whose birth on the Sixth had made of that day
> An unnecessary interim.
>
> . . . .
>
> Back, then, at last on a natural economy,
> Now His Impudence was gone,
> Looking exactly like what it was,
> The Seventh Day went on,
>
> Beautiful, happy, perfectly pointless . . .
> A rifle's ringing crack
> Split their Arcadia wide open, cut
> Their Sabbath nonsense short.
> For whom did they think they had been created?
> That fellow was back,
> More bloody-minded than they remembered,
> More god-like than they thought.

If finally I venture to say something about the master of them all, it is largely because recent criticism of him forces me to do so. There is little doubt that the younger generation of critics now finds T. S. Eliot a faded—if a one-time magnificent—figure. Here, for instance, is Wright Morris, talking about D. H. Lawrence; he pushes Eliot down so that Lawrence may come up:

> . . . to make the modern world possible in art is not the same, as Lawrence would have insisted, as making life possible in the modern world. . . . It is Lawrence, the Englishman in exile, who speaks for the brave new world, and Eliot, the American in exile, who speaks for the old. . . . In the poet from St. Louis we have

the classic example, carried to its ultimate conclusion, of the American artist's tendency to withdraw into the past, to withdraw, that is, from America. . . .

[Lawrence's] is the speech of a man alive. . . . It is this man of whom we can say—as Picasso said of Matisse—that he has a sun in his belly. The sun in the belly of Mr. Eliot is a mythic sun. It is a clinker to manipulate: the fire has gone out of it. The man alive in the present is that patient etherised on the table, awaiting burial.[19]

And Raymond Williams, a distinguished voice from England, describes how at one time he had been able to appreciate Eliot's "penetration of the varieties of illusion and self-deception" since he (Eliot) spoke about "the whole area of experience which . . . most masters of the Left seemed to omit or not even to know." But alas:

It seems now to be over. In 1950 Eliot's sensibility was still significantly directive in our literature, as it had been for the previous 20 years. In 1960 it is not directive at all. It may be that *The Confidential Clerk* and *The Elder Statesman* marked the decline; in dramatic intensity certainly, but also, for me at least, in feeling. Watching the last scene of *The Elder Statesman* in which the cold, conscious love talk seemed to go on and on while Monica knew her father lay dying in the garden, it was finally and unmistakably clear that one was watching an alien world. If it belongs to anyone still alive they are welcome to it, but the problem for others of us is how the reaction spreads back. . . .

It was, he says, "the weakened and trivial form of the late plays" which "made release" from Eliot's grip easy. And he insists that it is Eliot's movement into popular, middle-brow drama that revealed a weakness that had started long before.

I think we have not yet adequately noticed the nature of Eliot's attempt to take poetry to a wider audience, doing the wrong thing for the right reason, in an actual social situation. It was not just the bitch-goddess of Shaftesbury Avenue, though indeed she is almost the central character of the plays from *The Cocktail Party*

[19] Wright Morris, "Lawrence and the Immediate Present," in *A D. H. Lawrence Miscellany,* edited by Harry T. Moore (Carbondale: Southern Illinois University Press, 1959), pp. 10-11.

onwards. It is part of the real complexity of this extraordinary man that he could repeatedly and genuinely mistake that compromise for communication. It is as if—as in his later social writings, and as perhaps earlier in Henry James—he really does not know what country he is in; and if this is so it is perhaps as much our fault as his. "History is now and England," but when you turn this over it is only that familiar mellow dusk which has been used again and again to prevent even those who have grown up here recognising where and how they are living.[20]

These are serious judgments. I think we may demur at Wright Morris' sweeping condemnation: Eliot's battle for tradition was necessary and is still valuable—and it must not be forgotten that Dr. Leavis (the most distinguished critic to pit Lawrence against Eliot) first came into prominence with his book *For Continuity*. But both Morris and (still more) Williams are saying something important about Eliot's failure to hold us today. What we have to ask is: How much of this is Eliot's fault? Or how much of the weakness indicated is simply due to poetic decline, old age, or exhaustion of the seam; how much is due to the hazards of the Christian artist?

The accurate answer to this question could only be given by God—who else has the electronic scales that could measure such proportions? Our approximate conjectures will vary according to our presuppositions. I can only offer my own: that a sizable portion of the failure—and that means the failure in the last four plays—is due to Eliot's thinking that the necessity for Intercession is equivalent to a vocation to Ministry. I mean this: that with Eliot's growth in Christian understanding of the world has come an increasing tolerance for the wicked and the stupid. The wider compassion shown in *The Confidential Clerk* and *The Elder Statesman*—and even, though with some stiff-jointedness, in *The Cocktail Party*—has been noticed by several critics.[21] But this has led Eliot

[20] Raymond Williams, "Eliot and Belief," in *The Manchester Guardian*, December 9, 1960.

[21] Leonard Unger, *The Man in the Name* (Minneapolis: University of Minnesota Press, 1956); and David E. Jones, *The Plays of T. S. Eliot* (London: Routledge and Kegan Paul, 1960).

to a certain diffidence, an unwillingness to castigate (as in the early poems or in *The Waste Land*) dullness and vice. And, since drama can only be made from conflict, the protagonists in his plays have had to be sought, not in life—where charity must reign—but in the safe, invulnerable land of the cartoon. Hence the unreal figure of Gomez, the improbable villain of *The Elder Statesman,* to whom "motiveless malignity" applies more aptly than it ever did to Iago. The denunciations that occur now occur in the safe areas of generalization where no libel suits can be filed—Celia's remarks to Reilly about having been always taught "to disbelieve sin" are at a sadly pedestrian, almost parish-magazine level. The gravamen could be summed up thus: that just as *Murder in the Cathedral* carries echoes of *Ash Wednesday,* and *The Family Reunion* carries echoes of *The Four Quartets,* so *The Confidential Clerk* and *The Elder Statesman* have passages, disguised as poetry, which might have come from the *Notes towards the Definition of Culture;* portions of *The Rock,* and even some of *The Cocktail Party,* have sad affinities with *Notes after Lambeth.*

The delicate lyric talent bred with the magnificent intelligence to produce the *Four Quartets*: but they were not suited to the tasks Eliot then felt a calling to use them on. And this is perhaps a failure both at an empirical and at a theological level: the failure to achieve the different marriage of charity with imagination; or perhaps the failure to be content with the achievement that has been supremely Eliot's. For, as Auden says in "To T. S. Eliot on His Sixtieth Birthday"

When things began to happen to our favourite spot,
A key missing, a library bust defaced,
    Then on the tennis-court one morning,
  Outrageous, the bloody corpse and always,

Blank day after day, the unheard-of drought, it was you
Who, not speechless from shock but finding the right
    Language for thirst and fear, did much to
  Prevent a panic. . . .

VI

I have suggested some of the perils that face the Christian writer. Many of them are not peculiar to him. The non-Christian, too, is constantly threatened by dishonesty—pretending to believe what he merely repeats; by false ambition—thinking to scale ranges that are beyond his powers of endurance; by arrogance—mistaking a personal hunch for a public certitude; by cowardice—fearing to be "different" or (which is the same thing) fearing not to be "different" enough; by power-lust—playing hypnotist to his characters and so depriving them of their freedom. What is peculiar to the Christian is perhaps that all these threats assail him with a particular intensity because of what his faith commits him to, and assail him in public places because his profession makes concealment impossible. No doubt the non-Christian artist, too, has perils peculiar to him. But the believer must surely always be in the worse case because he has the less excuse. *Corruptio optimi pessima.* Yet if the corruption of the best is the worst, at least this tells us that man is not so far fallen that he cannot make this judgment—that *corruptio,* etc. Here is, at any rate, interim capacity; a modest one, yet valid. For

> Between those happenings that prefigure it
> And those that happen in its anamnesis
> Occurs the Event, but that no human wit
> Can recognise until all happening ceases.
>
> (W. H. Auden, *Homage to Clio,* I)

A Hope for Literature

BY CHAD WALSH

THAT LITERATURE will continue to be created, so long as there are men to create it, I am certain. In a time of utter catastrophe it might dwindle to the village bard and story-teller and be transmitted by word of mouth, but it would not cease. Its continuance is not the question. The question is whether it will be any good.

I shall confine myself to the English-speaking world, and shall not try to peer into the future more than a generation or two. With this limited perspective, my surmise is that which is suggested by the title of this chapter. There is hope for literature—if, and if, and if. . . .

Great literature seems to require a major talent living at a time suitable for its particular kind of genius. There have been centuries when these double conditions were apparently not met. The specialist happily immerses himself in the literature of fifteenth-century England, but what is there for the general cultivated reader except Malory and the Scotch Chaucerians? Between the twin heights of Chaucer and the Elizabethans, there is a low valley of humility. Possibly we are wandering toward such a valley now, or are already in one. I do not believe we are, but the point can be debated.

Literary geniuses are born, not produced. But the time of their birth can be favorable or unfavorable. If Shakespeare had lived three centuries earlier he might have been the greatest writer of rhymed romances, but it is difficult to believe he would have found in them the same scope that the theater offered. His birth was perfectly timed by the Muse, by the gods, by God, or by chance. When he grew to manhood the ground had been cleared for a mature theater. He did not have to invent blank verse or the five-act form; he had only to perfect them. The audience was already at hand. And the social and psychological state of London was just right. The Middle Ages, with their sense of human and divine hierarchy and an undergirding and overarching moral structure to morality, were still in the blood and bone of men. But restless doubts and questions were shaking the old implicit assumptions. There was just the right tension between the tried-and-true assumptions of an ageless, organic society and the thrust of new individualism and gnawing doubts, to enliven and complicate and loosen the old certainties but not destroy them.

Shakespeare had an audience whose responses he could predict, for he shared the attitudes that engendered the responses. But it was not an audience made dull and sodden by unchallenged faith in the inherited beliefs and patterns of living. The audience was part of a society in which men were beginning to stride, often more than life-size, shaking every wall erected by man or God. It was a society that produced real Macbeths and still believed, or wanted to believe, that the avenger would always be sent by the very nature of things, to restore the divine ordering of relationships.

Dostoevski had the same good fortune. After his youthful flirtation with advanced thought, he became a staunch disciple of the established order of Tsar, Orthodox Church, and the Slavic mission. All around him the old ties were being eroded by new ideas, but the masses were still faithful to a way of life that seemed an outcropping of the divine will. The same tensions were in nineteenth-century Russia as in Shakespearean England. Dostoevski knew well how to use them in novels that are the nearest prose parallel to the poetic tragedies of Shakespeare.

I take it that the Greek playwrights enjoyed circumstances somewhat similar. They had a public still living in a traditional and largely unexamined pattern of life, but the winds of modernity were blowing, and the old assumptions were no longer impregnable. The cultural situation into which Shakespeare, Dostoevski, or the Greek dramatists were born is not, however, the only kind that can be favorable to a major talent. Dante lived when the Middle Ages were crystalizing into their classical form; he was the younger contemporary of that great systematizer and exponent of the newest intellectual trends, Thomas Aquinas. Dante was in the position of a Soviet writer who feels himself part of the "coming thing," and can set his imagination to work exploring and presenting it. He had the joy of being, in his highly individual way, part of the wave of the future.

But what of Homer? His two epics—if he wrote them—are retrospective works, composed several centuries after the events they purport to chronicle. They are his *Gone with the Wind*, except that he sings the winning side. He lived in a time of breakdown and confused turmoil, when the past seemed a golden age of heroism and splendor, fit to be celebrated in ringing hexameters if hardly to be emulated. In this feeling for the past, Homer was one with his public. It looked backward to Achilles as the Dark Ages did to the fabulous Caesar and Alexander.

So far I have mentioned writers who stood inside their society rather than taking a vantage point outside it. Any quarrel they had with society was distinctly a family altercation. Dante advanced sharp views on many religious and political matters, but these were shared by many of his nonpoetic contemporaries. Shakespeare was, if anything, something of a conservative, even a "reactionary," to use the modern jargon. As far as we can judge, he loved queen, country, and the inherited social system as simply as any British regimental commander of the nineteenth century. He was no Jacobin, no leveler, no one out to remake the world that he observed with such unswerving accuracy.

At times a writer seems to draw strength from a lover's quarrel with his society. This I take to have been the case with Faulkner. Moving through an archaic world, at once benighted and yet possessing a depth of sensibility and relationship lost by most of the urbanized, industrialized, and rationalized North, he was fiercely Southern to the outside world and an *enfant terrible* to his fellow Southerners. One can perceive how flattened out his work would be if he had been merely the complacent Southerner or equally if he had chosen the position of the Southern expatriate who parrots the shallow certainties of Northern liberalism and loses all rooted relationship with the nuances of a society in which men still live by organic relationship rather than by the casual and cold bonds of the voluntary, social contract.

But what of the writer—and he is popularly supposed to be the norm—who is "alienated" from his society and writes in isolation from it? He is harder to find than one expects. Where he exists at all, he occurs chiefly in the nineteenth and twentieth centuries and appears to be the by-product of those great events and intellectual movements that have dissolved the old social ties and thrown the individual back upon his aloneness. The industrial revolution, replacing the rising and setting sun with the time and motion studies; the contractual relationship between employer and employee, instead of the inherited obligations of a feudal world; the weakening of the Christian creed and code and its replacement by nothing much; the rise of science and its inherent inability to supply the certainties that religion and custom once bequeathed from generation to generation—all these things, and many more, have left society a thing so little viable that the writer has scarcely known whether anything is left to be either accepted or rejected. Add to this the fact that all men have become specialists; the writer is regarded as one specialist among others. And specialists have not found the Esperanto that will permit them to communicate across the boundary lines of their specialties. Meanwhile, a low-level ordering of values has offered a kind of consensus—material possessions, gadgets, security, peace of mind—that hardly calls for strident rejection, since there is so little in it to tempt a perceptive and sensitive writer.

What I have just said applies more particularly to Great Britain, the southern United States, and parts of New England. In most of America there were from the start only traces and vestiges of the kind of organic society, ultimately feudal in its roots, that I have been describing. But its psychological equivalent was supplied in many ways by the frontier, which at its best called forth a society at once organic and equalitarian to meet its implacable demands. The passing of the frontier and its replacement by the assembly line and the public relations office have done things to America of which we are yet only dimly aware, though I think our psychiatrists could speak on this point. We are haunted by national memories of heroic achievements, of bitter challenges triumphantly surmounted. Meanwhile we punch the time clock or write copy for magazine advertisements and television commercials. Each year residential mobility increases, so that the colleges are filled with young people who have never lived five years in one community. No wonder there is a depersonalization of relationships. In the spawning suburbs one sees the desperate attempt to create a sense of organic community by committees within committees, planned playfulness, and that trinitarian cluster of institutions to bring people together: the Church, the country club, and the Parent-Teachers Association. I read recently in the *Milwaukee Journal* of a new housing development that intended to embody the values of "village life." The promoter promises: "The management also would help establish a way of life in the village by having a sociologist plan the leisure time for interested tenants. . . . There would be dances, entertainments, educational lectures, card parties, etc."

One wishes the promoter success, but doubts that he will have it. At any rate, the crumbling of many certainties and patterns of life has left society a vaguer and more confusing milieu than it used to be. Some writers have reacted by trying to hasten the process. Others have psychologically pulled away and created a private world.

Certainly many nineteenth- and twentieth-century writers have felt themselves out of step with Victorianism and its attenuated survivals. Thomas Hardy set himself in opposition to the rigid certainties of the late nineteenth century. Theodore Dreiser proclaimed a world in which man, no longer the sinful yet glorious image of God, was the blind plaything of "chemisms." Sinclair Lewis (though with more than a touch of the lover's quarrel) put the business and professional world of America under a microscope that magnified its great, open spaces. James Joyce dissolved and re-formed the language of a dissolving world. As for the poets, they have found patterns of meaning where they could. Robinson Jeffers took to the hawk and the rock and the dark, unloving God of natural processes. William Butler Yeats constructed his own mythology from eclectically borrowed materials. Robert Frost found in archaic rural New England a set of assumptions still viable for poetry. T. S. Eliot turned to orthodox Christianity, a decision almost as bizarre for his time as the current preoccupation of the "beats" with Zen Buddhism. In short, finding little meaningful order in society at large, the poets have found or created a local or private order, and thus have been enabled to write.

All these instances involve rejection of a sort. But one must bring in the qualifying terms. The writer who seems to be rejecting his society may actually be expressing the half-formed conviction of a minority which tomorrow will be the majority. He may be the first bomb thrower of the successful revolution. When Wordsworth and Coleridge led their early readers away from the geometrically planned gardens of eighteenth-century reason, to explore the cottages of peasants, the uncharted wildernesses by land and sea, and the inner world of the heart, they were not alone. They were the pioneers of a new sensibility, everywhere in the air, which lacked only the poetic voices that would give it words and power. Similarly, Hardy and Dreiser did not march as solitary rebels against Queen Victoria; rather, they composed the battle hymns that modern man, convinced man is "nothing but," mumbles today off key. Once Eugene O'Neill seemed very far out when he translated Freud into the tortured figures of his stage; today every college student can psychoanalyze himself and his roommate without having read a word of Freud. Or can one really say that the Zen-reading, beard-growing beatniks are solitary figures? They represent a subculture, a society within society. It is a world of conscious rebels, but within that world there are strict norms and traditions. One recalls the *New Yorker* cartoon of the man reading a copy of *Time* in a beatnik restaurant; the waiter apologetically requests him to leave.

The case of the atheist existentialist writers is particularly illuminating. They express man's agonizing sense of aloneness in a world where God is dead, and society is just one solitary figure after another, bumbling around in the darkened confusion that Matthew Arnold accurately portrayed and depicted. But to picture such a world is not a retreat from society; rather, it is an attempt to understand it. The physician who says, "I'm afraid it looks like cancer," is a realist, not an escapist. And it is noteworthy that a strong moral passion often infuses the books of the existentialists; they will not let man use his solitariness as an excuse for inner or outer anarchy. He is sternly commanded to create his own world, but that world inescapably involves others through his decisions. He is not permitted the pretense that he is the innocent plaything of impersonal forces.

All that I have so far said is a prelude to three conclusions. Great literature seems to involve, most often, three preconditions: (1) The birth of a literary genius. Since this cannot be brought about by any act of will or marvel of scientific manipulation, I shall say little more about it. At least, if a Shakespeare could be born into a nation of five million, there is the statistical hope that geniuses will continue to enter our teeming world. (2) A society with attitudes, values, and beliefs that are interesting and significant enough for the writer to embrace them, reject them angrily, or enter into a lover's quarrel with them. (3) An angle of vision, a way of looking at things, which the writer may share with society or which may be his supreme act of defiance. In any case, it gives him a means of ordering his observation and experience, so that he can make sense (and this includes aesthetic sense) of it.

Precondition (2) demands guesswork. I think it likely that during the next couple of generations the English-speaking world will not change beyond recognition its attitudes and implicit assumptions. A diffused Christianity and generalized religiosity will continue widespread, if often confusingly blended in the United States with "the religion of democracy" and "Americanism"—whatever one means by that; and alloyed with the values of "The Establishment" in Great Britain. For the greater number of persons, it is likely to be a Christianity without cutting edges, blandly tolerant not from charity but from ignorance of doctrine; a religion of comfort and psychological gimmicks rather than a revelation centering about salvation, sanctity, a Cross, and an empty tomb. Even diluted and diffused, Christianity is not to be despised. Diffused Christianity grows sweeter fruits than diffused fascism or diffused *laissez-faire*. But I question whether this mild and vague faith produces a society with which the writer can have either a passionate love affair or a bitter quarrel. It is too soft and rubbery; he can't sink his teeth into it. Certainly, very few writers will find this bland, adulterated Christianity adequate for *themselves*. They need something starker, more categorical, if they are to have a vantage point from which they can view the world about them, whatever that world may be.

If the prediction I have hazarded is at all correct, I expect to see another, complementary movement, not important in numbers but important in every other way. There are already some indications of it. Christianity is beginning to develop a core, an inner group. This consists of those Christians who are not content with the nebulous and undemanding faith that is offered in painless potions. Movements such as that centered in the Iona community are one indication of what I mean; the Quaker community at Pendle Hill is another. In most parishes one can find what is, in effect, an inner circle—much as the phrase is repulsive. By inner circle I mean not those who are the "pillars of the Church" and frequently its lay popes, holding the minister in subjugation, but rather the persons who take Christianity seriously by studying it, by constant prayer, and by specific efforts to do the concrete things that make the faith a weekday reality. These various tendencies may never become united in any sort of "third order"—it could be best that they do not—but they point, spiritually and psychologically, in that direction. Christians who mean business are a Church within the Church; they are Christian colonies in a society so vaguely Christian that the word has only a minimal meaning.

A writer of the near future, as now, will see around him a world that cannot be neatly schematized. He will observe many people living, apparently, for the proverbial television sets and split-level houses, for security and social standing, for a healthy and happy sex life, for protection against the lowering Communists. But if this is all he sees, he will be a superficial observer. Almost always there is a wistfulness. There is the diffused sense of anxiety, at times of futility, the wish to believe "there is really something beyond all this." Here and there the observer will see people who know precisely what the "something" is. The well-instructed and dedicated Marxist is not given to gentle wistfulness. The scientific humanist has a philosophy and a program of action. And the religious person, who takes his religion with life-and-death seriousness, will also know where he stands.

The one safe prediction seems to be that for some decades, at the very least, society will probably continue to be as blurred and confusing as it now is. Perhaps here and there, little islands of meaning will rise and take definite shape from the murky seas of vagueness. Marxism, scientific humanism, authentic Christianity—they may become more sharply defined, as scattered individuals find in them the key to making sense of life, and as such individuals discover one another.

What I have so far said is based on the unprovable assumption that the Cold War will continue, without substantial changes in the power positions of the two great systems. If Khrushchev should turn out to be a better prophet than I, and our grandchildren happily live under a system imported from the USSR, then the writer would find his task either enormously simplified or made impossible. He could throw himself into the new world being created all around him and become its bard and laureate, or—if he were out of sympathy with it—oppose it as long as he could and then fall silent. He would in either case at least have about him a society lacking the ambiguities that today so often make the writer feel he is touching a shapeless lump of wet clay.

I shall assume that Khrushchev is wrong. If so, we need to look now at the writer, living in a society whose values, attitudes, and beliefs are vague, fluctuating, and often trivial. Can he possibly find on one of the "islands" the vantage point from which he can make sense of his experience and observations?

Precondition (3) implies that a writer must acquire a pair of eyes through which he can view everything. But this figure of speech is too superficial. The writer needs to find meaning and significant order not merely in what he sees but in himself—in what he is and what he does. The first thing to be liberated into meaningful order is himself and his life. In trying to find meaning for himself, he is simultaneously seeking a meaningful way of relating himself to society, even though—in some cases—his relationship will appear to be that of the detached observer, chronicler, and interpreter.

We are born with physical eyes but we acquire metaphorical eyes. These give us our patterns of understanding: the key ideas and emotions by which we organize what we experience and observe, and make some sense of it. The metaphorical eyes are, in short, our philosophies, religions, and ideologies. These may be conscious and explicit or almost entirely unconscious and implicit.

One pair of metaphorical eyes is what I shall call, for lack of any more precise term, "naturalism." Man is "nothing but." He is a curiously developed and specialized animal; he builds temples and organizes symphony orchestras, and he makes of sex a ritual and an art. He lacks the charming and direct common sense of the other animals. But after the qualifying phrases have been conceded, man is still nothing but an animal. He bears no image of God; there are no angels for him to rival, and no real devils to tempt him. He is simply an animal that evolved in a direction as odd as that of the duckbilled platypus.

Naturalism can produce significant literature. Some of Zola's novels still have a massive impact that the reader cannot evade. Whether it can produce a literature of the greatest heights and depths, I question. One does not compose a *Divine Comedy* or a *King Lear* about dachshunds, not even about anthropoids that wear tuxedos or blue jeans. Mankind, viewed through the eyes of naturalism, is diminished and flattened. The words damnation and salvation lose their sharp meaning. It is hard to think of a hell or heaven for even the most highly developed "mere animals." Naturalism makes the human drama duller. No longer is the visible scene a battleground between the invisible Devil and the invisible God; the landscape ceases to be one of bottomless abysses of the spirit and soaring Everests. It becomes a flattened plain or teeming jungle. One need not be a Christian to recognize all this. Sophocles knew it perfectly well. Naturalism may or may not be "true" but, if it is taken as a complete way of viewing man, it makes him less complex, less fascinating, less memorable than he once appeared. In actual practice, as one would expect, the naturalistic writers have dealt with the instincts, impulses, passions, and in general the "animal-like" side of man, and have shown considerable embarrassment when confronted by his capacity for self-transcendence and altruistic nobility. At the same time—and this is a striking thing—many of the naturalistic writers, such as Zola, Dreiser, and Crane, have been aflame with a zeal for justice which to the observer's puzzled eye seems to come from some mysterious source altogether outside the naturalistic world view.

I have been speaking of naturalism in its old-fashioned, simplistic form. Indeed, its origin is closely linked with the partially outmoded science of the nineteenth century, a time when scientific certainties had a pat assurance they have now lost. Many of the modern scientists, such as Julian Huxley, now offer a considerably more subtle and adequate view, conveniently called scientific humanism. This is an effort to see in the scientific outlook a basis for man's finest intuitions and what could be called his spiritual character. Scientific humanism is not reductionist; it does not fall into the genetic fallacy. True, it refuses to leap back into the bosom or brain of any recognizable God, but it discovers in the life process, indeed in matter, a quality that is potentially spiritual from the beginning. Evolution becomes a progressive unfolding of the possibilities latent in a speck of dust. Man's arts, ethics, and even his religions are not accidental freaks in the history of a strange animal, but rather the line of development toward the full actualization of what has always been latent in the universe. The scientific humanist does not say "nothing but." His thought is really teleological, though he posits no traditional God as the goad toward the ultimate goal, and the goal is not one miraculously revealed in advance, but rather one to be discovered and created in the course of man's continuing evolution—an evolution that is decreasingly biological, and increasingly social, psychological, and ethical.

To an author, this pair of eyes reveals a much more interesting landscape than the eyes of simple naturalism permit him to see. He can look at a man such as Schweitzer and see in him, not a biological curiosity, but a person who is in the mainstream of the long epic from "lifeless matter" to the finest flowering of the spirit. Shakespeare is not a biological sport but a major means by which life in its unfolding has come to know itself.

Scientific humanism permits one to take the human story seriously and to recognize in it a beauty and a poignant grandeur. It is, from the Christian's viewpoint, an impressive attempt to put scientific foundations under very much of what the Christian has always believed for reasons other than science. The writer whose metaphorical eyes are those of scientific humanism will not be forced into reinterpreting human motivations so as to make them acceptable to the chimpanzee or lemur. Rather, he will look with something of the eyes of a St. Francis at all furred and feathered things, seeing in them the dawning hints of the progressive revelation of cosmic meaning—which, on this planet at least, has its standard-bearer in man.

Does a writer find anything lacking in scientific humanism? I am not referring to its ultimate truth or falsehood. Certainly it is a creed that demands an act of faith as great as that of the theistic religions. To see a Mozart latent in a handful of dust is as daring a leap of faith as to see God breathing upon a handful of dust. But the question is a different one. Can scientific humanism offer the writer a pair of eyes through which he can observe every scene (including his own inner landscape) and make sense of it?

It will open many more doors than mere naturalism. Where it fails, I think, is in lack of inwardness. There is something once-born, healthy-minded, about scientific humanism. It has a well-scrubbed quality, handsome teeth gleaming in an optimistic smile. It seems to be saying, "Buck up, the great human adventure is just beginning." Its buoyancy is exhilarating to the man who feels himself fit and ready to march forward with his fellows down the evolutionary highway. It cannot say much to the Kierkegaards of this world nor to the man whose advanced state of cancer prevents him from marching. Scientific humanism holds forth glowing landscapes for that collectivity, mankind, but so far as I can see it has little to say to solitary man, particularly solitary man in his incommunicable abysses and heights. The focus on the broader pattern and drama is just the opposite of the vision of most writers. To them, Tom, Dick, and Harry, Oedipus and Othello, have always been more interesting than mankind.

Speaking still and always from a writer's point of view, scientific humanism is weak where existentialism is strong. It is faithful to the intuition that we are part of a blundering but always marching army of fellow pilgrims trying to find the half-guessed shrine that is the goal of our drama. It is too healthy-minded for the tormented solitary, alone with his own consciousness. And part of mankind's evolution is the gift or curse of experiencing this aloneness and forlornness. Existentialism, for its part, is a solitary awareness reaching out in an agony of yearning to make contact with other imprisoned centers of consciousness.

I have so far mentioned Marxism only in passing. This is because, for the moment, it is a minor alternative with most English-speaking writers. The reasons for this are as much historical as theoretical. The enchantment with Marxism that enlivened and bedeviled the 1930's has been shattered by the harsh actualities of the Communist development in the USSR. Stalin, the purge trials, and the fading of Utopia as the commissars began to organize it, have resulted in widespread disillusionment among Western intellectuals who greeted the mild welfare state with approval but resisted a doctrinaire attempt to impose an ideology on all human activities. The cold war, calling into play the simplest emotions of fear and national self-concern, has made it still more difficult for writers to find in Marxism, at least of the Soviet variety, the metaphorical extra pair of eyes.

If the writers of the 1930's overrated Marxism, both as a world-view and a program for action, those of the 1960's underrate it. There must be something emotionally and intellectually compelling in a creed that has won a third of the world—and not wholly by force of arms and sly deceit. Marxism is a peculiarly potent amalgam of Old Testament prophecy, the apocalyptic hope, Hegel, and nineteenth-century science. It offers a view of history that makes some sense, at least, of humanity's dark agonies and dark deeds, as well as its creative achievements; it combines the conviction of inevitable fulfillment (found in a gentle form in the doctrine of inevitable progress) with a social passion that has unmistakable Biblical roots. A writer who is looking for some way to make sense of his observations will find in Marxism some very keen tools to be used in analysis. But he will find an additional thing. No more than Christianity does Marxism invite the writer or anyone else to use it merely as a pair of eyes. It professes to be the way, the truth, and the life; it is a call to action and commitment. It says, "Follow me, and be a part of the vanguard of history's movement forward, a movement that will reach its goal with you or without you." This commandment has a curiously Biblical ring.

Is Marxism, then, adequate to the needs of the writer? No, not finally. It also is too simple and too healthy minded. It lacks inwardness. In Russian painting, it produces the ruddy-cheeked peasant rejoicing at tractors. But a peasant can also mourn the scorn of the girl he loves, the death of his child, the coming of old age, the breakdown of understanding between friends. He can have purely private ecstasies that do not seem to serve a social purpose. Finally, the triumphant sweep of history is small consolation to the man who is assured that he will be dead, really dead, and never see the earthly paradise. The degree of disinterested idealism to which he is summoned is impressive, noble, and murderous to the very roots of his being.

Marxism explains much. It explains too much. It is too simple. And it demands too much. We have seen in the

USSR how writers are constantly probing the ideological walls, hoping to find a chink here and there. Being writers, and therefore men with a more than normal sensitivity, they perceive—consciously or unconsciously—that there are vast continents of human experience and yearning that simply have no significant point of contact with economics, production, and the unrolling of mankind's broad history.

It is significant that the decline in Marxist influence among English-speaking intellectuals has been paralleled by the rise of Oriental religion as a live option. The various strands of Hinduism and Buddhism that are packed for export all have in common an inwardness, and a relatively minor preoccupation with those events that loom blackest in the daily newspapers. When the individual is urged to lose himself, it is not to history, to the masses, to the economic process, or to the movement, but rather to the unconditioned Ultimate (words falter here) which, he is likely to be told, is akin to, or identical with, the deepest level of his own being. Thus in losing himself he finds himself.

It is perilous and also unfair to attempt any vast generalizations about the influence of the Oriental religions and philosophies on current and future Western literature. These faiths are not monochrome, and one must reckon also with Western misunderstanding, as well as understanding, of them. But one assertion seems safe. The inwardness that is lacking in Marxism is found in them. In a way, however, it is a provisional or momentary inwardness, if by inwardness one is thinking of individuality and sense of identity. The general imperative of imported Orientalism is—through individuality and then beyond it—back to the All. Liberation is escape from the nagging demands of the ego and the discovery that the most profound level of the spirit is one with the Ultimate. The logical upshot of this kind of religion is prayer, meditation, silence, and union with the Ultimate. History cannot have the same meaning that it does for the Jew, the Christian, or the Marxist. If all things are ultimately one, the diversity of the passing scene and the excitement and terror of the momentary abysses and heights of history is a secondary thing. In short, Oriental religion, at least as it is understood by the West, devalues the sense of individuality and the significance of history. In doing this, it partially devalues the usual function of the writer.

Some writers have discovered, and I think more will discover, that Christianity offers them the best pair of eyes. This is not the main reason for being a Christian—one should not worship Christ merely in order to write a *Hamlet*—but the discovery remains valid. To change the metaphor, the Christian lives in the roomiest house that seems to be available. The writer who becomes a Christian discovers that he has only his negations to lose. The affirmations that other faiths make, he can mostly second—with appropriate footnotes, of course. Their negations he must deny.

He can agree with the old-fashioned naturalism that man is an animal, but he cannot add "nothing but." He must rather add "plus." With the scientific humanist he has much in common, but his act of faith is a milder one, for he posits an intelligent and loving Will that wooed the miraculous dust and guided it until it became Michelangelo. He also sees a bigger place for individuality and the intractable oneness of the individual (thanks to God) than scientific humanism, engrossed with the collective march down the highway of evolution, easily accords. He has a view that makes room for neurosis as well as mental health, for crosses as well as schools and art museums.

With the Marxist, the Christian has much in common, more than with the traditional Hindu. He believes that history has meaning (though the full revelation of that meaning is not wholly boxed in by history); that the most grubby details of daily life, such as banking systems and modes of production, are to be taken with all seriousness; that the quest for justice here and now is the essence and evidence of enlightenment. But again, the Christian must negate the negations. He negates the atheism of Marx, and he negates the naive insistence that productive processes are always primary and "culture" is always an epiphenomenon. It must be quickly added that he negates this latter not by an equally false idealism, which would contend that disembodied ideas incarnate themselves in factories and counting houses, but rather by seeing all of man's activities as a broken and sometimes demonic—but occasionally magnificent—reflection of the image he bears within him. Neither "matter" nor "mind" is primary. God is.

At any rate, with the Marxist the Christian finds enduring and exciting meaning in the making of goods, the distribution, and the development of new processes—but his ultimate lies as much beyond these human achievements as it lies beyond the finest performance of *Oedipus Rex*. Christianity supplies a real ultimate, not a deification of history and process; it also gives the individual whereon to stand. His destiny is inseparably linked with the total, ongoing spectacle, and yet not wholly. God saves men one by one. One by one, at the last, we find whether we have accepted salvation.

I have mentioned the increasing influence of Oriental thought. I expect this to continue and grow. A Christianity worn threadbare by sterile moralism, old truths somehow shriveled into platitudes and clichés, and psychology dressed up in the faded finery of Christian theology, lacks the power to grip, heal, and illumine. To the Westerner, there is something crisp and clean about a religion from far away, one with great spiritual and psychological subtlety, one that restores his inwardness and leads him beyond it. And yet—one must make these judgments with all possible humility, but still make them—I am convinced that the various Oriental varieties of the "perennial philosophy" will not long provide, for many writers, the firm island of meaning on which they can plant their solid feet and make sense of their own lives and of what they observe. Too much is left out. If everything is somehow a part of the All, and the All is what matters, then why write novels? Unless the passing scene has some meaning in its diversity and perverse insistence on being what it is and not something else; if the passing scene is a half-illusory pageant, marking the retreat from the All and the return to the All—then it is hardly a fit object for prolonged identification or agonized and loving study. I am more likely to write a poem about a bluebird when it is intractably a bluebird; less likely if I consider it a pale reflection of the eternal, metaphysical, and invisible bluebird; least likely of all, if the bluebird appears to me as a momentary and insignificant aberration from the unity of all things. Nor do I see how the passion for social justice can be as deeply anchored in a religion that takes the material world and history lightly, as in one that regards history as the theater, here and now, of duty, love, salvation, and damnation. Marxism is too materialistic, and most Oriental religion seems too spiritual. Christianity, by its doctrines of creation and providence and by its sacramental mode of experience, manages to be both fiercely materialistic and fiercely spiritual. Again, it negates only the negations.

I need hardly point out the great amount of agreement between existentialism, even in its atheist varieties, and Christianity. There is the same sense of the uniqueness, and the aloneness of the individual, and there is the same inescapable necessity of making choices. But where existentialism can offer little way out, other than responsibly creating one's world (as though Adam had not already named all the animals!), Christianity assumes a world that already exists, a dimension of meaning whose center is God, and holds forth the hope that entrance into this world—now, this minute—can unite our separate lonelinesses into a communion that does no violence to any man's unique selfhood.

I come back to my prediction. I think a fair number of writers may turn to Christianity. They will do this, in most instances, after a process of trial and error, much of it unconscious—in an effort not so much to write better as to find meaning in their own lives. With writers, of course, these two yearnings cannot be neatly separated. They will often come to Christianity reluctantly and with a hangdog feeling, having experimented with many alternatives and discovering at some point that each alternative makes them say *no* to some experience or observation which they know in their bones to be meaningful.

Christianity is not an easy religion for the person who wants sheer logic. It is full of odd twists and paradoxes that do violence to logic and even to ordinary morality, but which ring oddly true. The mathematical absurdity of the Trinity leaves any theologian stammering when he tries to explain it to an intelligent (or stupid) university student, yet it tallies with actual religious experience. The assertion that the last shall be first outrages ordinary morality and justice, yet it is not alien to the deepest perceptions of a sensitive participant in life. The Hindu doctrine of Karma is a plausible way of viewing cause-and-effect in the moral life, but Christianity cuts violently across the rational diagram with a God who breaks the cycle of Karma by shouldering his way to the Cross and bearing on his shoulders the consequences of men's sins. And so it goes. The Christian faith has about it something of the off-beat, compelling quality that one finds in a very great writer, who knows how to break the ordinary rules of writing, and in breaking them fulfills them. It is like the violent liberties that Shakespeare takes with iambic pentameter in his plays. There the lord of all metrical feet affirms them by remembering them or forgetting them for a time: blank verse is made for Shakespeare, not Shakespeare for blank verse. Or it is like Shakespeare writing *Hamlet,* a play that has everything wrong with it from a formal viewpoint and is also the play that haunts mankind more than any other. In Christianity, man's neat schematizations of the moral and spiritual life must be broken and reshaped by God. And God has done this in Christ.

Ordinary life is full of similar odd twists, absurdities, and paradoxes. A man who falls five hundred feet from an airplane almost certainly dies, but he *may* land in a snowdrift and live. Architects who are failures at fifty usually remain failures, but sometimes they live to be a glory and an abiding influence. The best seller is forgotten; the book written by an obscure crank comes out in paperbacks a century later. Nations that are mortal enemies turn into allies. A chaste, water-drinking, and honest mayor can leave his city in worse shape than he found it; whereas his philandering, gin-guzzling, pocket-lining successor may build symphony halls, attract industry, and find ways to reduce juvenile delinquency. The unpredictability and downright ironic irrationality of real life seems more akin to the paradoxes of the Christian faith than to the more strictly rational assertions of most of the competitive religions and ideologies. Of these, only existentialism seems to have the same respect for the absurd.

What advantages are there for a writer in being a Christian? I am speaking now of advantages to him *as writer*, not *as man*. In the first place, it gives him whereon to stand, an ordering of his own personal life that makes intellectual and emotional sense. It also gives him a perspective on his work as a writer. He can honestly see himself as a kind of earthly assistant to God (so can the carpenter), carrying on the delegated work of creation, making the fullness of creation fuller. At the same time, he is saved from the romantic tendency toward idolatry. Art is not religion. A writer is not a god or godling. There is wisdom and illumination but not salvation in a sonnet. Thus the work of any writer is set in proper proportion. Just as a husband and wife have a deeper marriage if they see their love as a human reflection of God's love, but do not make gods of each other, and do not equate the ceremonies of the marriage-bed with the love upon the Cross, so an author writes better (for the inner setting of his work is founded on true relationships) if he gives himself to his work in a spirit of deadly serious playfulness and does not pretend to himself and others that he is a temple builder and the high priest and divinity of the temple.

Christianity offers also to the writer, as it does to every

man, a community. In the earlier part of this chapter I suggested that the old organic communities are visibly dissolving. I do not think this process can be reversed. Perhaps it should not be. In the organic communities, the individual was born into a world of inescapable relationships and duties. As the organic community crumbles into the vague society of the social contract and voluntary relationships, there is a gain in freedom. One must select, one must take the initiative to establish relationships, rather than merely inherit them. New dimensions of liberty—frightening, it is true—are opened up. In terror at their new freedom, men hastily erect clumsy substitutes for the old organic bonds: they invent ideologies and stage mass rallies; they organize interlocking committees and hire sociologists to create an ersatz togetherness. But a Communist rally or a community square dance planned by a committee with sociological goals in mind is not the same thing as the old organic community, which was like an extended family. One can be as lonely in a planned demonstration or a community-sponsored fun night as in a solitary cell.

Angels or demons with flaming swords bar the way back. The Church offers a way forward, beyond mere individualism, beyond mere organization. It is a voluntary community of those who have caught some glimmering of what God means in Christ and how Christ unites all who accept the Accepter. Thus in the Church, at its best, there is both the flowering of individuality and also the sense of belonging, of being accepted, of forgiving, of being forgiven, of loving and being loved.

Admittedly, the average parish church does not bear much visible resemblance to the community of voluntary love and acceptance and mutual responsibility that I have briefly sketched. It is too much like the world about it. It bears traces of the old organic society, now in decay; it is sometimes an anarchy of solitary individuals who come together and worship as though each were in a lonely, separate room; or at times it feverishly generates a synthetic sense of community by activities, activities, and activities. Those who have the peculiarly Christian sense of community are likely to be a minority, a kind of third order or *ecclesia in ecclesia*. Thus it may be that the writer will find his "community" not so much in the parish church as in that "scattered brotherhood" of persons whom he meets here and there, comes to know, and in whom he finds a hint of what it means to be centered in Christ and therefore members one of another.

Any genuine community, whether localized or diffused, is a home. Living in it, drawing strength from it, the writer can move back and forth into the surrounding and interpenetrating world, and yet always have solid ground under his feet. Paradoxically, the firmer his sense of community, the less fearfully he will throw himself into society as a whole. He will be enabled to love it more, to study it with more compassion and interest, for he will not be afraid of absorption and destruction by it. And, yet another paradox, he will find strong evidence that in the apparently non-Christian or very vaguely Christian society, the secret Christ is at work. The scattered brotherhood will come to include, for him, men and women who do not recognize the Master they nevertheless serve.

Most of the gifts I have so far mentioned are those equally precious to the housewife, the business executive, and the writer. But there are some gifts that are especially valuable to the writer. The poet, for instance, is reassured that his preoccupation with sensory observations is not a frivolous study of *maya*. Things are real; they are real because God made them; and, because he made them, they are important and worthy of study and even a proper portion of love. Not only did God make things. He built us so that we perceive them as much through our animal senses as our minds; the mind must turn to the senses to have something to feed upon. The color and smell of a rose are not irrelevant or illusory. We were constructed so that we come into communion with the rose through its color, fragrance, and the thorns that scratch. Compared to the rose that the senses perceive, the rose of the botanist—still more the rose of the physicist—is a construct or abstraction, true in its own way, but not the rose that we are built to admire and love.

The novelist and playwright receive the assurance that man's social and psychological life and his entire historical existence are meaningful. History becomes part of a cosmic drama, reaching backward to the moment outside of time when the command, "Let there be," was spoken into the void, leading forward toward a culmination that is destined but not compelled; a culmination that by some mysterious paradox lies both inside and outside history and calls forth man's deepest freedom in working with what will surely come to pass.

There is another gift that Christianity bestows. In some systems of thought, diversity dissolves into a totality of one kind or another. Sciences move steadily toward mathematics as the All. Hindu thought, so far as I understand it, has no meaningful place for diversity. The teeming variety of this earth is a strange and passing thing, eventually to be merged once more with the All. To Christian eyes, diversity is a good thing in itself, for God made diversity. He did not create "trees"; he created pines, oaks, and ginkgoes. The animals are as fantastically varied as the impish drawings of a surrealist. The temperaments of men are as varied as the forms of animals. Christianity aims not at the bypassing of individuality and absorption back into the All, but at fulfillment and redemption of the individual. Salvation is not absorption but relationship. If Hamlet and Lear are both in heaven, it is not because they have become indistinguishable nor because they have lost individual consciousness and are now merged as raindrops in the ocean of God. No, each is more himself than ever, but each self is a redeemed self, oriented to turn with love to God and his creatures. In sum, Christianity is concerned with the fulfillment of personality, not its negation. We are called to be sons of God, and a son is not his father. A novelist is not being frivolous when he takes his characters seriously.

Another way in which Christian eyes aid the writer is simply that he can make greater sense of the towering heights and dizzy abysses of the human drama. He does not have to explain them away. He need not elucidate Hitler as a throwback to the anthropoids or St. Francis as a complex manifestation of the herd instinct. He sees in man both the angels and the demons at work, as well as the simpler imperatives of the animal nature. And he observes, and experiences, a drama with eternal stakes. The stakes are not merely the welfare or destruction of society, but the drama of individual damnation and salvation. It is a drama with no foregone conclusions. In real life, as in a good novel, the spectator is kept guessing up to the end.

So much for some of the special gifts and graces that a writer can receive when his eyes are baptized. His faith is no substitute for talent, for genius. But if he has that, the new eyes can aid him in seeing more, understanding more, saying more.

But to whom shall he say it? Is the Christian writer of the near future doomed to be an esoteric, coterie figure, speaking only to those who share his pair of eyes? It is possible that this is the case, but I am hopeful that he can reach many others. If it is true that the soul is *naturaliter christiana*, Christian insight should not be without response among non-Christians. Many an agnostic is deeply moved by Dante; there is Graham Greene, whose novels are meaningful to thousands who reject his theology. If the Christian faith provides the roomiest dwelling; if Christian eyes can see more and see it more exactly, it should follow that the truth a Christian writer can portray will somehow get through, because it will ring true even in men who consciously reject the faith that offers the new eyes.

I could be mistaken in this. It may be that for the next few generations the Christian writer is condemned to write for a coterie. This is more likely to happen with the playwright than anyone else. He requires a certain community of reaction. The people sitting in the theater need to have enough in common so that they will respond with some unanimity to the play. If their assumptions and ingrained attitudes are too different, it may be impossible to arouse the spontaneous symphony of individual responses that great plays call forth when there is common ground between playwright and audience. Conceivably, the Christian playwright may have to develop his own audience in Church circles. I do not believe this is the case, but it could be so.

The case of the novelist and the poet is more hopeful. Except for public readings of poetry (almost a form of drama) these two types of literature are read by individuals in their solitude. There is not the necessity to arouse a group response. A man reading a novel or a poem can mull it over, let it sink in, and respond to it at his own speed. If the soul is Christian by nature, it can take its time and slowly grasp whatever insight is offered.

At this point I have the uneasy feeling that some readers may assume I expect Christian writers to produce "Christian literature." If by that they mean books in which such words as God, Christ, soul, etc., frequently occur; or books dealing with Church life, ministers, devout souls, etc.—they are mistaken. The Christian writer does not necessarily deal directly with anything that would be labeled "Christian." His plots and characters may be precisely those one would find in a naturalistic or existentialist novel. The difference is much more subtle and more important. It is again the angle of vision, the nuances that a different pair of eyes can yield, a way of understanding, not subject matter.

I have tried to state the "hope for literature" in modest and tentative terms. One must not claim too much nor hope too much. If there is to be a great literature, it will come about first of all because great talents arise. In the future, as in the past, many of these may be non-Christians. Their insights will often be more probing that those of devout but less gifted Christian authors. In a sense, a real sense, they may write books more radically "Christian" than many Christians have the skill to write.

But, for Christian and non-Christian alike, this is a world moving into a period when all foundations are increasingly shaken and new foundations are perhaps being built without our quite knowing the building material we are using. Science, for good or evil—that is our choice—is doubling and redoubling the wager. The old dream of world brotherhood is becoming a possibility, a mirage, an absolute necessity, all simultaneously. Mankind is called upon to achieve the impossible or perish. The nineteenth-century world order, as hierarchical with its distinction of "civilized" and "primitive" nations as the social hierarchy of the Middle Ages, is dissolving in fire, blood, and strident shouts for equality and dignity, in tongues only recently reduced to alphabetical form. Meanwhile, the space vehicles are probing the heavens, and who knows what adventures of the spirit lie barely beyond tomorrow's newspaper, when the first contact is made with intelligences independent of our parochial earth? Closer to home, all the advances of science make a human being more a marvel, more an impenetrable mystery, than ever before. The final frontier is ourselves.

It could be another Elizabethan age, a century of outer and inner explorations, while everywhere the relations among men and between men and whatever they call God are being reordered. Like the Elizabethan age, it is already a time dominated by voices of pessimism, at the very moment when men are acting with frantic energy and, for good or evil, are doing mighty deeds.

Writers will continue to write. They will have much to write about. It may be that the Christian faith will help some of them to see more, see it more truly. This is a hope, not a certainty, but when was hope ever the name for a sure thing?

A Selected Bibliography

Abrams, M. H., ed., *Literature and Belief*. New York: Columbia University Press, 1958.

Allsop, Kenneth, *The Angry Decade: A Survey of the Cultural Revolt of the Nineteen-Fifties*. London: Peter Owen, 1958.

Bethell, S. L., *Literary Criticism*. London: Dennis Dobson, 1948.

Buckley, Vincent, *Poetry and Morality*. London: Chatto & Windus, 1959.

Chapman, Raymond, *The Ruined Tower*. London: Geoffrey Bles, 1961.

Clive, Geoffrey, *The Romantic Enlightenment*. New York: Meridian Books, Inc., 1960.

Dillistone, F. W., *The Novelist and the Passion Story*. London: Collins, 1960.

Elmen, Paul, *The Restoration of Meaning to Contemporary Life*. Garden City: Doubleday & Company, Inc., 1958.

Esslin, Martin, *The Theatre of the Absurd*. Garden City: Doubleday & Company, Inc., Anchor Books, 1961.

Eversole, Finley, ed., *Christian Faith and the Contemporary Arts*. Nashville: Abingdon Press, 1962.

Every, Brother George, *Christian Discrimination*. London: The Sheldon Press, 1940 (A "Christian News-Letter Book").

Ford, Boris, ed., *The Modern Age*. Baltimore: Penguin Books, Inc., 1961 (Volume VII, "Pelican Guide to English Literature").

Gardner, Helen, *The Business of Criticism*. Oxford: Clarendon Press, 1959.

Greene, Graham, *The Lost Childhood*. New York: The Viking Press, 1952.

Hassan, Ihab, *Radical Innocence: Studies in the Contemporary American Novel*. Princeton: Princeton University Press, 1961.

Heller, Erich, *The Disinherited Mind*. Philadelphia: Dufour and Saifer, 1952.

Heller, Erich, *The Hazard of Modern Poetry*. Cambridge: Bowes & Bowes, 1953.

Henn, T. R., *The Harvest of Tragedy*. London: Methuen, 1956.

Hopper, Stanley Romaine, ed., *Spiritual Problems in Contemporary Literature*. New York: Harper & Bros., 1952.

Isaacs, J., *An Assessment of Twentieth-Century Literature*. London: Secker & Warburg, 1951.

Jarrett-Kerr, Martin, C. R., *Studies in Literature and Belief*. London: Rockliff, 1954.

Krieger, Murray, *The Tragic Vision*. New York: Farrar & Rinehart, 1960.

Lewis, R. W. B., *The Picaresque Saint: Representative Figures in Contemporary Fiction*. Philadelphia: J. B. Lippincott Co., 1959.

Lynch, William F., S. J., *Christ and Apollo: The Dimensions of the Literary Imagination*. New York: Sheed & Ward, 1960.

Maritain, Jacques, *Creative Intuition in Art and Poetry*. New York: Pantheon Books, Inc., 1953.

Mauriac, Claude, *The New Literature*, trans. by S. I. Stone. New York: George Braziller, 1959.

May, Rollo, ed., *Symbolism in Religion and Literature*. New York: George Braziller, Inc., 1960.

McCormick, John, *Catastrophe and Imagination*. New York: Longmans, Green and Co., 1957.

Mueller, William R., *The Prophetic Voice in Modern Fiction*. New York: Association Press, 1959.

Norton, Aloysius A. and Nourse, Joan T., eds., *A Christian Approach to Western Literature*. Westminster: The Newman Press, 1961.

O'Faolain, Sean, *The Vanishing Hero*. Boston: Little, Brown and Co., 1957.

Rougemont, Denis de, *Passion and Society*, trans. by Montgomery Belgion. London: Faber and Faber, 1940.

Savage, D. S., *The Withered Branch: Six Studies in the Modern Novel*. New York: Pellegrini & Cudahy, 1950.

Scott, Nathan A., Jr., *Albert Camus*. London: Bowes & Bowes, 1962.

Scott, Nathan A., Jr., *Modern Literature and the Religious Frontier*. New York: Harper & Bros., 1958.

Scott, Nathan A., Jr., *Rehearsals of Discomposure: Alienation and Reconciliation in Modern Literature*. New York: King's Crown Press, Columbia University Press, 1952.

Scott, Nathan A., Jr., ed., *The Tragic Vision and the Christian Faith*. New York: Association Press, 1957.

Speaight, Robert, *The Christian Theatre.* London: Burns & Oates, 1960.
Stewart, Randall, *American Literature and Christian Doctrine.* Baton Rouge: Louisiana State University Press, 1958.
Turnell, Martin, *Modern Literature and Christian Faith.* Westminster: The Newman Press, 1961.
Turnell, Martin, *Poetry and Crisis.* London: Sands, The Paladin Press, 1938.
Weidlé, Wladimir, *The Dilemma of the Arts,* trans. by Martin Jarrett-Kerr, C. R. London: SCM Press, 1948.
Wilder, Amos N., *Modern Poetry and the Christian Tradition.* New York: Charles Scribner's Sons, 1952.
Wilder, Amos N., *The Spiritual Aspects of the New Poetry.* New York: Harper & Bros., 1940.
Wilder, Amos N., *Theology and Modern Literature.* Cambridge: Harvard University Press, 1958.
Williams, Raymond, *Drama: From Ibsen to Eliot.* London: Chatto & Windus, 1954.

The Contributors

NATHAN A. SCOTT, JR. is Professor of Theology and Literature in the Divinity School, University of Chicago, and a priest of the Episcopal Church. He is a frequent contributor to theological and literary journals and symposia. His most recent books are *Modern Literature and the Religious Frontier* and *Albert Camus*; and his book on Samuel Beckett is scheduled to appear shortly.

JOHN MCGILL KRUMM is Chaplain of Columbia University. He is the author of *Modern Heresies*.

W. MOELWYN MERCHANT, Professor of English and Head of the Department, University of Exeter, has contributed many articles to books and journals. He is the author of *Shakespeare and the Artist*. Fr. Merchant is an Anglican priest.

RALPH HARPER is Rector of St. James' Church, Monkton, Maryland, and has taught English at Harvard University. Author of *The Sleeping Beauty*, he frequently contributes to journals.

PAUL ELMEN is Professor of Moral Theology at Seabury-Western Theological Seminary. He is author of *The Restoration of Meaning to Contemporary Life* and many articles in theological and literary journals.

KAY BAXTER is best known as playwright of *Pull Devil, Pull Baker* and *Gerald of Wales*. She is an Associate of Newnham College, Cambridge, and has lectured at Union Theological Seminary, New York City.

E. MARTIN BROWNE has directed contemporary poetic and religious drama in London and in New York. All the English productions of T. S. Eliot's plays have been directed by Mr. Browne. He was Visiting Professor of Religious Drama at Union Theological Seminary, 1956-1961.

RALPH J. MILLS, JR. is Executive Secretary and Assistant Professor in the Committee on Social Thought, University of Chicago. He has written articles for literary and religious journals, and is a contributor to *Poets in Progress*.

MARTIN JARRETT-KERR, C.R., is now engaged in educational and pastoral work for the Community of the Resurrection in Cardiff, Wales. He is the author of numerous books and articles, his most recent book being *African Pulse*.

CHAD WALSH is Professor of English and Chairman of the Department, Beloit College; and he is a priest of the Episcopal Church. Among his recently published books are *Campus Gods on Trial, Behold the Glory, Eden Two-Way*, and *The Psalm of Christ*.